A RAZOR FOR

A Razor for a Goat

A DISCUSSION OF

CERTAIN PROBLEMS IN

THE HISTORY OF

WITCHCRAFT AND DIABOLISM

Elliot Rose

UNIVERSITY OF TORONTO PRESS

© University of Toronto Press 1989
Toronto Buffalo London
Printed in Canada

Scholarly Reprint Series
ISBN 0-8020-7055-8

First paperback edition 1989
ISBN 0-8020-6768-9

Canadian Cataloguing in Publication Data

Rose, Elliot
A razor for a goat

(Scholarly reprint series)
1st paperback ed.
Bibliography: p.
Includes index.
ISBN 0-8020-6768-9

1. Witchcraft — Europe — History. I. Title.

BF1584.E9R68 1989   133.4′3′094   C89-094546-2

Acknowledgments

THE PRESENT WORK was begun in a somewhat frivolous spirit seven years ago. Its survival and any serious merit it may possess are due to the continuing interest, encouragement, and advice of more people than I can now name—more, I fear, than I can now remember. Among these the first place, both in importance and in time, belongs to Dr. Peter Green. He and his wife, Lalage Pulvertaft, were a patient audience in the thinking-aloud stage, and at every subsequent stage I have made, with justified confidence, the most exorbitant demands upon his time and trouble as well as on his wide-ranging knowledge of ancient superstition. If, as I suspect, other friends in England have been pestered to help check a reference or the like, I must confess with shame that their services have slipped my mind. This, of course, is because they are such nice people that particular kindnesses of theirs do not stand out in retrospect.

Many of my colleagues at Toronto have shown an interest in my subject that threatened to reveal the extent of my ignorance. My gratitude is due especially to Professor Karl Helleiner for the quiet persistence with which he resurrected a project I had thought dead and for several of my more abstruse references. Professor R. C. Dailey gave generous help in a hunt for the frontispiece.

I must express my appreciation for the unfailing courtesy and professional zeal of the readers and staff of the University of Toronto Press. These have been such as to make the collaboration of author and publisher a pleasure.

It should go without saying, but it seems to have become the custom to say, that none of those who have offered me advice is responsible for any errors or rash opinions the book may contain. These are, of course, my own responsibility, as are any failings in the index.

Lastly, my thanks are owing to the Humanities Research Council and to the Canada Council, the former of which, on the latter's behalf, made a grant towards the cost of publication.

E.R.

Contents

A RAZOR FOR A GOAT

CHAPTER ONE

Which Witch Is Which?

FEW PEOPLE NOWADAYS are witches; or, if they are, they are not often ready to admit it. This is a pity, not only because there are many occasions in modern life when a witch might be useful, but also because it means we have, most of us, no chance of finding out anything about witchcraft by positive and direct evidence. Indeed, when there are, for practical purposes, no witches, and when everything written about them is so vague, contradictory, or conjectural, we have not even a steady peg to hang the word "witch" on. In default of such a peg, the word is free to wander, and does wander, among a bewildering variety of mental associations; so that it is by no means certain—I speak from bitter experience—that any two studies of the subject that stand side by side in a bibliography are really about the same subject at all.

The same applies to the word "magic"; and it will be readily agreed that we can get no forwarder with an examination of witchcraft unless we have some idea what we mean by both these terms. I do not propose, here on the first page, to produce out of my sleeve a definition I should thereafter use exclusively throughout the book. That would be necessary in discussing many vexed questions, but here it would actually be worse than useless. Obviously, what one can prove about witches, or anything else, depends on how the terms are defined; when the word in common use is imprecise, one can prove what one likes by nothing more strenuous than imposing a hard and fast definition upon it. My purpose here is to prove nothing, but to enquire with a free mind; and the meaning the word "witch" ought to have (if indeed it ought to have one meaning) is itself open to enquiry.

The word "witch" has been used, in England, in ages when almost everybody believed in witchcraft and in ages when almost nobody did so. It has been used by people of all degrees of education and intelligence, and in the nature of the case those with most education have often been those with the least knowledge of witchcraft; it has been used in gravity and in mockery; and our understanding of it is built up out of all the former uses. For the educated, the wanderings of the word do not even end there; anthropologists have exported it to remote parts of the earth, and archaeologists have projected it far back in time. The word is not my property or my invention, and I can hardly venture to define it; but undefined, it rides its traditional, sub-literary, pantomime broomstick over the wide compass of the heavens, and in hell also the weird sisters cackle and gibber.

I propose to avoid this dilemma by singling out for consideration a manageable fraction of the subject. In the first place, I shall confine myself to the Western European "culture complex"; Latin Christendom as it came to be defined in the Dark and Early Middle Ages, and the modern nations directly derived from it. This is an obvious convenience; the word "witch" has had many meanings, but *hexe, strega, sorcière* translate all of them. The cultural unity of Western Europe is strong enough to secure that much; witchcraft may have varied enormously within that unity both according to place and time, but throughout that unity the same people would be regarded as witches and most of the same popular and literary traditions about them have been repeated, mingled, and spread. When we read of witchcraft in other cultures we cannot be anything like so sure. The Bantu and the Babylonians did not use our word "witch"; modern scholars have proceeded on the assumption that they would have done if they had spoken English. It is a fairly safe assumption, and the thought processes behind primitive magic show remarkable similarities the world over, but this is a generalization which cannot be depended on in detail.

Further, I shall not attempt to deal with all aspects of witchcraft and witch-superstition as they have been understood within this one culture. An encyclopaedia could not cover them all, and most of them hardly present a historical problem of any interest. I suppose I need not apologize for ignoring black cats and horseshoes and mandrake roots, which are the business of folklore specialists, and for almost ignoring pixies, gnomes, and creatures of that kidney. (As will be seen, I cannot quite ignore them.) In superstitious communities quite ordinary people, and not only witches, employ the simpler kinds of magic; and these therefore are only "witchcraft" for want of a better word. With these, and with fairies also, there is a common mental link with witches through "superstition," but we cannot afford to draw our categories so wide. If witches were simply people who knew about the charms and omens everybody knew, everybody once was more or less a witch. If they are people who associate with elves and goblins, nobody is a witch. In either case there is no problem.

I am concerned with witches who may have existed and about whom non-witches believed things that may be true but are not obviously true. Within these limits, and within the limits of Western Europe already set, the main problem leaps to the eye. What reality, if any, lay behind the great witch-scares of the Renaissance and Reformation?

Of course, half this question can be answered at once. We need hardly pause to discuss whether the victims of the scares had actually been employing malign magic. (As a matter of fact I shall later discuss the question whether they could theoretically have wielded powers in one sense or another supernatural; because, as I shall have to make plain, there is here a case of sorts to be answered. The discussion has been relegated to the latter end of the work, where the reader can more conveniently skip.) On the other hand, we need have no doubt that in all ignorant societies in all times, and, among others, in European villages in the Middle Ages and much later, some have imposed upon the credulity of their neighbours, and probably also on themselves, with pretensions to supernatural knowledge and power. Both men and women, but women it seems especially, have made a surreptitious trade in spells and charms, or used the threat of them as a satisfaction of malice. A folklore expert who should happen on such a person today and gain her confidence could learn a great deal about the ways of thought of that particular community; but the witch, in this sense, is still hardly a historical subject. It is a fair guess that she has always existed, and that may suffice to give her her covering dates. Her devices may have changed from time to time—they certainly vary widely from place to place—but their changes are without thought and without meaning. She herself has not changed essentially. Witchcraft in this sense shows no development; it is not an institution that has grown with the growth of the culture that contains it, but a permanent fact with variable manifestations. Change is the course of Nature; only change that can be seen as development is matter for History.[1]

[1]Some historians may question that last assertion, and we must be on our guard against the idea of "progress." But development is not necessarily growth in size or merit; it is that kind of change that is conditioned by all former changes and will, however slightly, condition all changes thereafter. Where causes of change are purely irrational, development cannot be traced nor History serve any purpose.

The case is quite otherwise with the witch considered as a religious rebel, diabolist, or idolater; and with the witch as a member of a permanent community of witches. The village wise-woman had existed for centuries, even in the culture we are considering, before Sabbats and covens and Black Masses came to be spoken of as adjuncts of sorcery. In the witch-burning times, witches were burned partly because any dabbling in sorcery was supposed to involve a real and conscious alliance with the Devil, further involving alliance with other witches, and symbolized by obscene and horrifying rituals. Here we have something that might be investigated. Here we have an alleged sect, practising certain very remarkable customs, also practising magic not only as individuals but on occasion collectively, possessing a common fund of knowledge and capable of organizing instruction in the craft; which may, according to some, have altered the course of ordinary history whether by natural or by occult means; which is alleged, with a fair show of probability, to have been numerous and powerful, and certainly gave rise to a great deal of public alarm, in one period of history and not in others; but which is generally and colourably held to have existed, in one form or another, from a much earlier date. Its origins, by universal agreement, are hidden in the mists of time; its end can be roughly dated, unless it still exists covertly. A great deal about its history is not now perfectly known, and probably never will be; but at least it *has* a history, which it remains the historian's task to discover if he can. Unfortunately the majority of historians will not handle the subject with tongs, for incidental reasons that may be imagined. As a result the task has devolved upon those less fitted to perform it, and a high measure of confusion has been achieved thereby. Counsel has been darkened with words without knowledge, and new and irrelevant associations fastened upon an idea which, as I have tried to indicate, is already over-clogged with them.

I hope, in the following pages, to clear a little underbrush and try to make out, more or less crudely, a practicable way through the wood; though I am bound to say I do not know where it will lead. My qualifications are that I am a historian of sorts, not wholly unfamiliar with the background; I have had, for other purposes, to give some attention to the appropriate countries and period; I can read Latin, and possess the ordinary layman's knowledge of anthropology and kindred subjects. I had perhaps also best make my bias clear; I am, as an Anglican, uncommitted on most issues of theology and philosophy, but as will emerge I disbelieve in the physical powers of the Devil and also in the kind of supernatural effect that is most readily called "magical"; this in spite of the fact that I am if anything a Thomist. I might perhaps add that I am, through my paternal grandmother, a distant descendant of the god Woden and therefore not provoked by any deep-seated prejudice against paganism, although of course I think pagans mistaken.

The reader may not think all these details germane; but details of the kind are sometimes a help in assessing a writer's reliability, and they are far too often omitted. I do not, however, rely greatly on the fact of having studied and taught history. If I can say one thing for certain as a historian, on the present question, it is that the history of the "witch-cult" can never be written. At least it cannot unless some quite unsuspected material comes to light; at the moment we have ludicrously little to go on. The best I can hope to do is to apply the resources of an ordinary intelligence to sort out the possible from the impossible and the colourable from the wildly unlikely.

I will, however, make one small point at this stage, in defence of taking up such a task. The claim is sometimes made, and *prima facie* it is plainly impressive, that since written records are inadequate someone, not a historian, should take over and apply some other, more appropriate, technique. This would be a good and reasonable claim if the search did not still take us through historical time, so that the anthropologist, psychologist, or whoever attempts it must still be a historian also. The problem cannot be treated in isolation from its time-context, and no solution will work which, perfectly convincing in itself, cannot be made to fit into the general history of the age when it is supposed to have taken place. I may add that a great deal more is known about the Middle Ages than many people imagine—more than is positively known about most of classical antiquity. We must also reject the idea, sometimes aired, that the newer-developed Social Sciences, being specially "modern," have superseded and can correct an old-fashioned branch of learning like History. This is pure *idolum theatri*[2] and must not be allowed to detain us. These disciplines are not, in the sense implied, more "scientific" because more recent in origin, nor is there in fact any hostility or any hard and fast line between the various studies that all have to do with the infinite variety of man. Historical theory can only be tested by the historical approach, which, however, it is the general liberty of all literate men to employ.

---

[2]"The phantom of the theatre": Bacon's phrase for the fallacies that arise out of the temporary dominance of a system of reasoning devised for one purpose but applied, on account of fashion, to all purposes indiscriminately.

It cannot be said that there is at present any historical theory of witchcraft in existence; at least if by that we mean a theory that gets into the history books and which any party among historians is prepared to accept until disproved. The subject, it would be broadly true to say, does not get into the history books at all, or not in its own right. Of course, the panic of the late sixteenth- and early seventeenth-century trials, when there was a great and quite unprecedented witch-scare that swept through central and northwest Europe, is a fact of general history and has been studied as such. The episode is of some interest from the points of view of the historians of thought, of law, and of religion.[3] But the interest lies almost wholly in society's attitude to the witch, not in the witch herself. The history of witchcraft has, in fact, been studied for one short period externally, but not otherwise, much as an English scholar might study Anglo-Spanish relations in the reign of Elizabeth I without claiming to have studied the history of Spain. Of course, those who have dealt with the subject have generally presumed some hypothesis about the reality behind the panic; but they have seldom felt any need to do more than presume, and in this they are not to be distinguished from the ordinary reading public.

It is time to consider the schools of thought, or of thoughtlessness, that exist. There seem to be (very broadly) four in number. I shall distinguish them as the Bluff, the Knowing, the Anti-Sadducee, and the Murrayite. Most writers on the subject can be fairly easily classified according to the oversimplification of their choice; but some are to be met with[4] who complicate matters by paying lip-service to one view while adhering to another.

The Bluff or Fiddlesticks school is almost solely concerned with the pantomime picture of a witch. It is an ancient and respectable body of opinion, which even existed to some extent during the great panics; but it now lacks leaders, nor has it ever attracted theorists, and it is not well represented in debate. Unquestionably its views are those of the majority and have been implicitly shared by many academics; but it has generally relied, in argument, on its hearty masculine unreadiness to listen to the other side.

The Bluff school dismisses the whole thing as one among the many benighted delusions of the credulous Middle Ages. Some go so far as to suggest, in the teeth of evidence and probability, that no one ever

---

[3]See Bibliography, s.v. Ewen, Kittredge, Lea, Notestein.
[4]E.g., R. Trevor Davies (cap. 9 below) who professes to accept Murrayism but argues on an assumption that excludes it.

tried to practise witchcraft; that there only ever were innocent victims of popular superstitious hysteria. There are traces of this curious attitude in the otherwise useful work of Mr. Trevor Davies, and it would probably be fair to say that the majority of serious scholars who have dealt with the witch-persecutions, while remaining non-committal on the question, incline to the Bluff position as the safest, the nearest to sober common sense. There is much to be said for sober common sense, but it used to teach that the earth was flat and is never to be relied on absolutely. The main strength of the Bluff party is drawn not from the scepticism of scholars but from sheer lack of imagination on the part of the multitude. The Bluffs have a common mental attitude but scarcely a theory worth discussing. To their honour be it said, before we leave them, that in the age of neurosis they alone braved the universal hysteria and their incredulity did sometimes suffice to save innocent lives.

There are at least two other attitudes possible to the materialist and currently in the field. There is, first, the Knowing. This is the kind of view aired in works of "Secret History" and the magazines intended mainly for men. In contrast to the Bluffs, to whom the witch is an old woman on a broomstick, the Knowing school is mainly interested in Sabbats and Black Masses. It is eager to lap up any accusation of depravity, and the explanation favoured is as nearly Freudian as any explanation can be in the very limited vocabulary members of this school normally have at command. The appeal of the Knowing approach, apart from the fact that it enables us to read as heavy non-fiction matter not in the ordinary way permitted to be exposed for sale, is its gratifying hints that, if the truth be told, our ancestors were as immoral as we should sometimes like to be ourselves. It is characteristic of history as written by medical men.[5] It also bears a strong resemblance to the more primitive forms of denominational propaganda, such as Protestant pamphlets about the confessional and Roman Catholic pamphlets about Freemasonry.

To the Knowing school, the main thing about witches is that they worshipped the Devil, and that the ritual by which they worshipped him was obscene. In this the second school shades off into the third, the Anti-Sadducee. It resembles the first, in that worship of the Devil is construed as mere delusion, and in that both appeal to the hearty materialist and generally excuse themselves on that ground from the obligation of producing any evidence—holding they must needs be

[5] I do not think this is altogether unfair to the respectable profession that produced Ploss and Bartels and Cabanès.

rational, being rationalistic. Like all except the Bluff, the Knowing school is quite capable of making contributions of its own to the corpus of witch-traditions. It is, I think, wholly responsible for a belief I have found to be common: that in the ritual of the Black Mass a naked woman always serves as the altar. The Knowing school is particularly interested in the Black Mass.

The Anti-Sadducee, or *Bien Pensant* school has, as I have said, certain points in common with this last, and is sometimes hard to distinguish from it. Indeed, it might almost be said that it includes the Knowing view and builds upon it. The Anti-Sadducees are another ancient and respectable body of opinion; they are probably the oldest of all and at one time definitely wrested the supremacy from the Bluff party. However, they suffered a decline, in the eyes of the educated, in the eighteenth and nineteenth centuries, and their more recent revival has been brought about by the determined efforts of individuals. As a result, they possess a much more explicit body of doctrine than we have yet had to notice; though, at the same time, their basic views are shared by an innumerable body of humble supporters quite incapable of understanding the published works of the leaders and even ignorant of their existence.

This is the school that accepts the supernatural element as a fact, and in the case of the leaders is prepared to argue the point. As it is a view that was right out of favour not so long ago, and still is with the majority of educated people, it is obliged to be militant and circumstantial; this is an advantage to us, as enquirers, and must ultimately weigh in its rivalry with the Bluff party. On these grounds, and because its views have got into print more often, I shall give it more attention than the two preceding. It is not, however, for these causes that it enjoys the widespread popular support it can probably claim. The party includes, potentially, everybody who has ever said, "All the same, you know, there's generally something in these old tales," and everybody who has ever felt a glow of smugness in repeating, "There are more things in heaven and earth, Horatio. . . ." Together these amount to a large part of the human race. With prodding, with careful feeding on tales of Mystery, Horror, and Imagination, these may arrive at the outright credulity of a Montague Summers.

Our age has seen, in many different fields, a revival of belief in the supernatural. Not long ago it was rather daring for an educated person to believe in God; nowadays it is almost possible, in pious circles, to believe in leprechauns and astrology. When G. L. Kittredge, in

Witchcraft in Old and New England, disclaimed personal belief in magic, he was referring in irony to this trend.[6] Superstition seems to live as a parasite on orthodoxy, and flourish with it. An early example of this association is to be seen in Huysmans, and specially in his novel *Là-Bas.*

Huysmans can hardly be said (though sometimes he *is* said) to have started the intellectual move back to Catholicism of the late nineteenth century;[7] but it was he, more than any other in his age, who saw the value of witchcraft as an external support, a flying buttress, for the Church. Except for Mr. Dennis Wheatley, who if he is anything is I suppose a theosophist, most moderns who have been prepared to take Satanism *au sérieux* have been Romans or High-flying Anglicans; and the most celebrated, the late Mr. Montague Summers, was both. (I of course except those, such as Mr. Aleister Crowley, whose actual religion was diabolism; and I must ignore as marginal any real-life Enoch Soames who may have contrived to combine the two extremes.) This is odd, because in the great days of the party, in the late sixteenth and early seventeenth centuries—the time of the great scare—it was usually linked, at least in England, with the more extreme forms of Protestantism; which has been rather an embarrassment to the leaders in modern times.

The technique of persuasion, as exemplified in *Là-Bas,* is adapted to the medium of the novel and therefore does not absolutely rely on documentation; but more than one writer of the school has directed different works to different levels of intelligence. The aim, in novels, is to create an impression that a mass of evidence exists, with which the author for the time being will not bore the reader. A central character who starts off as an incredulous rationalist is gradually brought into contact with the manifestations of the occult; as his *scorto* through the Inferno there is another main character, a believer, who gradually reveals a mass of learning on the subject of Satanism, and who bears down the rather simple-minded scepticism of his young friend by sheer weight of instances. His extremely well-informed conversation, combined with the ordinary suspension of unbelief in the novel-reader, is calculated in the end to convince the reader that something has been, or could have been, proved. Typically, however, the author makes his task easier by aiming at a public more or less predisposed to believe;

[6]Preface to *Witchcraft in Old and New England* (p. vii).
[7]The move back to Catholicism, in France, is as old as the Romantic movement itself, and began with Chateaubriand.

he presumes in the reader, and ascribes to the sceptic with whom he is expected to identify himself, the common brand of unthinking adherence to Official Christianity.

The pattern appears fairly clearly in *Là-Bas*, in Wheatley's *The Devil Rides Out*, and (to take a more recent and middlebrow example) Michael Burt's *The Case of the Angels' Trumpets*. R. H. Benson's *The Necromancers* is broadly analogous.[8]

The most prolific writer of the school, however, and the one whose name is most often associated with it, was not a novelist. The Reverend Montague Summers was a High Anglican clergyman converted to the Roman church, who continued thereafter to style himself "Father" and was presumably reordained, but who devoted himself wholly to literary activities. His earliest works were verse of an extraordinarily "decadent" flavour; later he became a literary historian, celebrated for his work on the Restoration comedy and the "Gothick" novel. His works in this field are useful to specialists as reprints and catalogues, but show no trace of critical sense; which could also be said of his work on witchcraft and demonolatry. He published a good deal on these subjects; much of it would pass for studies in a curious bypath of literature or folklore, but his own view of the reality was never in doubt. In his *Popular History of Witchcraft*, he moved so far from mere bibliography as to quote no references at all. What he said there is given out simply as fact and conveys a very complete picture of the extreme views of his school. Certainly he made some reservations; he denied those stories of non-Catholic writers that did not square with Catholic pronouncements,[9] but that is about all he denied.

Even this cannot be said of Dennis Wheatley. I am at a loss to describe his religion; but certainly *magia* (as opposed to *goetia*) forms a part of it. His approach to every subject he touches, in a novel or not, is that of the self-educated man who is burning to educate others. His method, giving the public a drop of adventure and a dollop of sex to help down a digest of useful or remarkable facts, is reminiscent of Jean de Meung in the Middle Ages (like whom, he writes at enormous length); but Jean de Meung regarded witchcraft as a delusion.

---

[8]The novels of Charles Williams present a different and more puzzling approach. Despite the fact that he also wrote non-fiction on the subject (and in his youth belonged to a society of would-be white magicians) his real attitude is peculiarly difficult to discern, credulity and scepticism being combined in him in very unusual proportions.
[9]In his *Popular History of Witchcraft* he contradicts, but does not refute, Miss Murray's assertions regarding Joan of Arc.

Mr. Wheatley reaches a wide audience and is a powerful ally of the Anti-Sadducees. He is hardly a typical member of the party, but he did put on record, in *The Devil Rides Out*, the classic argument of the party in a conveniently extreme form. The well-informed character points out to his young friend that he believes in miracles and he believes in the Devil; if the forces of Good can set aside the course of Nature, why not the forces of Evil? One would have supposed that an orthodox Christian could think of several reasons why not; but this is roughly the attitude of the Anti-Sadducees as a body. The Devil, under the Divine Permission and therefore saving God's Omnipotence, retains powers over Nature that belonged to him as an archangel, and these he imparts to his sworn adherents on earth. It is not for us to ask why God gives him this licence to trouble mankind; the possibility is plain, and there are innumerable instances to testify to the fact, as soon as we have banished mere unquestioning incredulity from our minds.

It will be seen that the Anti-Sadducee party is thinking mainly of the witch as devil-worshipper, but in opening the door to the Devil it is prepared to let in the hobgoblins as well. Holding that all sorcery stems from the Devil's intervention in human affairs, in a sense it makes belief in magic unnecessary while retaining belief in witchcraft. The witch is directly the Devil's worshipper and subject; there may be those outside the coven-system who have a private pact with him, and he may be able to use less conscious agents, but the coven is the real menace. The Anti-Sadducee's pious concern is to emphasize both the reality of the marvellous and the witch's moral turpitude. He concentrates therefore upon the Sabbat; on the witches' flight to the meeting-place (generally by means of an ointment whose secret the Devil imparts to them, the broomstick being an inessential accessory); on the physical presence of Satan at the assembly, and on the obscene service paid him. Representations of the Sabbat in art generally derive from this school and show as its presiding genius a creature unmistakably supernatural. The Anti-Sadducees also stress the blasphemous element and are inclined to confuse Sabbat and Black Mass; and they insist upon the witch's compact with Satan, the "selling of souls." The associations of this act, however, are with such stories as "Faust"; and it is a further point of contrast between this school and the Bluff that to it the witch is much less exclusively female. The word is, in fact, applicable to men and is frequently so applied by the Anti-Sadducees, although unlike all other parties they are not obliged to believe in the presence of any male human being at the Sabbat.

For reasons which I have sketched, the Anti-Sadducees are on the whole the most *informative* party; they are more active in giving the public the details than those who do not consider witchcraft a real menace, and the works of such as Summers contain remarkably complete accounts of the central body of traditions. In this connection it is worth noting that, as a result of the Anti-Sadducees' greater anxiety to spread information, most other writers in the field have been largely dependent on Anti-Sadducee sources; and one way or another this must affect the credibility of the material itself and any theory founded upon it.

Useful as their material is, one is bound to complain at their disposition to believe *everything* and lump *everything* together, both as following from the same evidence and as forming a connected system; because it seems likely that some things included in their picture of witchcraft have strayed in from some other department of the Devil's activities, and some witch-practices they describe were not practised by the same witches as others. I say, "it seems likely"; it would at any rate increase one's idea of a writer's discrimination if he showed himself conscious of the possibility.

Even so, the arguments of the Anti-Sadducees have much to commend them to the less analytic believers, and their array of abstruse knowledge much to impress, as compared with the two I have already touched on, which are hardly based on argument at all. The first two, indeed, are hardly nowadays rivals (above the journalistic level) to the third and fourth, with one or another of which they might be reconciled at a pinch. They are largely instinctive reactions to a rudimentary scrap of the facts, and as instinctive reactions go they have the serious disadvantage of not appealing to human nature's deep-seated will to be convinced of the marvellous. Most of us want to have the credit and comfort of rationalism and the thrill and last resort of superstition as well. The Man in the Street does not, of course, believe in all that nonsense, which Science of course has disproved; you do not fool him so easily; but all the same—all the same, he is standing in the street, rather than on the sidewalk, because he hates walking under ladders. If its literature can only be widely enough spread, the Anti-Sadducee school is likely to prove much the most formidable rival of the fourth, and currently the dominant, party.

The Murrayites seem to hold, at the time of writing, an almost undisputed sway at the higher intellectual levels. There is, among educated people, a very widespread impression that Professor Margaret Murray has discovered the true answer to the problem of the history of European witchcraft and has proved her theory. Whether her theory is in fact the correct one we shall have to discuss at some length; but I feel confident in saying at this stage that it has not yet been proved. The general readiness to accept it, however, is not hard to explain. Its author, an Egyptologist by training, rose to a Chair in Social Anthropology in the University of London and therefore possessed much more imposing credentials than most writers on the subject. The theory, when first put forward, came to the rescue of the sceptics at a time when the Anti-Sadducees were writing all the books, but when Michelet, outside his own country, still had some shreds of a reputation. On him, it must have seemed a vast improvement. It appeared to embody all the newest research in the newest techniques, and to unlock in the name of anthropology the door at which history might have hammered for ever in vain. Neither the anthropology nor the history involved is actually of the kind now regarded as "modern" by those who practise the arts in question; but this was not obvious in the nineteen-twenties when the theory first found utterance, nor is it now to that numerous body of intelligent people to whom the last word in anthropology was Sir J. G. Frazer's *Golden Bough* (or perhaps some of its progeny, such as Mr. Robert Graves's *The White Goddess*) and to whom mediaeval history is a distant memory of the schoolroom. To anyone in that situation the Murrayite view is attractive, as fitting in with the general picture of pre-Christian Europe a reader of Frazer or Graves would be familiar with; and the facts put forward in evidence are not such as he would find it easy to check.

Professor Murray's theory was adumbrated but not argued in her first work on the subject, *The Witch-Cult in Western Europe*, in which she presented her picture of the witch, as extracted from accounts of trials; I may say that more than any other theory hers concentrates on the witch as cult-member (as her title suggests). Later, the evidence was put in its general historical background in *The God of the Witches*, which was intended for a less specialized audience than the earlier work but actually contained much of the same evidence as well as all the argument to link it with (nearly) the same conclusions, which had formerly been almost omitted. On the strength of these, Miss Murray and a number of admirers took the case as proved and adopted a more dogmatic tone and larger ambitions. Apart from odd articles, the fruit of this was *The Divine King in England*, in which was revealed how thoroughly England's Rough Island Story, unbeknownst to those whose trade is to study it, has been permeated by witchcraft, almost to the exclusion of the other factors normally present in political and religious affairs.

The theory, to summarize (I hope not unfairly), is that the witch was essentially a member of a cult-organization, which was not in revolt against Christianity but a wholly independent and older religion, in fact the paganism of pre-Christian Western Europe surviving for centuries after a nominal conversion. Its worship was directed to a two-faced, horned god, identifiable with Janus or Dianus (who is fully described in the early chapters of *The Golden Bough*) and with the Celtic Cernunnos; inquisitors in their ignorance and bigotry confused this deity with the Church's Satan, but his claims in fact were hardly less respectable than Jehovah's and locally had priority. Indeed the cult was the real popular religion of England and several neighbouring countries throughout the Middle Ages; Christianity was a mere official veneer, adopted from policy, to which rulers enforced an outward conformity. Even rulers who did so, however, could not really afford to suppress the witch-cult (or, as Miss Murray preferred to call it, Dianism). For its practices, far from being malign or anti-social, were generally considered necessary for the well-being of the community, as they had been in the days of open paganism; and for this cause they were secretly encouraged, down to the time of the Reformation, by the highest persons in the state and precisely those who were publicly committed to abhorrence of the horned god and all his works.

We are told that the cult, which seems to have been monotheistic, had an elaborate organization based on the coven of thirteen, which ran through all classes of society and included kings and their ministers, and even nominally Christian prelates. The part these played had, of course, to be heavily camouflaged and is never made explicit in contemporary chronicles because of the bias of their monastic authors. (The fact that monastic chroniclers are often biassed appears to be claimed by Miss Murray as a discovery.)

The most important part of the rituals, from the public point of view and to these distinguished supporters, was the periodical sacrifice of the king, or a king-substitute. This took place according to a seven-year cycle, and the prosperity of the kingdom depended on it, for reasons that Frazer and Graves have made familiar. The witch-cult, or the Dianic religion, was in fact a pagan system of the same general type as is described in *The Golden Bough*, and which is sometimes held to have been universal at a certain stage of man's development. It was the cult of a god perennially dying and ever reborn, representing the crops or the seasons, himself represented by a king who must also die violently in his prime in order to renew the vigour of the deity on whose recurrent revival after death (as corn, or summer) the whole people depended. This rite had therefore still to be performed after the nominal conversion of the Western European nations, and (we are told) it actually was so, in conformity to the ancient sacrificial cycle; though in these last days of its strength it always had to be contrived under cover of some official, non-pagan explanation. The victim, who had to die at a stated season of a stated year, might actually be the king; of this, William Rufus supplies an instance. More often, however, the real king might be spared for another seven years of usefulness by choosing a substitute, who must be someone specially close to the king whether in blood, in public honours, or in the coven-hierarchy. Thomas à Becket was one such substitute; and so were both Joan of Arc and Gilles de Rais ("Bluebeard") in France. Both these two last were active members of the cult, and Joan's title of "la Pucelle" ("the Maid") refers to her position as "Maid" (an essential officer of all covens) in the Supreme Coven of France, to which the Dauphin Charles belonged. There are many other examples; in England the succession of ritual victims was preserved down to the reign of James I.

The element of human sacrifice and the virtual universality of the cult at all social levels are the two most startling of Miss Murray's claims. As regards the village witch, the coven, and the Sabbat she is mainly concerned to emphasize the status of "Dianism" (so to call it) as a religion, comparable with Christianity and wholly independent of Christian influence. Dianism borrowed nothing from Christianity; it did, however, offer many parallels in its observances, and in some respects the coven was able to influence the Church (which seems, if I have understood Miss Murray aright, to have borrowed details of its organization). Certainly, the hold of the coven over the public mind was so much firmer than the Church's that the latter's efforts to destroy or resist it were of the feeblest kind until, with the Reformation, Christianity at last—though still not all at once—became a popular religion and could dare to launch a vigorous persecution.

Miss Murray's views have received praise and imitation, but she hardly founded a school of Dianic studies, and I do not know how far I am justified in speaking of a "Murrayite" party. I must make plain that I do so merely for convenience, to include those whose works show them to have been strongly under her influence, not necessarily those who acknowledge her as an authority. Indeed, these two categories bear no resemblance to one another. I understand it to include, for example, Mr. Pennethorne Hughes and Mr. Hugh Ross Williamson, whose writings though less wild on the historical side have obviously taken a good deal of colour from hers. I would exclude Mr. Trevor Davies, who seems to recognize Miss Murray as authoritative but actually favours the Bluff party. I would, however, include Mr. Lewis Spence, whose independent work on fairies and related questions has filled in some of the background to Miss Murray's picture; in general outline these two were agreed, and while I am treating of her subject I suppose I need not justify my allotting Miss Murray the priority.

Fairies indeed enter into the creed of Dianism. The party would have it that they were the dwindling remnant of a former ruling race, displaced and driven into hiding by invaders of inferior culture. In their retreat they retained their special skills, in manufactures and so forth, and probably they were of small stature; hence the general characters of the legends their supplanters concocted about them. They were naturally worshippers of Dianus, and their closest contacts with the ordinary population were with the witches; indeed, it is highly probable that the secret lore of the witches was derived almost wholly from such contact and was rooted in the traditions of the elder race as well as the elder gods. Theories on these lines have a familiar ring and have been aired since the latter part of the nineteenth century at least, though the connection with witchcraft is more narrowly a point of Murrayism. I believe similar explanations exist for much other folklore, Robin Hood and Arthur and so forth; but I do not think these will prove relevant to our main purpose.

It is broadly characteristic of all these suggestions that they would be perfectly credible (with reservations) if they happened to deal with an imaginary country or one without historical records, and are therefore credible, when applied to Britain, to those who have concentrated their attention on other fields of study than history and its ancillary disciplines. They plainly belong to the sphere of the possible, even if it is on occasion an "improbable-possible"; while as against the other naturalistic explanations in the field they have the merit of actually explaining something.

There are probably other schools of thought in existence, of a more obviously eccentric character. I should be surprised if nobody has put forward a theory that would make witchcraft the last degenerate trace of the spiritual sciences that came to us from lost Atlantis. But the weirder kinds of Pharaonic fancies and latter-day gnosticisms can fitly be regarded as Anti-Sadducee splinters; and in any case they only normally touch our subject through White Magic, so called, and will have to be discussed, if at all, under that head. I propose, so long as I remain argumentative rather than speculative, to reduce the range of alternative opinions to two, those two that have been most vehemently urged in recent years: that witches really served Satan in the flesh, and that they really worshipped "Dianus," with all the corollaries that are held to follow from each view by its supporters.

Now some of these corollaries may with convenience be set aside at this stage, because they concern details only associated with witchcraft at all by one school or the other, and if the other or the one is right they have no place in our purview. We can thus attempt to determine how far both of them understand the word "witch" in the same sense, even if both of them are wrong.

We can drop off the Black Mass, and the *contractual* relation between the Devil and his devotees, which whether or not they occurred at all are only associated with witchcraft by those who assume witches consciously worshipped the principle of Evil; and the selling of souls, of course, if it actually took place, must have been to a real, not an imagined, Satan. On the other hand, the periodic cycle of human sacrifice is specially a feature of the Murrayite interpretation, never dwelt on by others; and of course the identification of the victim as a "divine king" on Frazer's lines is even more exclusively an "anthropological" hypothesis. Moreover, such a custom, like the Black Mass, could imaginably coexist with witchcraft in one society and not be a part of witchcraft. It will be convenient to set apart the questions whether such practices were followed at all, and by whom; and to turn for the moment to what supporters of both views would agree to be characteristics central to witchcraft, however each might choose to interpret them.

In the first place, both the Anti-Sadducees and the Murrayites think of witches primarily as members of a cult. Both accept pretty much the same *external* picture of the cult; both, I mean, would give much the same description, with a different choice of adjectives, of what witches *did* on their great corporate occasions. They would not find it so easy to agree what witches *were*. Both would accept the picture entertained by judges and pamphleteers in the great scare period, of the organization, the coven, and its major festival, the Sabbat. The details of this last would naturally appear more lurid in an Anti-Sadducee account, and perhaps more uniform, certainly more solemn, in a Murrayite; but a substantial measure of agreement would remain.

They would agree that it was primarily an act of worship; they would
give similar accounts of the kind of worship paid and of the outward
appearance of the god. Both, moreover, would be prepared to go
beyond the trial evidence in ascribing to the cult a very ancient origin
and very distinguished support. (Both would probably agree, for
instance, that Gilles de Rais had been a member.) It may be added
that both parties are concerned to represent the cult as an intelligible
and connected system of belief, however horrible or however mistaken;
witchcraft, to both, is *logical*.

This leaves, apart from marginal matter, some few central and
basic points at issue between them; but some of these are not so
crucial, for our purpose, as they must appear to an adherent of either
party. There is, first, the question whether witches really enjoyed
supernatural favour. Of course, we are apt to assume they did not,
and that is my own opinion; but as I have said, the Anti-Sadducees
can put up a case and later this case will have to be answered. Still,
the question of theoretical possibility can wait for the moment and in
my opinion should; it can only be discussed from a very private standpoint, and we ought first to seek what measure of agreement we can.
In any case, supposing *per impossibile* that the Devil in person was
really supplying the witches with supernatural powers, he clearly may
have done so under the cover-name of a pagan god, and been worshipped, if at all, as such.[10]

There is next, of course, the question of the *moral* standing of the
cult; but this again is scarcely crucial. The attempt to clear it of all
obscene, anti-social, or blasphemous elements, which appears to be
private to Miss Murray in her later works, could be dropped and still
leave the "anthropological" explanation unscathed. There is no need
to prove that the "Dianic" religion was not priapic, in order to prove
that it was a religion; nor even that it inculcated any particular morality. Witchcraft could be proved utterly loathesome without telling us
whether Margaret Murray or Montague Summers were right on any
other point.

There is lastly the question that most concerns us: did the cult
originate right outside Christianity, probably long before Christ, or
is it a rebellion, a parody, consciously counter-Christian? This also is
not quite so absolute a difference between the parties as might appear;
for, this time, the Murrayite view might be accepted without finally

[10]Logically, I will admit, this is back to front; I am adopting a subjective order of
importance that would, I think, be acceptable to the majority of enquirers in our
own day.

silencing the Anti-Sadducees. If the Devil was the cult's inventor, he may have designed it as a Christian parody *before* Christ (supposing, as generally has been supposed, that he can foretell the future); and in any case he had time, after the Incarnation, to frame and establish his rival sect in unconverted Western Europe. Actually, I think most Anti-Sadducees would rather favour this view. It would, after all, establish that, *if* witchcraft was Satanism, it was the work of a real Satan and not just something concocted by nasty-minded human beings. It is not really in controversy between these two parties that witchcraft and Christianity have certain elements in common, either because the Devil is the *simius Dei* or because Christ is just another variant on the *Rex Nemorensis*.

The basic question, whether witchcraft was Dianism or diabolism, emerges from these three. One ought perhaps to add a fourth, what witches *thought* it was; but I am not sure that this, if answered, would be generally regarded as conclusive either way, or whether the Murray-ite party would be prepared to accept any evidence on the point as free from ecclesiastical prejudice.

I think we can now see that the common ground between the Murrayite and Anti-Sadducee parties is more considerable than might have been expected. It would not be an impossible task to reconcile them, though in doing so one would make enemies on both sides. In any case it gives us something to work on; if we have not quite got a definition even now, we have at least the chance of being able to tell whether the evidence as to fact refers or does not refer to the kind of witch we are considering. Henceforward I shall refer to her as "the witch" simply. I shall also speak of her as "her," in deference to common custom, though one of the points of detail in our common ground is that the witch is, in fact, by no means necessarily a woman. Another detail of the common ground is that the modern works of both parties are based, to the point of cribbing, on the same evidence. To this evidence, and the picture it actually reveals, it is time to turn.

CHAPTER TWO

Light from the Obscure Men

THE DIRECT EVIDENCE for the practices of the witch-cult is derived almost wholly from a single type of source, and mainly from a relatively short period. This, of course, is the judicial material produced in the great scare of the sixteenth and early seventeenth centuries (which I shall call for the sake of brevity the Age of Neurosis). It is important to note that this period was the only one in the history of Christian Western Europe that has produced any bulk of such material; and not only do most of the known trials fall within it but so also do most of the outbreaks of popular hysteria. Witchcraft, of course, has been believed in and feared before and since; but only in that age has there been any widespread panic or one that infected the educated as well as the ignorant classes throughout a European nation. I am bound to say, however, that this is much more the case with Britain than with the Continent; in France, in Germany, and in Switzerland the late Middle Ages had seen minor outbreaks of a hysteria which seems to have passed Britain by till after the Reformation.

I should make it clear at this point that when I talk of "hysteria" and of "infecting the educated" I am not seeking to prejudge any issue that is genuinely in controversy. There can be no serious doubt, whatever view of witches we take, that the fear of them at this time was enough to distort men's judgement. Nobody need deny, and probably no thinking person would, that many who died for the crime of witchcraft were unjustly condemned, not necessarily because witchcraft does not exist or, existing, is not a crime, but because they, individually, were not witches. Indeed this can be shown on evidence at least as good as witchcraft itself can afford. We know of witches who confessed; we also know of perjured accusers who confessed, of witch-suspects who retracted confessions extorted by torture or prompted by despair, and of a very few judgements that were reversed and miscarriages of justice detected too late. It is fair to assume that there were far more such cases than ever came to light. Some of the fullest accounts of trials betray in the minds of the judges utter confusion of thought and a rooted prejudice against the accused. Even if we had no record of this, it would be fair to expect it when so learned and influential a jurist as Jean Bodin allowed his judicial sense to be so far warped on this subject as to lay down that only the strongest proofs of innocence should be accepted against an accusation of witchcraft. It is clear, moreover, that those few who could furnish such proofs remained permanently stigmatized in the popular mind, sometimes in the official mind also, from the fact of having been accused. This kind of thing is not unfamiliar in the modern age; and it serves to explain some apparently free confessions. A suspect if she got off with her life would probably lose her livelihood; an old woman dependent on the charity of neighbours would lose her hope even of alms and might well wish rather to die.

It seems only too clear that justice for suspected witches in the Age of Neurosis was vitiated by the idea, common in Congressional committees, that when a crime is very dangerous and very horrible society cannot afford the risk of a fair trial. And there are, of course, other reasons for taking the evidence produced by these trials at something less than its face value. In most countries affected, except England, torture was normally employed to extract confessions. In all countries the courts recognized tests of witchcraft which rested on no sound knowledge but only on popular tradition; and these tests could be made a very effective substitute for torture where this was not legal. A more technical, but quite crucial, point has often been overlooked: much of the contemporary material on which investigators have relied is itself secondary; not the official record of a trial but a horror-pamphlet purporting to tell the story. Some of these have been shown fairly conclusively to be mere sensational fictions.[1]

Other similar caveats will call for a mention; and there remains more to be said about the great scare. As, however, this is the one aspect of the history of witchcraft which can be, and has been, written

---

[1] E.g., the "Campden Wonder," for which see the collection with that title edited by Sir G. N. Clark (also discussed by Hugh Ross Williamson in *Historical Whodunits*, but less reliably).

For the general subject of exploded scares, see R. Trevor Davies, *Four Centuries of Witch Beliefs*, especially caps. 4 and 5.

as history properly so called, there is little need to go into it here at length. Even so, there are several points of interest about it, which may be dealt with more appropriately as they become relevant, and some of which we shall need to bear in mind and had best set out now.

The origins of the panic are obscure, though some of the agencies by which it spread can be guessed at. The main question is, of course: why should a period generally hailed as the dawn of modern enlightenment have much worse trouble from the fear of witches than earlier ages? To this the age itself had an answer: that the malice of the Devil had singled it out, and there was in fact more witchcraft about than there had been. It is plainly conceivable also that there had been no increase, but the danger had newly come to be recognized for what it was; or, as the Murrayites claim, Church and state now for the first time dared to exert power and propaganda against it. Or it may be that the intellectual history of the age, more closely examined, will reveal the seeds of new error as well as new truth. But we are not ready to discuss this question adequately as yet.

The geographical incidence is curious. If one were to plot the panic on a map, giving a dot to every person known to have been executed in the material time (taking this either at its widest, c. 1300–1700, or at its narrowest, c. 1550–1650), the storm-centre would probably be about Basel, where France, Germany, and Switzerland meet. There would be a considerable blot at that point, and at Lyons, Geneva, Nuremburg, and other places in their general neighbourhood. A trail of blots would run across Switzerland and some way beyond, east and west, and another at right angles up the Rhine to Amsterdam. From this main concentration the speckling of the map would shade off, north, east, and west into blankness (most gradually to the east), with minor blots in eastern Scotland; in England the speckling would be slight and mainly concentrated in the east. Southward, the map would be white; there was almost no significant heightening of witch-mania in Italy, and on Spanish history of the time the panic seems to have left no trace at all.

It will be seen that there is no correlation between witchcraft or the fear of it and "superstition" in matters of religion generally; nor between witchcraft and backwardness in other spheres. As the intensity of the panic could vary remarkably between one part and another of the same country, it is impossible to account for the variations entirely on the ground of different policies in different states; and though at first sight the area of the Black Mass seems strangely divorced from the area of the Mass, there were centres of repression both on Roman Catholic and on Protestant soil. It is, however, worth noting that, taking both time and place, there is a kind of correlation between a virulent witch-hunting temper and a weak or popular system of ecclesiastical discipline. Wherever a strongly authoritarian hierarchy was firmly in the saddle, as in the Lutheran states of Germany, England till the time of the Civil War, and most countries that remained subject to the Papacy (especially Spain), there witch-hunting was kept within bounds. It became a massacre where ecclesiastical affairs were in a state of chaos, as in France, or where discipline was imposed from below upwards, as in the Calvinist states and generally in free cities; and broadly wherever two or more religions were struggling for the mastery. This does not hold good quite universally; Sweden at the material time was as rigidly Lutheran as she is today, and she suffered at least one bad scare; while Hungary and Bohemia were ravaged by religious dissension but not noticeably by witches; and one might say roughly the same for Ireland, Wales, and the west of England, where the fate of the Reformation was long in the balance. But it is to be remarked that the generalization holds good at the centre and breaks down at the periphery, which is on the whole a good thing for a generalization to do.

Broadly, we might expect to find that the witch-scare was the work of the same kind of people who took to Protestantism (not always the same people); that it first took hold of the educated laity of the new Middle Classes and the have-not minor clergy, and later spread in simplified form to the mass of the People by means of conscious propaganda by the two former groups. This, indeed, is more or less what we do find. One could search long before one found, in this period, a witch-hunting bishop. The most energetic and vocal Anti-Sadducees were mostly lay lawyers or popular preachers of Reformation. This is, I think, specially clear in England but there is a general tendency that way. In France, Bodin, the judge who formulated the most drastic set of rules for witch-hunting in the courts, was a sceptic in religion and incidentally a man of unquestionable learning. All the main reforming theologians, Luther, Melanchthon, Zwingli, and especially Calvin, lent the weight of their authority to the growing fear of Satanism. It was, of course, strictly with Satanism and not with any more or less amoral spell-casting that these were concerned. Any of the intellectual leaders of the day, on the Protestant side, would start out with a bias against belief in the efficacy of ceremonies and forms of words to work a supernatural effect. But equally their bias against these in religion predisposed them to believe that the Devil might be ready to make use of them for purposes of delusion. The Devil himself was very far from a delusion in their eyes.

The people at large naturally made no such distinctions; nor do the educated laity, amateur theologians as they often were, seem to have troubled about them overmuch. Information rather than thought seems to have been the goal of the new reading public, then as later. Indeed, when we consider the history of the "mass media" of Public Opinion, from the printing press to television, we are bound to ask ourselves whether any advance in the technique of spreading information and discussion further afield does not necessarily involve, at least at first, vulgarizing and lowering their mental level. The prophets and columnists of that age were capable as never before of collecting and disseminating fact or fancy about witches, but not (it would seem) of digesting it.

It must be remembered that one of the classes of literature involved was translations of the Bible. The word "witch" itself, and references to related ideas, occur fairly frequently in the Authorized Version. In no single instance is the translation not open to question, and it becomes of importance to note that this translation was made when Anti-Sadducism was at its peak in English academic circles. This is only one example, and relatively late, of what was going on throughout the Protestant world; the verbal inspiration of the Bible was being stressed at the same time (and by the same people) as the words themselves were being given, in all good faith, a party slant.

The Bible can hardly be cited as a witness against the supernatural; but actually nearly all its references to "witchcraft" can be interpreted in a naturalistic sense, as referring either to poisoners or to *pretended* soothsayers. The Jewish translators of the Septuagint seem on the whole to have favoured interpretations on these lines where we cannot, and probably even they could not be sure of the full implications of the original Hebrew. Jerome, in the Vulgate, habitually gives *veneficus* or a derivative where *maleficus* would be less ambiguous. *Veneficus* certainly came nearer the Greek and had the double sense; the ideas of poison and witchcraft are fairly closely related, and by the Renaissance period the word was generally used in the sense the Protestant translators gave it.

It may be added that it would hardly have been less "superstitious" of them to translate "poisoner." The Renaissance was an age when poison was regarded, with deep interest and profound ignorance, not indeed *as* magic (they drew the distinction, though it would not be easy to say where), but as something nearly as potent and nearly as mysterious. By some it was regarded with much more horror. Thus, in England, a poison scare under Henry VIII produced panic legislation that defined murder wrought by this means as high treason and prescribed boiling alive as the punishment. Much later, under Elizabeth, witchcraft for the first time became a capital crime against the state, but only when it was used to procure a death; later again, under James I, all witchcraft was made a felony, but neither of these acts distinguished it from other felonies in procedure or penalty.[2]

It must, of course, be borne in mind that poison and sorcery could easily be employed by the same people, and to those who believe in sorcery the distinction between them is not easy to draw. This may perhaps be allowed to moderate the horror we ought to feel in the face of the persecutions launched under the influence of the great witch-scares. The relative mildness of the English courts was only relatively mild; in Europe generally, civil governments in this age were only too ready—in heresy as well as in witchcraft—to learn and improve on the worst lessons the old Inquisition could teach. Between them, the printing press and the Reformation had made theological speculation available to the Million; and, as theologians for some time previously had been moving towards the Anti-Sadducee extreme, the ordinary rustic fear of hobgoblins suddenly became respectable as abhorrence of Satan and all his works. This may be allowed to serve for the moment as a capsule thesis to explain the panic. It is not fully adequate, and of course it has itself to be explained. What put theologians on this course is a point that will be touched on later; for the moment I am still anxious not to prejudge the issue between the parties. We are still concerned to discuss where the parties got their facts from.

Whatever one thinks of witchcraft, there is no doubt that the minds of the witch-hunters were in a state of alarm and confusion; we need to be cautious how we accept the evidence they extracted from their suspects either as the evidence of real witches (people, I mean, who would have given the name to themselves) or as true answers to the right questions. Given that torture was used, it is more important to know why a question was asked than how it was answered. The judges were investigating crime, not folklore; inevitably they brought to their work a picture already formed of what they were looking for. We have to consider what factors went to the making of the picture of witchcraft-as-crime that courts in the panic period would entertain.

[2]Acts against witchcraft: 5 Elizabeth I, cap. 16, and 1 James I, cap. 12. Cf. Act against Poisoners, 22 Henry VIII, cap. 9.

It is important to understand that, in other respects besides being more generally feared and more often subject to the lay courts, the legal status and usual mental picture of sorcery had profoundly changed since the High Middle Ages. Up to about the time that the Inquisition began its activities in the thirteenth century, the secular law if it took account of magic at all made a sharp distinction between White and Black. It was sometimes felt that sorcery might be employed by the courts themselves to determine matters of fact, though this—not surprisingly—remained a speculative opinion (trial by ordeal was not regarded as magical). The systems of law native to Western Europe made a large allowance for the supernatural, and the progressive lawyers of the twelfth century and later, deriving their ideas from Roman Law, accepted the reality of magic both beneficent and malign. But in practice this was a very recondite branch of legal studies, with which the lay courts had little to do. The Church courts enforced the Church's own legislation on the subject, but with no great severity so far as we can tell; and neither Church nor state seems to have felt any lively alarm about the danger of sorcery.

By the end of the Middle Ages a great change had taken place. All sorcery was held to be criminal and widely felt to be the most dangerous of all crimes. Hysterical fear of it was general among the public at large and usually shared, even if it was not actually encouraged, by the authorities. This fear drove civil governments into pursuing witchcraft in competition with the churches. Ironically, the Inquisition lost a near-monopoly by the very magnitude of its own success; for there is little reason to doubt that the Inquisition was mainly responsible, if not for the panic, at least for the official change of attitude.

From the thirteenth century on, the Holy Office had been taking cognizance of accusations involving sorcery and diabolism, as special cases within its normal field of religious infidelity. The Inquisitors were therefore the experts; though actually such cases accounted for only a small part of their work, at least until the reorganization of the Reformation period. This was not for want of trying. Like any other great organization, the Inquisition was less monolithic than it looked; it contained its internal parties and cliques, and right at the end of the Middle Ages there arose within it something like a witch-hunters' lobby. This launched the first propaganda drive of the Anti-Sadducee movement—backed, of course, with evidence acquired by the Inquisitorial process.

The Inquisition was developed as a kind of Papal Scotland Yard to deal with the first popular heresies. It was meant to supplement, assist, and streamline the normal authorities, not to replace them; it had no overriding powers and wielded its vast influence solely on account of its prestige. It was not the only machinery for pursuing heresy, but it won the reputation of being the best. Its methods were admired and its aid was sought by local authorities faced by the kind of problem it was adapted to deal with, though never automatically; it was never invited to establish itself in England, for example, and without invitation, without the positive encouragement of the state, it was powerless. As a further result, it was imitated. The closest as well as the most celebrated imitation was the Spanish Inquisition, which operated in nearly the same sphere, but the most important instance for our purpose was the widespread adoption of its procedure by lay criminal courts.

It was its innovations in procedure that principally distinguished the Holy Office among the ecclesiastical courts and gave it its reputation as a specially efficient protection against Dangerous Thoughts. The Inquisition did not depend on informers to bring accusations, but maintained its own prosecutions staff, then a rarity. It interrogated the accused, and subject to certain limitations it could employ torture in doing so. Witnesses for the prosecution were not (normally) subject to cross-examination except by the court itself, and at the court's discretion could remain anonymous. The court also maintained strict control of the defence; whereas in most courts in the Middle Ages the accused had the choice of several procedures for establishing his innocence, the Inquisition need hardly leave him any way open to do so. Virtually it conducted both prosecution and defence at its own unfettered discretion and then judged between them. The accused was supposed, if possible, to be advised by his own confessor or by an advocate appointed by the court; but even this could be refused, and about the only line of defence recognized as legitimate was an accusation of malice against the witnesses.[3]

It is essential to bear in mind that as against the ordinary criminal process the object of the Inquisition was to secure repentance rather than retribution. From the personal point of view of the accused, this was an advantage that ought not to be overlooked; from a judicial point of view it had a disastrous influence on that and other courts,

[3]Lea's *History of the Inquisition* is of course the main authority, but the point is specially borne out in the *Malleus Maleficarum*.

from the tendency it encouraged to regard the extracting of confessions as practically an end in itself, inducements, as well as threats, being a permissible means thereto. Moreover, the Inquisition's responsibility in the very subtle matter of heresy made it inevitable that the court should sometimes suggest to the accused what it was he was required to confess. When it is added that the regulations, in practice, left the court ample oportunity to use torture or physical coercion of one kind or another, it will be seen that some caution is necessary in handling evidence derived from these confessions. It is only just to add at this point that such caution must be doubled in dealing with matter accepted by secular or Protestant tribunals that took the Holy Office as their model; these unprofessional searchers of souls generally acted with a great deal less restraint and under a great deal more pressure from government or from hysterical public opinion.

For the Inquisition was widely imitated, not always with understanding or even consciously; and for reasons outside our present subject this was especially the case in the sixteenth century. Witchcraft was about the most important factor in direct and conscious borrowing, at least reckoning by the mere bulk of cases. Here the eager champions of True Religion in the Reformation period had the benefit of a handbook—the *Malleus Maleficarum* of the fifteenth-century Dominicans, Kramer and Sprenger. This work became the classic authority on the subject, in an age when every department of knowledge still required a classic authority; it was the Bible, the Aristotle, the Code of the Anti-Sadducees. It was accepted both as an academic defence of orthodoxy and as a guide for the courts; though its claim to be either was not so strong as on the surface it might appear.

Heinrich Kramer, or Institoris, was an unusually credulous man for his age; as Inquisitor in the Tyrol he had taken it on himself to combat the direct intervention of the Devil in that province, and by his most un-judicial ferocity had earned himself powerful enemies. He left the Tyrol suddenly and under a cloud; but he gained the ear of Pope Innocent VIII, a native of Genoa and therefore of a region where the wilder stories about the Waldensians were particularly current. The Pope commissioned him (by the Bull *Summis Desiderantes* of 1484) to put the world right on the danger of sorcery, in collaboration with Jacob Sprenger of Basel, Prior of the Dominicans in Cologne. As the work was to vindicate Kramer, he was presumably the main author; but Sprenger being the more reputable, it was represented as his. Anybody might have supposed that Sprenger's office implied a close connection with the Theological Faculty at Cologne, which in fact it did not. But he had unofficial influence in the University, which he exerted to persuade the Faculty to license the *Malleus* as dogmatically sound. This, unexpectedly, the Faculty would not do; the junior members supported Sprenger, whom doubtless they did not care to offend, but the senior did not care whom they offended. Now, Cologne was the centre of Dominican studies in Germany and otherwise a school of no importance; its declaration of independence on the witchcraft issue was a grave defeat for Sprenger and for witch-hunting, and had to be disguised from the world. A most disingenuous notarial act was composed, designed to give the impression that the book had been approved by the Faculty to anyone unfamiliar with the forms usually employed; and this was appended to all editions *except* those issued at Cologne itself. This involved actual perjury only by the Yeoman Bedell, in his deposition to the notary that the rest of the Faculty agreed with the deponents (who were the juniors, but the outside world would not know this). Kramer and Sprenger presumably followed the established custom of the Holy Office and absolved each other. The ruse succeeded beyond its deserts; the Inquisition itself seems never to have adopted the text, but few in after ages were to observe that the work stood recommended to the world by a Papal Bull issued *before* it was written, and by a tissue of evasions purporting to be the act of a minor university. Nor did the world understand that neither author held senior academic office, and, while one had been an unsuccessful Inquisitor, the other had not been an Inquisitor at all.[4]

The *Malleus* was accepted at its authors' valuation; what later judges knew or thought they knew of witchcraft was what it told them. It remains then to examine what it says.

It does not attempt a definition of the word *malefica*, nor any justification of the use of the feminine gender. Its argument, as a result, is largely vitiated by the Undistributed Middle, the authors taking for granted the existence of a uniform category "witch," or, in terms that would be more familiar to them, a Real Universal. While the abstract part of the argument is at fault in this, it may be allowed that the concrete examples go some way to excuse it, as they are drawn from a single geographical region in which uniformity might well be presumed. This is the region to which both authors were native—roughly speaking, German Switzerland. If the *Malleus* is trustworthy

---

[4]Lea, *Materials toward a History of Witchcraft* (building upon Hansen), here considerably modifies the impression given in his earlier *History of the Inquisition* (cap. 6).

for nothing else, it is good authority for the sense in which the word *hexe* was understood in that area in the fifteenth century.

There is nothing at all about the coven in the *Malleus*; neither is there anything directly about the Sabbat, but on the whole the arrangement of Part II, Question I, makes better sense if we suppose the authors had it in the back of their minds. They do speak of witch-assemblies, of supernatural means of transport thereto, homage to the Devil in bodily form, and subsequent copulation (subsequent in the chapter-order) with *incubus* or *succubus* according to sex.[5] The next subject treated is the part played in sorcery by the Christian sacraments perverted from their proper use. The "Black Mass" is only one example of this, but it seems to be the reason that the matter is raised at this point. The arrangement strongly suggests a picture of the Sabbat as an assembly to which numbers of witches came from a distance, being transported through the air; where new members of the sect were initiated as the first ceremony, or preliminary private business; and where this was followed by the orgiastic element of the rites and finally by the Black Mass, which might be considered a part of, or be confused with, the witches' own ritual feast or *agape*. This gives broadly the Anti-Sadducee view of the essentials.

It might be said, though the *Malleus* of course does not say so, that while the Sabbat would include all these elements they could each occur separately. This I imagine was the authors' view. As to riding through the air, they plainly considered it was confined to attendance on the Devil, or nearly so; but this was the least important element from a ritual point of view. Moreover, they recognized that it could be a delusion on occasion. I believe it was not till later that the Holy Office could produce case-histories of such delusion; Kramer and Sprenger considered themselves bound, probably wrongly, by the "Canon *Episcopi*" (see pages 106 f.), which appeared to condemn such a belief as a delusion arising from dreams. The initiation of new witches, the embrace of the Demon Lover, and the Black Mass could all take place in private. Indeed, the tendency of the examples quoted is to emphasize the *secretiveness* of the cult, and to that extent the *Malleus* is inconvenient material for the Murrayites, though almost anybody else, of course, would expect it in an assembly of sorcerers.

The investigators of sorcery in the sixteenth and seventeenth centuries, unlike those of the two previous, had academic authority to go on, even if it was in many ways besides its Latin the kind of academic authority that the *Epistoli Obscurorum Virorum* held up to

[5]For these terms, see appendix C.

ridicule. One effect of its scholastic origin was that the *Malleus* imposed on witchcraft an order and a uniformity that quite possibly did not belong to it by nature. Indeed, I suppose some such order in the judges' minds was a necessity if judicial investigations were to be made on the grand scale. It was no use putting a suspect on the rack if you did not know what questions to ask, especially if the suspect did not know herself what answers were required. The *Malleus* was exceedingly helpful in this respect.[6] Nevertheless, the appearance of uniformity thus imposed on the cult, and the appearance of a cult imposed on the practice, were, as we must recognize, wholly artificial. Many Renaissance writings on the subject, as well, probably, as many trials, were rendered worthless by the tendency, which is still with us, to presume the whole of the cult where one of its elements exists, counting everything down to talisman-peddling and the Evil Eye as such an element. It is perhaps unkind to say that the age of the Counter-Reformation herein was applying what was in the days of Frazer the "anthropological" approach.

However, far more important than any idea of witchcraft that the *Malleus* conveyed was the seal of orthodoxy it conferred on the *fact* of "witchcraft" undefined. It persuaded the educated classes that sorcery occurred; and thereby persuaded the secular courts that it was a particularly dangerous crime. The courts were therefore open to receive charges framed by mere popular superstition and owing nothing to Kramer and Sprenger except the chance to be heard. We have no means of knowing how ready the common people in former times would have been to bring such accusations; but there is every reason to believe that, once started, the panic increased itself, by mutual infection of judges, preachers, pamphleteers, and the public. Our problem is not made any easier by the fact that the media of this infection, the propaganda pamphlets, form the bulk of the source-material on which such as Miss Murray have relied; and probably the writers of these were more prone than judges or people to the error just alluded to, of presuming the whole of a hypothetical unity wherever a part was present.

How, then, ought these parts to have been distinguished? I myself would break the cases down into five main classes, while admitting that probably it would have saved no innocent lives if this had been done at the time, for the five classes each involve a conceivable crime though a different crime. The first would include all cases that turned wholly on the "Evil Eye" and induced diabolic possession. These,

---

[6]The whole of Part III refers.

which were linked together at the time, do not on any theory pre-
suppose either spell-casting or membership of a counter-Christian
movement, though they would generally be taken to indicate a *private*
pact with the Devil.[7] Belief in the Evil Eye seems to have been responsible for a very large part of the popular hysteria, especially that part
which was inspired by the fears of neurotic children; and a high
proportion of the cases where perjury and faked evidence were afterwards discovered were of this nature. In wholly false, that is wholly
insincere, accusations it would be natural to find some borrowings
from other trials, and in Sweden and New England it is clear that
even children were capable of this; but it seems only to have occurred
in communities specially open to the propaganda of Puritan alarm-
ists. In general, it seems to have been fear of the Evil Eye above all
other fears that could be used by malice to work on the popular mind.
On a more sophisticated level, the Loudun case, on which Mr. Huxley
has told us rather more than is known,[8] was a case of supposed induced
demoniac possession afterwards recognized to be false. There is next
the class of cases that turn on positive, deliberate sorcery (which of
course might be beneficent in intention) but are silent on cult practices. Third and fourth come those that offer evidence of association
with the Devil ("pact" evidence) or with other witches ("coven"
evidence), the last of course requiring some other evidence to make
it witchcraft. Lastly there is the evidence that purports to give a
full account of the Sabbat, which naturally includes the third and
fourth classes.

The order in which I have placed them is roughly the order in
which I guess they would rank for quantity, had this division been
made at the time. Actually, evidence of the third class was never considered necessary and evidence of the fourth class was always sought,
whatever the original character of the charge. The fifth class, which
is the one we are concerned to look for, is the rarest and the most
suspect. It is mostly very late, and many admirably full accounts are
on one ground or another obviously inadmissible. On the whole, the
stories about the Sabbat come to us with poor credentials. We need
not assume on that account that the Sabbat did not exist; but the

[7]That is, a friend of the Devil's could "ill-wish" an enemy, who would then be
"possessed." This was the usual form of the belief in the sixteenth and seventeenth
centuries, and was probably a *rationalization* of the primitive feeling that anyone can
effectively curse anyone else; specially, of course, such persons as are ritually con-
taminating or for any other reason spiritually to be feared, which in some societies
would include *all* women.

[8]Aldous Huxley, *The Devils of Loudun* (see Bibliography).

credibility of the accounts must depend very much more on their content than on their external authority.

Witchcraft was investigated, as a crime against the Church, from the early fourteenth century on; but until the age of the great scares the material produced was hopelessly confused and confusing as regards coven and Sabbat. It became explicit and detailed only as culprits, witnesses, and the judges themselves learned, with the increasing volume of trials, sermons, and pamphlets, what kind of crime they were expected to confess, reveal, or unmask. Even so, it never became uniform. The tendency of the judicial process was both to stimulate any latent superstition in the people, making for confusion, and to fix in the public mind the picture of the witch as a diabolist, making (ultimately) for talk about goats and dark strangers and wild orgies and parodies of the Roman Mass. It may be remembered that in the latter part of the period, over much of the territory affected, the Roman Mass itself was a subject for the wildest misconceptions and for superstitious abhorrence to the simpler Protestants; and dark strangers who roved the country and presided at the meetings of secretive religious groups were often common-or-garden Jesuits or even the prophets of proscribed sects such as the Anabaptists.

(A further related point may as well be made here. Masses are often classified according to their liturgical colour, and of these black is one. The phrase "Black Mass" is rare in this connection, but it does occur; it refers to a private requiem, naturally a not uncommon type of mass in times of persecution.)

But as there is little ground for the view that either the Sabbat or the Black Mass presupposes the other, as the most intelligible accounts would have it that if they co-existed they were always at least notionally distinct, I shall confine myself for the moment to the Sabbat and the worship of the witches' god or devil. The Black Mass may have been a form of such worship, but such indications as we have go to show that it was not the only form nor was that its principal purpose.

Evidence[9] from the fourteenth century describes assemblies of witches; and at these assemblies homage was paid to a god who may or may not be identifiable with the Church's Satan. Previous to the fourteenth century even the vague and suspect indications the Late Middle Ages can supply are wholly lacking. Now, for the general history of the two or three hundred years before we have less evidence than we should like but more by a great deal than many non-historians

[9]Summarized in Lea, *Materials*, p. 230ff.

who have written on the subject have supposed. For the six centuries or so that remain between that and the collapse of the Western Empire, we have good information for some countries in some periods but have to put up with serious gaps. In England we have history that can be so called for all but the century after the Romans left, for which interval we are almost wholly dependent upon a combination of archaeology and guesswork. For the next age, moreover, the narrative is thin to start with and not perfectly reliable. In the Dark Ages our knowledge of English history is below the Western European average, though for the High and Late Middle Ages it is distinctly above it. The age of conversion to Christianity is everywhere a problem, naturally so, since everywhere it either coincided with the dawn of literacy or was followed by very destructive invasions. One of the consequences is that the one age in which we could account easily for any gap in the records is also the one age in which it would not be controversial to say that paganism survived underground. By the time that we have a bulk of evidence really sufficient to challenge such an assertion, it would be conceivable that paganism had had time to die out; and all that bulk leads us to suppose that it had. In particular, one class of evidence is good and relatively abundant for every age after the conversion, namely, the records of the Church. We can trace the history of churches with much more certainty than that of states, because churches were from the first more prolific of the written word. This may well give us a slanted picture of the Dark Ages, but in many ways such material is nonetheless useful evidence of the condition of religion and society. As soon as devotional writings are addressed to the laity, they tell us a good deal about the laity. As often as clerks mention paganism or pagan gods they tell us something of their own attitude to paganism, whether they regarded it as fraud, menace, devilry, or pretty legend. As often as they inveigh against the vices of their age, they tell us what vices they were *not* alarmed at. And there are matters of style, matters of the *total* impression conveyed, that ought not to be altogether disregarded. The history of a universal Church, even of a would-be universal Church, must be to some extent the history of the society it works in.

It is thus fairly safe to say that, when the belief in witchcraft as a form of devil-worship begins to leave literary traces, the belief itself is relatively new among the educated. This occurred much later than the Age of Conversion, or perhaps I should say of official conversion, to Christianity, and our sources of knowledge are much richer and more varied than those I have just mentioned. Certainly we should be very circumspect in approaching any argument which rests on our ignorance of the Middle Ages. How ignorant mediaeval observers were of major social facts of their own day is another question, and perhaps the main question of the book. We have seen that in the fifteenth century men had a picture of the witches' Sabbat which would be recognizable to an Anti-Sadducee or a Murrayite of today. According to the former view, not only their picture of what went on but their interpretation of it was substantially correct. According to the latter their interpretation was wholly misconceived and their knowledge of facts inadequate, men in earlier ages having unluckily failed to observe, or neglected to record, the perpetuation of paganism in their midst. As I have indicated, this view is not altogether easy to maintain; we shall later consider whether there are any grounds for it at all.

In any case, observers of the great scare period have bequeathed to moderns of all parties their picture of the Sabbat and of the witches' cult-practices in general. In considering this picture it is, of course, necessary to bear in mind that the only actual *evidence* for it was derived from confessions, almost all of which were the products of torture or mob-violence if they were not the products of mental disease (as in the notorious case of Major Weir[10]). The vast majority of such evidence is quite worthless, yet there do remain some indications of a fire behind all this smoke. The victims were of the same community as their accusers and must have shared the same system of folklore, so that if they were witches it is probable they understood the term in much the same way. Morever, some have left confessions that irresistibly carry conviction, confessions so graphic and circumstantial that they bear in their *style* the stamp of authenticity. This is a risky kind of criterion, and such plums are rare,[11] but the rarity itself is a kind of corroboration. If the cult did really exist, it would be likely that the drag-net would bring in, besides many innocents, a few, but not less than a few, who were genuinely its members.

It may be as well to say again at this point that we are only concerned with evidence of organization, and of organized worship, among witches. That old women peddled spells, and indeed still peddle them today, is not in dispute. But in the age of the witch-hunts witchcraft was believed to involve something more than this, and it is

[10]For Major Weir, see especially Scott, *Letters on Demonology and Witchcraft*, Letter 9.

[11]Far the best is Isobel Gowdie of Auldearne, extensively quoted in Murray, *Witch-Cult, passim.*

on the nature, and reality, of this something more that the various parties join issue. Our concern is with the Sabbat.

Miss Murray distinguishes two kinds of occasion both ordinarily called "Sabbats"—the Sabbat proper and the "Esbat." There may be some value in this distinction, though the evidence that witches recognized it is inadequate, to say the least. The word "Esbat" occurs in De Lancre's account of witchraft in the Pyrenees, and nowhere else; it occurs in the confession of one suspect, and this confession was not only extracted by torture but given in the Basque language. The probability that De Lancre was mistaken is nearly overwhelming. Still, the fact that "totem" is not really a word in Ojibway has not prevented it from becoming quite a useful one in English. We can use "Esbat," though not quite in Miss Murray's sense, without accepting her whole thesis. To her, the Sabbat was a meeting attended by the general public, while the Esbat was confined to the "coven"; the former was a religious occasion, the latter a session for ritual magic (not an easy distinction to maintain in the circumstances); Sabbats took place on major feasts of the cult, such as Hallowe'en, while Esbats were held according to convenience—they might be held regularly, but their date had no special significance. Since popular tradition does consecrate certain days in the year to the assemblies and high revels of witches, this last distinction is probably worth preserving. There is no reason to suppose it entails the other two.[12] Sabbat and Esbat, however, are *not* distinguished in any account as different types of ceremony, and in discussing the various elements of the Sabbat as ordinarily described we must not presume a particular date for it.

In the general belief (reflected, though not fully developed, in the *Malleus*), witches rode to their assemblies through the air, the exact means of flight varying. The Sabbat was celebrated out of doors and in the presence of the Horned God himself or one who impersonated him. It might begin with initiations or other private business; according to some accounts the presiding devil interrogated his devotees on the harm they had wrought since the last meeting, dealing out rewards and punishments and issuing any necessary instructions. The rites proper would begin with a general act of formal homage to the Devil, the *osculum infame*. The main ceremony would seem to have begun with a round dance and ended with a feast, the details of both varying considerably. We can reasonably place between them, at the moment of highest emotional intensity, the sacrifice or Black Mass, if any such

[12]Murray, *Witch-Cult*, p. 97, quoting De Lancre, *Tableau de l'inconstance des mauvais anges* (Paris, 1613), evidence of Estebene de Cambrue.

took place; also an act of sexual intercourse between the devil and some or all of the female initiates present, which is a detail more uniformly dwelt on in descriptions of the cult than any sacrifice. Miss Murray suggests that this was performed by means of an artificial phallus, and if it actually took place I suppose no one would dispute the suggestion.[13] Either this intercourse or the banquet closed the proceedings, passing without further ceremony to the return flight.

This is the standard picture, and it will next be necessary to consider the different elements in more detail. In doing so it behoves us to see whether, at any stage or on any point, we can safely eliminate from consideration either the Anti-Sadducee or the Murrayite view. By this means we ought to be able to establish, within limits, both how far these two opinions are coherent within themselves and how deeply they really differ from one another.

[13]*Witch-Cult*, p. 179ff.

CHAPTER THREE

Dianus *versus* Diabolus

"DIANUS," according to Frazer, and the Hebrew "Helel," which we translate "Lucifer," both mean "The Shining One." This is a trivial coincidence, but may serve to illustrate what enormous differences of opinion may be at the bottom no more than variant interpretations of a word. Many of the differences between the Anti-Sadducee and the Murrayite views of the Sabbat may appear, or could with a little ingenuity be shown, to be differences about names rather than things. There remain one or two possibilities which would clinch the argument one way or the other. If it could be shown that the witches really did exercise supernatural powers or enjoy the favour of a supernatural being, the matter would be settled; and it would be almost settled, if not quite, if the rites exhibited clear signs of a pre-Christian origin, including the *conscious* worship of a being identifiable as a pre-Christian god. (It would not hurt the essentials of the Murrayite position if this god turned out not to be the god of *The Golden Bough*, provided that he was native to the local soil.)

The central point at issue between the parties is the true identity of this god. Its importance may, perhaps, be exaggerated. If the witches thought their god was the Devil, this may have been a corruption of an earlier belief in Dianus; and if they thought he was Dianus, and always had done so, this belief may still have been inspired by the Devil. The first of these is a possibility to be seriously considered, the second perhaps less so. It is now my purpose to see how far the question can be resolved by examining the details of the Sabbat.

To begin at the beginning, with the witches' means of transport to the meeting, it is perhaps needless to state that there is no objective evidence for flight through the air. What is perhaps more remarkable is that it seems to have been highly unusual even to invent such stories. Nobody seems ever to have observed witches in flight, and, considering that this was the one aspect of the Sabbat which reasonably might have had an eye-witness, it is strange that no more use of it was made by false accusers during the scares. It would seem that this whole subject has acquired more prominence in later folklore than it enjoyed in the panic period. In particular, the idea that witches fly *on broomsticks* appears to be modern. The association between witches and broomsticks may be ancient, but is not anciently connected with flight. (It is sometimes suggested that they used broomsticks as hobbyhorses in some of their dances, and this would explain how the idea of riding on broomsticks arose; this is an ingenious speculation, but speculation merely.) In the time of the great witch-hunts, broadly three methods of transport were recognized: by natural means; by flight on the back of an animal (surprisingly rare; we may include with it the very exceptional instances, confined I think to the Blokula scare, of riding on the ground but on a paranormal steed); and flight by means of an ointment supplied by the Devil, applied to a stick or to the person.

Inquisitors and judges were prepared to admit that such flight might be a delusion in the minds of those who claimed to have experienced it, and on occasion this could be proved.[1] In the early stages of the hysteria, it remained fashionable to be sceptical on this one point, for reasons we shall consider later (see cap. 6). However, there is almost no part of the subject that occupied more of the theologians' attention, and few aspects of witchcraft have been more authoritatively pronounced possible by the Roman church.[2]

Several alleged formulae for the ointments have been collected;[3] they vary, and they have probably been distorted in the interests of

[1]E.g., during the Blokula scare (appendix A below), and cf. Lea, *Materials*, p. 449.

[2]For the discussion, see, e.g., *Malleus*, Pt. II, Question I, cap. 3; Lea, *Materials*, pp. 187–98. For the authoritative pronouncement, Bull *Summis Desiderantes*, Innocent VIII, 1484.

[3]Especially by the rationalists Wier and Reginald Scot; see Murray, *Witch-Cult*, appendix 5.

Wier gives three formulae, viz.: Aconite, Parsley (? or Hemlock), Poplar leaves, Soot; Belladonna, Water parsnip (? or Hemlock), Cinquefoil, Sweet flag, Bat's blood, and oil; Water parsnip, Aconite, Belladonna, Cinquefoil, Baby's fat, Soot (all presumably *quant. suf.*).

Scot has the first two, and includes oil in the first, which of course would not be an ointment without it; he makes it clear that it was added separately. Gardner and Leland (see cap. 10) both regard vervain as the principal ingredient, and it has a considerable reputation as a witch's herb, but it seems not to occur in this context before the nineteenth century.

making them appear gruesome, but it is clear that their effect would be narcotic and (in the only legitimate sense of that misleading word) aphrodisiac; and like many quite ordinary intoxicants they would impair the sense of distance. The question is one to which we shall have to return, but in passing it should be noted that if these ointments were really employed they might help to explain the element of honest self-delusion in the confessions.

We need not dwell upon the "private business" which may or may not have preceded the rites of the Sabbat proper, but the initiation of new members is a matter of some importance. It is mildly surprising to note that witch-finders and judges seem not to have looked for a formal bargain with the Devil on the lines of the Faust legend. The novice supposedly vowed herself to the goat-god's service, and an implicit contract was presumed by such as Kramer and Sprenger; but there seems to have been no talk of a term of years, no contract signed in blood, or anything of that kind. It is true that witches were popularly supposed to make such a bargain, but even manufactured evidence is almost entirely lacking in this particular. The Faustian compact, indeed, as Dr. E. M. Butler has shown,[4] grew out of a quite independent tradition and belongs to the Magia of the study, not of the blasted heath.

The two elements of induction into the cult that bulked large in the public mind in the scare period and before were the "Devil's mark" and the gift of a "familiar." These are to some extent related. The Devil was believed to set his mark in some secret place of the witch's body, which was thereafter insensible to pain (though the marking process itself might be painful[5]). The ideal spot was sometimes held to be the left arm-pit, and the ideal form of the mark a dwarf, supernumerary teat; but there is no reconciling the variety of views either on the proper position or the proper form of the mark. It could even be on a finger, though in theory it ought to be hidden; and it need not actually be a visible mark in the skin, though witch-finders regularly searched the bodies of suspects in the hopes that it was so. The discovery of this point of local anaesthesia that all witches were believed to carry was indeed the classic evidence of diabolism, and great stress is laid upon it in the *Malleus* and its derivatives. In view of the general vagueness about what the searchers were supposed to be looking for, it is easy to concur in the usual opinion of our day that reliance on this ludicrous test represents the nadir of judicial sense

[4]See Bibliography, *Ritual Magic* and *The Myth of the Magus*.
[5]*Witch-Cult*, p. 87f.

even for the panic times, and it is clear that it was a powerful weapon in the hands of the professional delator. Any natural mark might be taken for the thing sought, probably often without pricking to test insensitivity. Even where a suspect was duly pricked, and an insensitive point found, the anaesthesia could be of hysterical origin (or the evidence faked). It is likely that many actual witches, and many suspects, were hysterical subjects, and the circumstances of the physical search would be calculated to provoke such a condition. This explanation was tested and found to work in one celebrated instance in the seventeenth century.[6] For our purpose the only value of the witch-mark is that it is genuine popular belief explicitly linking witchcraft with the Devil.

This also applies to the gift of a "familiar," an attendant subordinate devil in the form of an animal. The two are related because the familiar was supposed to draw nourishment from the mark—to be suckled at the witch-teat, or in its absence (and in most suspects, of course, it was absent) to draw blood from the insensitive point. This belief was fairly general, though the statement is often met with that it was confined to Britain. It was, however, rather vague. Familiars were supposed to run errands for the witch, bring her messages, and behave as no natural pet could. They were also often (by no means always) described in terms that suggest more or less chimerical creatures. Yet no animal unknown to biology was ever physically produced in court, nor any act of theirs reported, by a credible and untortured witness, that would have been impossible to a natural animal. Tradition on these points, genuine as it is, is woefully unspecific and very little help.[7]

So far, we have been considering whether something supernatural may have occurred, and I think it is plain that there is nothing here to shake the faith of a materialist. Neither—failing evidence of the supernatural—is there much on which the Murrayites and Anti-Sad-

[6]In the celebrated case in Newcastle in 1649, where a Scots witch-finder selected an hysterical subject, threw her skirts over her head, and rammed in his pin when she was anaesthetized by shock. Lt. Col. Hobson, the Roundhead commandant, insisted on a second test when the woman had calmed down, and to this she responded normally and was released (Ralph Gardiner, *England's Grievance Discovered in Relation to the Coal Trade*, London, 1655; quoted R. Trevor Davies, *Four Centuries*, pp. 159–60; Pennethorne Hughes, *Witchcraft*, p. 87).

[7]Miss Murray casually mentions an alleged initiation ceremony wherein the postulant placed one hand on her head and one on the sole of her foot and vowed to "Dianus" everything between. (This seems to come from the very late evidence of Isobel Gowdie of Auldearne.) She also suggests that new names were bestowed on initiates at a kind of mock baptism. This clearly may be so, but her reasons are no

ducees can differ. Returning to the Sabbat proper, one of its most prominent and debatable features was the act of formal homage to the presiding god or devil, the *osculum infame*. This ceremony perhaps might be combined with the initiation of a postulant to the sect, but was performed by all. Nearly ever account concurs on the nature of the ceremony. The worshippers are held to have kissed the hind-quarters of the Devil in the form of a goat, that is, either of the actual Devil *in propria persona*, of an actual goat (possibly sacrificial), or of a man, a witch-master, representing the goat-god in a horned mask and disguise of skins. To the Anti-Sadducee the obeisance is appropriate to the Devil, as being obscene, and its intention is to emphasize the utter subjection of his dupes. It is a deliberate act of self-degradation, extorted from the Satanist in imitation (hardly in mockery) of the humility and self-surrender expected of the Christian. To the Murrayite the point of the ceremony is lost by salacious reporting; the horned god, being identifiable with two-headed Janus (Dianus), wore two masks, fore and aft, and was kissed on both, expressing the completeness, but not the abjectness, of the worshipper's devotion.

The evidence, slight as it is, says nothing whatever of any hinder mask. But in any case, the possession of supernumerary faces, in the Late Middle Ages, would not imply that one was Janus; it would rather imply that one was the Devil, who was then often so provided. In view of the absence of evidence this point need scarcely delay us,

---

reasons at all. Assuming that all known suspects were guilty, she finds certain names significantly recurring, but as she fails to discuss the comparative popularity of the same names in society at large at the time, this proves nothing.

It should be noted that the relative indifference of the investigators towards ceremonies implying compact with the Devil is to be explained by the fact that no such ceremony was held to be necessary. The compact virtually and morally existed if a sorcerer had consented to receive the Devil's assistance.

A witch's initiation, moreover, might take place (for all anybody knew) at other times than the Sabbat. It was commonly held that the children of witches were inducted into the cult at a very early age, when they could have taken little part in the ceremonies although perhaps they attended them. For this reason, efforts were generally made, at the trials, to persuade suspects' children to testify, and the child of a convicted witch was often punished along with its mother, though usually less severely and merely as a caution.

(Accounts of children whipped round the pyre, and so forth, even where the witch's own children are in question, need not however be taken as indicating a presumption of guilt against these children. In the sixteenth century—and much later —children might be beaten simply to drive home the point of a lesson. In Germany especially, it was a common practice of the courts to order *all* the children in a town to be beaten at a public execution, to impress upon them the solemnity of the occasion and make sure they did not forget it. Cf. the action of Benvenuto Cellini's father on seeing a salamander in the fire.)

but it introduces an important consideration. Modern representations of Satan are obviously inspired by the classical Pan (as is also the Renaissance, non-classical, satyr), but it does not follow that Pan and Satan are, or ever have been, one. It is possible that the mediaeval devil physically resembled some older god, but the Church's picture of the Church's Satan was more familiar to everybody's mind and bodily eyes than any pagan idol. If a being is represented in (say) the fifteenth century with horns, tail, gigantic phallus, and two or more faces, then that being is the Devil until proved otherwise. Admitting for the time being the possibility of the Murrayite contention that the witch-cult was in origin a pagan cult independent of Christianity, the *osculum infame* in the age we are considering can hardly have been regarded, by anybody, as anything other than Satanism. If witches really kissed the buttocks of the goat-god, or anywhere near them, the effect on the adorer's mind would in any case inevitably be to create a sense either of consenting humiliation or of rather perverse sexuality. The original motive might be different but the tendency is obvious.

It is, of course, possible that the *osculum infame* was not originally part of the rites. In that case, either the practice itself or the belief that it existed must have originated elsewhere. I shall have to return to suggestions along these lines (see cap. 6).

The question of homage to the goat-god or witch-master who presided at the Sabbat (for whom I propose to adopt the name "genius" as a technicality) gives rise to two further questions dividing the parties: whom exactly did the worshippers themselves suppose the object of their worship to be, and, were the rites, in their essentials, obscene? The second is perhaps marginal enough to dispose of summarily. Miss Murray herself has shown a disposition to represent the Sabbat as something entirely innocent, with nothing orgiastic about it, but as much primitive religion is orgiastic this does not help her case; she could agree, on this point, with the Anti-Sadducees and give away nothing. The question of fact remains open, but it need not be treated as a party issue.

Whom did the witches suppose their genius to be or to represent? Dianus (or some such) or the Devil? I must repeat that a final answer to this question would not be a final answer to the whole debate. The Devil might choose to disguise himself as a god of pagan antiquity—a question for theologians—or, more probably, a god formerly Dianus and mistaken by witch-finders for the Devil may also have been mistaken for the Devil by witches themselves. It would be out of all reason to expect that a pagan cult surviving in a Christian society for a thousand years or so should survive unchanged and uncorrupted.

However, in fact it is very hard to determine what witches believed about their god's identity. They were perfectly ready to confess that he was the Devil, but this proves nothing in view of the circumstances in which they confessed it. On the whole they seem to have referred to him, in their own circles, as "God" or "Lord," and perhaps by nick-names to avoid actually naming him, which of course is a taboo common to much primitive religion. All this points to paganism, or would do so, if we could argue that they would not have called Satan so. This is too much to argue, however, of people living in an age when it was commonly assumed that Satan desired the honours paid to God. (This is to pass over the fact, probably irrelevant though mildly curious, that "Lord" translates "Archon," a common name for the Evil Principle in gnosticism, and "Adonai," the ordinary Hebrew synonym for the "unspeakable name," *Jahveh*; and Jahveh—the God of the Old Testament—was identified with the Evil Principle by some mediaeval dualists.)

There is little hope, we may agree, of determining *exactly* how the witches regarded their god, or where they considered him to stand in relation to the Christian Trinity—in which, in a sense, they almost certainly believed also. It is most probable, whether we regard them as sorcerers or as pagans, that they looked upon the Christian god and their own as two rivals among many possible deities. It is worth noting here that if their god was not in fact modelled upon the Church's Satan, they must have regarded the representations of Satan in churches as portraits of their own Dianus-or-whatever.

Carvings and paintings, rather than the canons of Lateran Councils or the works of St. Thomas Aquinas, would be the main source of information about the Devil to the general public from which witches sprang. The outward form would be more familiar than the doctrine, and the name merely a question of names. An Inquisitor would hardly be surprised if he was told that witches worshipped the old pagan gods; he would be surprised, and bewildered, if he was told that *therefore* they did not worship the Devil. That witchcraft contained a tincture of paganism was common form, being attested by the respectable authority of the Canon *Episcopi*. A more extreme view, that pagan deities can be equated with devils and therefore do exist, is of imposing antiquity though it has never been orthodox. Witchcraft does not appear to have been mainly or typically a cult that attracted the more learned classes of society, and, though as I shall show I am inclined to believe that the learned took a hand in its development at more than one stage, their object would be to shun the limelight. The ordinary victim of the scares would certainly be incapable of explaining, as Frazer explains in *The Golden Bough*, just what kind of a god was Janus and how he stood related to Jupiter and the rest of them.

After the *osculum infame*, dancing seems to have been the main occupation at the Sabbat. We should expect the dances to be magical in intention, and therefore probably imitative, but actually what little there is in the way of description lays more stress on the loose and immoral character of the revelry than anything else. We should not be too hasty to regard this as evidence for orgies. It seems to be common ground that the witches' dances were ring-dances, widdershins (anti-clockwise) in direction at least usually, and as compared with other dances of the time informal in pattern—all characteristics of the ordinary ballroom dance of our day. Indeed, the waltz derives from a dance, the *volta*, generally associated with witches. Some dances may have been (from our point of view) more eccentric than others; there is talk, for instance, of couples dancing back to back, though this was certainly not confined to witches.[8] It must be understood that the Church viewed *all* dancing with disfavour[9]; that is, it started with a prejudice against it and admitted special cases. Later, when this was considered old-fashioned, Church and state in many places continued to regard certain dances as a danger to morals; the rhythm of the saraband was too relaxing, the partners of the waltz embraced too closely, and in our own day rock'n'roll is equally alarming to the pious though presumably for the opposite reasons. In Austria, where it originated, the waltz was banned until the late eighteenth century on prudential grounds, not because of any connection with witchcraft, and the ban was only removed by accident.[10] One should perhaps add that the Church's disapprobation of dancing as such may have been, probably was, partly inspired by the feeling that it tended to paganism; but except in very late attacks on the maypole[11] this is not a point usually made by the moralists.

[8]The "dancing backwards" in a confession quoted by Lea, *Materials*, p. 239, is probably the same thing. The Flemish miniature reproduced in Pennethorne Hughes, *Witchcraft*, obviously shows a public occasion, not one of witchcraft.

[9]Coulton, *Five Centuries of Religion*, vol. I, appendix 23 (c), p. 531.

[10]A Spanish peasant dance of similar character was included in Martin y Soler's fabulously successful opera, "Una Cosa Rara," and was encored by the Emperor Joseph II.

[11]E.g., Phillip Stubbes, *Anatomie of Abuses* (London 1583), quoted Frazer, *Golden Bough*, p. 123.

One point to consider under this general head is the question of how witches were dressed at the Sabbat. The common impression that they were naked is actually supported by little contemporary testimony. It occurs in some confessions, but is not a usual feature. Miss Murray, in her least exceptionable work,[12] reviews this evidence and plays down nudity, probably rightly. It is reasonable to suppose that practice-varied, though probably nakedness was usual, as this would be natural in a priapic or phallic rite, natural if the "flying ointments" were employed, and useful for many purposes of magic.[13] I may add, to anticipate, that what little and questionable modern evidence is to be had supports this. An alternative view, that witches for some purposes wore green, is not hostile to the supposition that they were naked at the Sabbat, as the grounds for believing they wore green are divorced from the context of the Sabbat. The view is to be found in the *Malleus*, and otherwise is drawn mainly from dubious affinities with the cult, in Robin Hood games, fairy legends, and so forth, which may perhaps be quite unrelated to witchcraft.

The Sabbat also by general agreement included a meal. There is no such general agreement on what was eaten, and it seems clear that it must have varied widely. This presents certain difficulties, not perhaps insuperable, in the way of regarding the meal as a religious *agape*. If it was not a religious act, then it holds no interest for us.

If it was the witches' *agape*, however, the Black Mass was not also. Actually there seem to be no grounds for supposing that the Black Mass, or any kind of sacrifice, was regularly associated with the Sabbat, even in the popular mind. The Black Mass should rather be considered as an alternative form of religious rite performed by sorcerers, though a combination of the two is by no means impossible, and may even be counted probable, as a syncretic development, in the last ages of organized witchcraft.

Mention of the Black Mass raises the question whether any part of the witches' ritual was so closely modelled on Christian usage, by way of parody, as to necessitate the view that its intention was blasphemous. I think it is clear that unless the Black Mass formed an integral part of the Sabbat, which it does not seem to have done, no such view can be entertained. The genius of the Sabbat may, as I have suggested, have been modelled iconographically on the Church's Satan, but this figure in its turn owes a great deal to pagan mythology and shares, or

[12]I.e., the *Witch-Cult*, where references to clothing are commoner than to nakedness.

[13]Frazer, *Golden Bough*, first five chapters, contains numerous instances.

shared, attributes with a wide variety of pagan gods. Here the converse applies of what I have said earlier; a figure who, in the witch-hunting times, was almost certainly identified as Satan may originally have been "Dianus"—any horned god, or god of a phallic cult, or Lord of the Dead might easily develop into a devil.

If a sacrifice other than the Black Mass took place at the Sabbat, it could hardly be regarded as a parody of the Mass; the actual slaughter of an animal or human being is obviously much closer to the pagan analogies. The rest of the Sabbat, as it is commonly described, bears no resemblance at all to the rites of the Church. If the Devil intended it as a parody of Christianity, the Devil is a thoroughly incompetent parodist. Borrowings there may have been, but they are not apparent on the surface and cannot be regarded as mockery.

There remains only the Black Mass itself as possible evidence that sorcery involved Satanism. However, it is by no means necessary to assume that, even if the Mass was profaned by witches, it was profaned as an act of worship of the Devil. The authors of the *Malleus* clearly believed that some kind of profanations did occur, but that their purpose was magical, not religious, so that however reprehensible they might be they did not imply the repudiation of Christianity but only the sin of superstition. The Mass might moreover be profaned in many ways, not all of them equally objectionable. At the lowest level, the sorceress might purloin the consecrated host as an ingredient in a charm or witch's brew; this was a danger ever present to the minds of clerical moralists, and incidentally the original reason why, in the Roman Catholic Church, the host is placed in the mouth, not the hands, of the communicant. Again, the Mass might be regularly performed, if a priest could be found, on the supposition that this would force God to grant its "special intention." This would differ from the ordinary Mass only in the moral status of the intention; the attitude of mind involved would not be very different from that of an ignorant Catholic in any age. Or, by an extension of this last, the Mass might be irregularly performed in the same hope, because it was not possible to arrange a valid Mass (if, for example, the celebrant was not in full orders). In none of these usages, which are well authenticated, is there any element of "blackness" except the moral obliquity of the motive. Even when these are set aside, there remain varieties of blackness. A Mass might be Black because it contained obscene or horrific accompaniments (like the Mass of St. Sécaire[14]), or because it was adapted as a service of veneration to Satan, or because it was made the occa-

[14]Frazer, *Golden Bough*, p. 54.

sion of insulting Christ's substance in the consecrated host. The second of these might be either imitation or parody; the synthetic Black Masses of modern dilettante diabolists such as Aleister Crowley would fall into this class. The third (abuse of the host, not to release supernatural power supposed to be stored in it, but to injure or humiliate the Christ supposed to be "really present" in it) might alone put the *Satanism* (as opposed to paganism) of the worshipper beyond doubt. Accusations of the kind were made in the Middle Ages, but unfortunately for our purpose they were not made against witches but against Jews, and for that reason they are manifestly false, for to a Jew such an action would be meaningless. The Jews did not believe in the divinity of Christ; it is essential to bear in mind that neither a devil-worshipper nor a sorcerer nor in all probability a pagan would share their unbelief.

Even if the ritual of the Mass or the consecrated host or any other Christian symbol was on occasion treated by witches in such a way as to suggest not imitation of another cult but loathing and contempt for it, there is an explanation, other and I think better than the Satanistic, which I should have said leaped unbidden to the mind if I knew of any writer on the subject who had mentioned it. Put it that the witches considered their religion and that of the Church as the cults of two independent gods, at most rivals and not inevitable adversaries (which is what their attitude would be if it was truly pagan). Faced with persecution by the followers of Christ, they might easily take the desperate resolve to bewitch Him. Where magic is really believed in, it is natural and not uncommon to believe that the gods themselves are not wholly free from its control, though to ill-wish a god is of course a very risky undertaking that one would hardly contemplate in any lesser emergency than the danger of the Inquisition's fires.

I suppose the general technique to be followed in such a case is common knowledge. Much the same principles are recognized by sorcerers the world over; this is, indeed, one of the most widespread of all magical practices. The life and fortunes of the victim are bound up with those of his *exuviae*, the emanations and traces of his personality, such as nail-parings, cast-off clothing, the remains of his food, and even his footprints. It is necessary for the magician to obtain some of these, as many and as intimate as possible, and then—broadly speaking—treat them as he would wish to treat his victim. (The familiar wax-image technique is a variant, since the image, ideally, should contain *exuviae* in order to identify it with the victim.)

In the case of Christ, the usual kinds of material objects through which a man could be cursed are not available, but instead we have the most perfect of all *exuviae* in the form of the consecrated wafer, which according to the priest, who ought to know, *is* actually His flesh. It is thus an obvious expedient to stab, soil, or burn the wafer if the power of the god locked in it is becoming a menace. If sacrifices are made to that god, which presumably increase His power, it is an obvious precaution to try the effect of *undoing* the sacrifice (as by reciting the prayers backwards or reversing their sense). In general, the techniques employed by the Christians are presumably the proper techniques for coercing the Christian god or for adding to His strength. If you wish to weaken Him or coerce Him in the opposite direction, you must rely on the same basic methods. None of this implies that you believe the god concerned to be the exact opposite of your own god. In that case, you would naturally rely on your own god, merely seeking to increase his power by the normal means. If that failed, you would abandon him, seeing the case to be hopeless.[15]

Before leaving the subject of the horned god's character altogether, a word should perhaps be said about his sexual prowess. This was a subject treated in great detail in the *Malleus*, and which not unnaturally preoccupied the judges to near the point of obsession (as it has done the Anti-Sadducees from that day to this). It would therefore be difficult to accept evidence for it extorted under torture, if there was any reason, on any view, to doubt that it occurred. So long as we are not asked to believe that a single man had real coitus with about a dozen women, there is nothing far-fetched in the view, common to all parties, that the Sabbat partook of the nature of a sexual orgy, or at least involved phallic rituals. One detail of direct testimony may be quoted, tending towards probability; a detail that would hardly have leaped unbidden to an overheated imagination. Confessions are unanimous that the Devil's embrace is *cold*; and while this would hold good for any embrace in the open air by night, especially if the genius relied on an artificial member, it is hardly what one would expect of a visitant from hell. It is for this reason a detail that carries conviction. The theologians' view of such illicit unions was that no true coitus took place, but that semen stolen from men, doubtless onanists, was

---

[15]The later history of the Black Mass is admirably covered in H. T. F. Rhodes, *The Satanic Mass*. Unfortunately, for its origins he relies on the wholly imaginary account of a Sabbat in Jules Michelet, *La Sorcière*. This latter should be noted as a variant of the picture we have been considering.

employed by Satan to impregnate his followers. The children thus monstrously begotten would of course be recruits to the cult from birth, and this partly explains the customary judicial attitude towards a witch's offspring.

While so far we have been discussing the organized worship of witches, if any, we should spare a thought for their organization in general. Only the Murrayites profess to be able to describe a regular system of covens, and even a primitive coven system is only authenticated for a part of the area affected and at the end of the persecutions. Professor Murray has given the coven a good deal of attention, apparently in the hope that the coven pattern might be more easily traced in other ages than the Sabbat, and thus help to establish the continuity of the cult. In Scotland in the seventeenth century it would seem that members of the witch-society were organized into local cells having their own regular sessions, and which properly should be thirteen in number though we may presume this was not always possible. Miss Murray presumes also a standard internal organization, headed by the male "Master" who might on occasion be described as "god" or "devil." Each coven would contain a female leader, whom she calls the "Maid," and the Master might have a personal assistant, the "Officer," whose functions are left vague. The Master would be subordinate to some further Master in the hierarchy that linked and supervised all covens, and the suggestion is that these upper ranks were also grouped in thirteens with an ultimate Supreme or Royal Coven for the nation. This at least is Miss Murray's theory as I understand it. She also holds that coven-membership—meaning by "coven" any group of thirteen—is a *test* of witchcraft, and tends to claim that thirteen is a number so intimately connected with the cult that wherever and in whatever context it occurs it shows either actual witchcraft or at least "Dianic" influence. This is a point to which we shall return; if sound, it would certainly make her general thesis easier to prove. But perhaps the thing to be chiefly borne in mind on the subject of the coven-structure is that *all* the evidence is very late and all derived from one country.

This lateness is disconcerting to the historian. It would scarcely worry the two leading parties, since the Murrayites dogmatically assert continuity with the pagan past for all features of the cult, and the Anti-Sadducees take their standpoint not in time but in eternity and assert only that, whenever Sabbat and coven took their rise, the Devil was their author. Once again, the two parties though wholly out of sympathy are not *directly* opposed to each other. Neither school gives more than perfunctory attention to the problem of origins, and in considering those origins we shall have to formulate our own questions and not simply conduct a debate between the forces already in the field. The most we can hope to do is first to discuss what questions ought to be asked, and then try to fit the possible answers into their context in general history. I think it will be found that we can by these means somewhat narrow the field of conjecture; but to tread safely in this quagmire we must refuse the added burden of a theory to prove. Steering by dead reckoning, from the known to the unknown, is the best we can do and the only respectable course; the usual error has been to take witchcraft itself (or its non-existence) for a charted point from which one might steer. I propose for the moment to regard the existence of the cult as a hypothesis, tentatively accepted. If we can keep this in mind, and if we can learn to tell the corposants and jack-o'-lanterns from the predictable stars, we may not arrive at our goal, but we shall know the failure does not lie at our door.

What physical shape the god took, in the last days of the cult, or what kind of worship was then paid him, are not questions which, if they could be answered, would tell us anything very conclusive. They are therefore not the best questions to ask, unless indeed the cult only existed in the days of persecution or from a very little before. This leads us to the question: when did the cult originate? This, if it could be answered, would be quite a good question. If we had the great good fortune to find that it all started in an age whose general history and ideas about religion were tolerably well known to us, we could indeed make a pretty confident guess *why* it started, and at least what ideas were likely to be present in the minds of the first members. But it will be readily agreed that this is too much to hope for. In the first place, to "find that it *all* started" at a given time would be very surprising. If the cult as it appeared in the age of persecutions was not an amalgam of successive accretions (and probably it was) even so it must have inherited earlier religious or magical ideas. In any case, almost all parties would agree in ascribing to it a prehistoric origin. To believe it a product of the age in which it first became prominent would go badly against the grain, as not being the kind of thing he is used to, either to an Anti-Sadducee or to an anthropologist of the rather old-fashioned (and, it must be said, rather amateur) school in which Murrayism took its rise. It is, however, a possibility to be seriously considered. If the evidence for the existence of any institution can be traced back to a certain point, and no further, and the earlier period falls within the sphere of history, there is a *prima facie* case for taking that first known point as the actual beginning, and some kind of positive reason for supposing it to be much older must be produced. It would be such a reason if it could be shown that the institution embodied ideas that could have had no source in that age, or for any other cause had not then a reasonable chance to grow up. It would also be a reason if the institution showed particularly close parallels with some known earlier institution, parallels too close to be spontaneous; but this would only be conclusive if we could afford to exclude the hypothesis that there was any conscious borrowing involved. If witches around 1300 did something that was done in, say, 300, *and* nobody knew in 1300 it had been done in 300, *and* if it was an odd thing to do, that would be a solid ground for believing that somebody had done it in the intervening time, unbeknownst to historians.

Still, if no evidence at all could be put forward for continuity with the distant past of our culture-complex, the absence of evidence would not quite amount to evidence for the contrary; we may as well accept that we have virtually no expectation of proving a negative. We can only compare probabilities; unless indeed some positive indication of continuity is forthcoming, and this the Murrayites claim at least to be able to supply. I imagine they would also claim that History has nothing to offer to the discussion and should be left out of it; and on both sides of the question professional prejudice has every chance to rear its ugly head. But any fancied hostility between the "historical" and "anthropological" approach can safely be ignored where both disciplines are equally in the dark, and equally deprived of the kind of material they are used to.

The historian and the prehistorian need not quarrel either; doubtless some elements of the cult fall into the province of the one, and some into that of the other. Almost certainly we shall have to seek separate origins for separate elements; in which case we need to adopt a provisional scheme for breaking the cult down into its component parts. This, of course, is very dangerous, for we shall be apt to ascribe an absolute validity to our subjective division; but we can hardly avoid the attempt, and the best we can do is to bear the necessary reservations in mind.

I should favour a break-down into the following details: the outward aspect of the god, or whatever element was common to it in all ages; the kind of homage paid *regularly* (not only on initiation), if any common element in this can be assumed; any detail that seems to be general in initiation and peculiar to it (*rite de passage*); the dances at the Sabbat; the *agape*; the sacrificial element, if any; the phallic or orgiastic element; the ointments; the word "Sabbat"; the coven organization; the word "coven"; sacrifices, if any, associated with the cult but not with the Sabbat; any magical practice of witches that may seem to have been widespread inside the cult and not well established among independent sorcerers; and any other problematic element that we may have to accept as having formed a part of ritual witchcraft.

I have not tabulated these, and I do not guarantee to treat them in any particular order. I merely set them forth as things for which, for any one of which, I should not be surprised to learn of a separate origin. Postulating a secret society of some kind, which took on one or another of these at different times, the society presumably came into being *by virtue of* taking on the first in date; that is to say, the first in seniority as a detail of the cult, for some may be older than the time of their adoption or even than the cult itself. It is also possible that the society might have previously existed with other characteristics; but if this should be so we have even less hope of establishing the fact beyond doubt than most of the facts we are seeking.

I may as well say that I believe we can narrow the range of the possibilities for some of these but not all. For some, if not for all, it may be our duty first to widen the range of possibilities; for that range, as I do claim to be able to show, has been artificially narrowed. The Murrayites in particular have narrowed it unacceptably by cutting out the whole zone of time between the quite unknown ages where the fancy is free to roam at will and the *terminus ad quem*, if indeed it is one, of the first actual trials. We must now examine what the historical case for very early origins really amounts to. In doing so, we must watch ourselves, remembering always that other kinds of cases have still to be considered; remembering also that the case that has so far been made is not necessarily the only one that history can supply.

CHAPTER FOUR

1066 and All That

MISS MURRAY'S PRESENTATION of English history, in *The God of the Witches* and *The Divine King in England*, is not likely to deceive anyone who checks it by the authorities she quotes, let alone by recent works of scholarship; but it may mislead him in the other direction. It leaps rapidly to the eye that these books contain an incredible number of minor errors of fact or of calculation and several inconsistencies of reasoning. It would be unwise to leap as rapidly to the conclusion that they cannot also contain genuine insights; there have been historians of respectable eminence (Froude, I suppose, is the classic instance) who were practically incapable of getting a fact right, and everybody makes some errors. Her picture could still be broadly true, though I maintain that in fact it is not; a habit of inaccuracy does not indicate either the presence or the absence of the historical imagination, though, of course, it is a fatal disadvantage if one has an unlikely case—or any case—to prove. Miss Murray's case could, perhaps, still be proved by somebody else, though I very much doubt it. And I willingly acquit her of dishonesty; if I insist, thus ungallantly, that she is not to be trusted, it is without any intention of blame, and only because at the time I write no one is more often treated as an authority on our subject or has committed more nonsense to print. This having been said, her theories remain to be examined.

If a pre-Christian origin for the later witch-cult is to be proved, then in almost every region affected there is a gap, from the conversion to the first trials, of something of the order of a thousand years. In every country, we know a good deal about the condition of the Church for at least most of that time. The enclosing dates vary; in England they are unusually late, falling in the late sixth and late sixteenth century, whereas for France they would have to be placed in the fourth and fourteenth (as also in Germany—otherwise an exception—if we can take the panic there to have stemmed from the Rhineland and Alps). This might seem, in itself, a factor narrowing the gap. However, in the first place the gap that is left is still regrettably wide, and in the second place it will not really wash. Miss Murray took it upon herself to establish her case for England alone, and rightly, for if her case is good it should work for England viewed in isolation from other countries. It is, of course, a possible theory that the witch-cult was continental in origin and an importation into England, but this would leave the gap as it stood (unless it had previously been exported *from* England), and besides, this is a view utterly hostile to Murray-ism. About the only point that school has in common with modern professional anthropologists of the school of Malinowsky is its strong preference for integrated cultures with all their institutions native to the soil. So, England in the Middle Ages did not really accept a foreign religion; she did not really acquire a new social or political structure with feudalism; but her religion, constitution, and social system remained all of a piece, different facets of the same fact, and this fact was the survival of the old Celtic paganism and the whole *Weltanschauung* that went with it, fairies and all. The theories of the Murray school contain at least some hint of wishful thinking.

In any case, Miss Murray has been bold enough to tackle that gap. But before we attempt to follow her, it may be well to ask: what gap? A gap between the later witch-cult and precisely what else? We have been talking as if some element of the cult could be presumed to exist in the days before the conversion. But have we any grounds for this? There is no known method of constructing a bridge to a hypothetical bank that may be any distance away or not even there. Note that any odd scraps of evidence the earlier Middle Ages might afford of ideas that cropped up again in the witch-cult would prove absolutely nothing about its antiquity without pre-Christian corroboration; because, supposing it was, say, a thirteenth-century concoction, it would have to take its ideas from somewhere, and odd bits and pieces of the cult may easily have a longer history behind them than the cult itself.

It is not altogether easy to criticize Miss Murray's own views on this point, because her writings leave one with no idea whether their author was or was not aware that the ancient Britons and the Anglo-Saxons were two different races. She always seems to talk about England before the days of St. Augustine as if it had been occupied by one of those integrated cultures since time immemorial; whereas, of course, St. Augustine landed while the Angles and Saxons were still hacking out their little kingdoms at the expense of Christianized and Romanized Britons.

Of course we could abandon that conversion and go back to earlier ones. The witch-cult was the real religion of Britain under the Druids. Was it? If so, most of what we have always believed about the Druids must be wrong, or else the witch-cult was already then an underground movement, smeared over with a thin layer of Druidism as it was later to be with the cults of Augustus and Roma Dea, of Christ, of Woden and Thunor, and then again of our Cold Christs and Tangled Trinities. The Druids were plainly priests of a tree-cult, animistic at least in origin, that concentrated on the oak and mistletoe; and while the exact nature of their worship remains obscure, it was not anthropomorphic. They did not, therefore, encourage man-gods or semi-beast-gods. It is certain that a degree of anthropomorphism did come to exist in Celtic religion; but in Roman times this is the new, the rising fashion, and in Britain was consciously fostered by the conquerors. There was Cernunnos in Gaul; we know the names of some gods of Britain, and though Cernunnos, the Horned God, does not happen to be one of them, an altar of his may yet be discovered. It remains *prima facie* unlikely Britons ever of their own motion went in for anthropomorphism, beyond the little that is implied in giving a god a name and praying to him as if he understood you, which is very little indeed. The official and dominant cult did not employ representations (or it is at least very unlikely), and where that is the case they are not to be looked for in more primitive cults of wood and field. Archaeologists have discovered singularly little reason to suppose that the Britons even in Roman times represented their own gods as men or half-men. They will not willingly accept even the gorgon-mask at Bath as the work of a native craftsman; and it would prove nothing that a people already Hellenized, the Romans themselves or the Gauls, should adopt a British god and ascribe him a human form, nor yet that Roman-type temples, presumably intended for Roman-type images, should be dedicated to Sul or to Bran in centres of Roman settlement or under the official pagan reaction of Julian the Apostate. No archaeologist would be glad to find room in his picture of pre-Roman Britain for a god of major importance or wide popularity who was imagined as half-man, half-goat. It would give him a new set of problems; it would solve nothing. If there was an anthropomorphizing tendency in Celtic religion at this time—a tendency either to humanize gods or to deify men—it was most probably the result of, and certainly encouraged by, Roman syncretism.

The Romans were hostile to Druidism because the Druids were considered to be magicians and to have a politically dangerous hold over the popular mind. This does not suggest that any other cult was more important, or more magical, immediately before Roman times. The Romans imported their own official gods and their own unofficial mysteries, but as a matter of policy they were everywhere anxious to identify local deities with those of the Olympian Pantheon (and in fairness to the Romans one should not overstress the politic factor in this; it did also appeal to the real religious feelings of those who still held the Olympians in high regard). They would therefore be specially disposed to encourage the worship of any local god who already closely corresponded to one of their own, in an area such as Britain where they had found themselves obliged, much against their normal inclinations, to suppress another native cult that was not thus to be assimilated. If this took place in Britain, it would of course serve to stress those elements in the adopted cult that were closest to Graeco-Roman religious ideas, and indeed it might be wholly responsible for any such elements appearing. Roman syncretism, however, was hardly scientific and in many instances a local god was identified with a Roman on analogies too remote to be even perceptible to us. If a Celtic divinity was assimilated to Janus it does not follow that he had formerly been Janus. The single, universal, coherent system of paganism in the region of Mediterranean culture-contacts which is described by Mr. Robert Graves in *The White Goddess* was a product of Mr. Graves's fertile imagination, quite apart from not being the witch-cult. But there is no evidence for a specially important Janus-cult in the Celtic provinces of the Empire. The task of bridging that gap may be impossible, or it may be much easier than we had supposed.[1]

While we are about it, however, we ought also to consider Nordic paganism. English evidence for this is exceedingly slight, consisting mainly of a few references in the Venerable Bede; but we need not doubt that it differed only in detail and in language from the religious systems of pre-Christian Germany and Scandinavia. For these, information is fairly abundant; Scandinavia produced a rich and uninhibited body of literature in the actual age of conversion, and in Germany the ancient myths long continued to furnish themes to Christian poets. As a consequence, we are accustomed to rely, for Nordic myths, on material rather later in date than the *known* survival of any Nordic pagan practice in England. It is possible—indeed virtually certain—that there had been development in the meanwhile.

[1] In all this section I rely mainly on Collingwood and Myers (q.v., Bibliography).

But we do at least enjoy a fair knowledge of the inhabitants of Valhalla as they appeared to *some* of their worshippers. Only one of these gives any hint of encouragement to the Murrayites. Woden, Wotan, Odin, or Grim, as he is variously known, was associated with royalty, human sacrifice, and the oak tree. As many people know, he "hung on an oak nine nights, sacrificing himself to himself"; and he was the ancestor of nearly every ruling family in the Nordic world. In fact, he represents the clearest case anywhere to be found of the king-priest-victim-god complex, with the possible exception of Jesus Christ, and he has a special connection with the oak, as according to Frazer had Janus. Moreover, he was usually though not always considered the chief god of Valhalla (Thor-Thunor was his rival) and therefore could still be worshipped if the cult should develop in a monotheistic direction. His only possible rival, if one is thinking in terms of *The Golden Bough*, was Baldur; and Baldur was a dying god who stayed dead. The Baldur myth could, of course, be combined with Woden's, on the hypothesis that they are related as substitute and substantive sacrificial kings. This does look promising; but there are difficulties in the way of believing that Woden was the god of the witches. In the first place, the only reason for supposing he was is the connection, postulated by Miss Murray and still to be discussed, between the witch-cult and a cult of a dying divine king. In the second place, human sacrifice is in the Nordic legends a very distant memory, and probably no such custom was still a part of their worship by the time of the *Völkerwanderung*. (They made sacrifices, but these were of cattle and horses.) In the third place, there is nothing in Woden's myths to make him out a fertility god or to link him with a horned animal. Fourth, there seems no likely means whereby his cult could ever have spread to the common people of France. Fifth, it does not seem to have taken any very firm root in England, except as a family tradition of the Anglo-Saxon aristocracy. On the evidence from place-names and from archaeological finds, it appears that the Nordic paganism was only a strong force among the English in the actual age of invasions; the known temples all fall within the areas of early conquest, and by the middle seventh century Christian syncretism as a first step to conversion would seem to have been established where Christianity itself either in the Roman or the Irish version was not. Of the Scandinavian fertility gods—Frey and the Vanir—there is in England no trace at all.[2]

[2]Syncretism is at least the suggestion of the Sutton Hoo ship-burial finds. My general reference for this section is to Stenton (q.v., Bibliography). Cf. *Encyclopaedia Britannica*, s.v. "Teutonic Peoples: Religion."

I think, in view of the fact that the later witch-scare hit Wales hardly at all, and in view of what I have said about Celtic religion, we need say little about the Welsh in the age of invasions. Their traditions for the period are a great deal richer than the English, though of contemporary historical writing there is only the vague and ill-tempered fragment of Gildas. But the literary culture of the Triads is one highly conscious of traditions that are Roman and Christian at the same time, whatever of folklore it may also enshrine; and the forces that held Mons Badonicus were Christians facing a horde of heathen.[3]

The view that England as a whole was not predominantly Christian for most of the Middle Ages is a view grounded on ignorance alone. This is not to deny that the conversion of a nation is a process rather than an event, and is not accomplished in a day. No one denies this much. But it has been maintained that Christianity was for many centuries an official veneer on a pagan foundation; and this is nonsense. We may allow that the ordinary worshipper was ignorant of much that he was supposed to believe and retained many ancient superstitions. But he was at least as ignorant of his forefathers' pagan beliefs (as were even the learned, and as are we to a large extent); while Christianity was worked inextricably into his superstitions, and into his language and daily life. To maintain that loyal churchmen are never superstitious is to flatter the Church unduly.

Already within two centuries of Augustine's landing, the English church had produced Bede, Boniface, and Alcuin; it had become celebrated, even above Ireland, for classical scholarship and for missionary activity in the remaining pagan parts of Europe. It had, therefore, a Christian population to draw on. By the time of the Norman Conquest, reformers could complain of the excessive number of unauthorized cults of native saints, and the stubborn persistence of a married and hereditary clergy; but they did not complain of surviving pagan worship. The parish priest had become an indispensable functionary in the customary law-courts. All Anglo-Saxon legal codes assume universal Christianity, though it is interesting to trace through them the developing ideas—fairly crude ideas, we may admit—of what this implied. In England and France kingship had taken on a new meaning with the introduction of the coronation ceremony, inspired partly by the Old Testament, partly by the East Roman Empire, and fully Christian from the first. As for the kings themselves, that they were (by this time) Christian at least in intention, and in the case of an

[3]For the condition of Christianity among the Britons at this time, see *Studies in Early British History* (ed. N. K. Chadwick *et al.*).

Alfred or an Edward in much more, is surely too evident to require serious discussion.[4]

For later ages, we know more altogether and we know more about popular piety. What evidence for a sneaking sympathy with the Elder Gods is to be found, for example, in the works of Langland or Chaucer? These are perhaps late examples; but they are earlier than the witch-scares. Before their time it must be admitted that the great bulk of relevant literary production was in Latin, by ecclesiastics, for ecclesiastics; and, as far as historical writing goes, they had the absolute monopoly. It has been objected that such writers had a bias, and rather suggested that historians had not noticed this. But what effect are we to ascribe to this bias? Ecclesiastical bias against witches did not limit the output of witchcraft-material in the age of hysteria, to say the least; why should it have done so before? Monastic chroniclers were not shy of mentioning the Devil; and what they had a bias against, they were fond of denouncing. Why did they not denounce paganism? It is suggested that prudential considerations held them back; that they did not care to offend the susceptibilities of kings, or to acknowledge, in admitting the people were not Christians, the weakness of their own claims to authority. This is a valueless suggestion if ever there was one, as the most cursory reading of the best-known chroniclers (say Matthew Paris) will show. They did not care whom they offended, or what crimes they imputed to the people at large. Doubtless there were tactful monastic chroniclers; but, as a class, historians in later ages have seldom been so sturdily independent, not to say rude.

Of course, this material is to be used with circumspection, though Miss Murray herself has treated some such works as objective evidence for their most obviously bigoted and emotional statements.[5] But in practice bias is about their least serious disadvantage, because it leaps at once to the eye. It is obvious which side they are on; what one needs to know is where they got their facts from and what chance they had of getting them right. Their sources of information were limited, and moreover they were not always interested in quite the

[4]We may perhaps discount those obscure princes of the heptarchy who achieved canonization, such as Kenelm of Mercia and Edward the Martyr of Wessex; but there can be no doubt of the Christianity of a king who translated Boethius (as Alfred did), or who like Canute made the emotions he felt on a pilgrimage to Rome the subject of a proclamation. (Canute was the *last* king of England to go to Rome as a pilgrim.)

[5]Most notably on the subject of Thomas à Becket. But a worse fault in her authorities is her preference for writers of the Tudor period, rather than contemporaries, on mediaeval questions. These of course would also tend to have a bias of one kind or another, though it would not be monastic.

things that interest us; but I think we can safely say that they would
have known if Dianism was the prevailing religion among the people
and would have favoured us with their biassed views on the subject.
It is not the custom to accept their word blindly; their assertions need
to be checked where this is possible. Unfortunately on the subject of
Dianism they seem to assert nothing whatever.

We should expect to check them against the records of courts. But
until an act was passed against witchcraft under the first Elizabeth[6]
it was not a problem that the courts viewed with any alarm. It was,
indeed, an ecclesiastical offence; a trickle of cases had passed through
the Church courts, mainly just such trivial quackery and fortune-
telling as would still be illegal today; for which reason we should be
cautious what we take them as proving. These cases seem to have
been regarded, as they would be today, as simple fraud, and received
penance without the invocation of the "secular arm." There was no
general belief, in England, in Devil-worship and Sabbats, in the intervention of Satan in human affairs by means of witchcraft, until this
belief was put about by conscious propaganda, mainly by Puritans
under strong continental influence, in the middle and late sixteenth
century. Whether the cult was a foreign importation or not, there is
little doubt the scare was. In Scotland the same seems to apply, though
when it had once started the terror took firmer hold there.

Apart from her theory about the periodic sacrifice of kings, Miss
Murray appears to rely, for the "intervening" period, on three cases,
one from England, one from Scotland, and one from Ireland. They
do little to bridge any gap, as they all fall in a brief and relatively late
space of time, 1282–1324. It may be allowed that they present points
of interest, not least the fact that just about this time the first hints
of the later panic appear on the continent also.

In 1282, in Scotland, the parish priest of Inverkeithing incurred
penance for having led the lassies (*puellulas*) of the village in a dance
of phallic character, in Easter week. The Lanercost chronicler leaves
room for no doubt about the obscenity of this frolic, though his erudite
references to Priapus and Liber Pater need not be taken *au pied de la
lettre*. In any case, it is clear that the Church authorities were not
under the impression they had a case of paganism to deal with; the
priest, after penance, was allowed to keep his benefice (though in the
event he was fatally stabbed by an enraged parishioner). Probably the
fact that he had danced, rather than the nature of the dance, was
the chief point against him. But even if the dance was actually pagan

[6]5 Eliz. I, cap. 16 (1563).

in nature, the incident can hardly be dragged into the general argument. Of course, many popular festivals, and perhaps all dances, were survivals *from* paganism; this is not the same as a survival *of* paganism. The maypole is such a survival; if it has no necessary connection with witchcraft, neither has this case, and if it has one, this case is altogether unnecessary to the Murrayite argument.[7]

The second instance has a more direct bearing on pagan, or diabolic, worship. In 1303, Miss Murray tells us, the Bishop of Coventry was accused before the Pope of worshipping the Devil in the form of a sheep, "like other members of his diocese."[8] The last phrase is pure camouflage, and seems designed to suggest, without actually saying, that a *public* ceremony was here involved. I am at a loss to conceive where Miss Murray got this from. Neither the reference she quotes, nor the many she does not, have anything to say about a sheep or any other horned animal, though they do supply the correct date, 1300.[9] The Bishop was alleged to have had a pact with the Devil, and to have kissed him *a tergo,* from behind. This is all the detail I can discover as to Satanism. The charges, laid by one John Lovetot, also included the murder of Lovetot's father (the judge of that name) and adultery with his stepmother. An element of personal malice cannot therefore be wholly excluded, though otherwise it would be tempting to suppose a political motive. For the Bishop, Walter Langton, was a very important man; he was Treasurer of England and, at that time, chief minister to Edward I and one of the best-hated men in the country. This, and the fact that Edward gave Langton his full backing against Lovetot, rather suggest that the charge of Satanism may have been added in order to induce the Pope to intervene. Boniface VIII did indeed summon Langton to Rome (Edward, to save his face, appointed

---

[7]*Lanercost, Chronicle of* (q.v., Bibliography); *sub anno* 1282. The crucial words are:

Insuper hos tempore apud Inverchethin, in hebdomada Paschae, sacerdos parochialis, nomine Johannes, Priapi prophana parans, congregatis ex villa puellulis, cogebat eas, choreis factis, Libro patri circuire; ut ille feminas in exercitu habuit, sic iste, procacitatis causa, membra humana virtuti seminariae servientia super asserem artificiata ante talem choream praeferebat, et ipse tripudians cum cantantibus motu mimico omnes inspectantes et verbo impudico ad luxuriam incitabat.

On a hasty reading, it is not hard to form the impression, with Miss Murray, that the dance was "around the phallic image of a god," but this is not quite what the author is describing.

[8]*The God of the Witches,* p. 18.

[9]Her reference is Rymer, *Foedera,* II, p. 934 (ed. of 1705); oddly enough, II, p. 932 also refers; and cf. *Flores Historiarum,* III, p. 305 (Rolls series); *Lanercost Chronicle,* p. 200; the English *Calendar of Papal Letters,* I, 600, 605, 607; *Registres de Boniface VIII* (pub. French School at Rome), nos. 4626, 4627, 4637, 4849, 5012, 5239.

him to a diplomatic mission there) and waited many months for Love-tot to bring his evidence. This he was unable to do, partly it would seem because of skulduggery by Langton's retainers. Finally the Pope lost patience and ordered the case to be heard in England by a special commission, the Archbishop of Canterbury and the local heads of the Dominican and Franciscan orders. Archbishop Winchelsea was not among Langton's political allies, and the court cannot be suspected of partiality either for Langton or for the Devil. However, it reported, in 1303, that the charges were fabricated and old Lovetot died a natural death; they seem to have regarded the murder charge as much the most important. The author of the *Flores Historiarum*—a well-informed chronicler in a tradition on the whole hostile to the Government—records with pleasure how young Lovetot came to a bad end shortly after these events, having (it seems) himself been accused of homicide.

Later, Langton fell foul of Piers Gaveston;[10] in 1307 he was thrown into jail, and accusations against him were invited. They came in shoals, but the charge of Satanism was not revived; which is curious, for this time it would have been a help to the Government to find him guilty of an ecclesiastical offence (for it had sequestrated his bishopric, which had to be returned). Neither then, nor later when he returned to public life amidst a storm of abuse, was any attempt made to implicate him in witchcraft or demonolatry.

It was an age when party feeling was enough to explain an accusation of just this kind. Our third case is an instance. The political importance of Walter Langton ought to be obvious to anyone who has given any attention to the period. The political background to the case of Dame Alice Kyteler is less well known, and anyone may be excused for overlooking it, though it is remarkable how often her story has been told and how seldom this aspect of it has been noticed.[11]

The party troubles of England in the vexed reign of Edward II were reflected, as in a distorting glass, in the clan-feuds of the Anglo-Norman aristocracy of Ireland, *Hibernicis ipsis Hiberniores*. Here, however, the real issue was not constitutional but a matter of deep, ancient, and appallingly tangled family grudges, and was brought to a head by the rise to dominance of the FitzGeralds. Dame Alice

[10]Miss Murray, not being aware that the Bishop of Coventry was also Bishop of Chester, unfortunately missed what might have been an intriguing addition to her theory here; see *The Divine King in England*, p. 97.

[11]I do not claim this as a discovery, though I regret I have been unable to trace who first pointed this aspect of the case out. *Proceedings against Dame Alice Kyteler*, Camden Society, 1840, is the main source for the episode, but undoubtedly conveys bias, consisting mainly of the narrative of a participant.

Kyteler of Kilkenny was a lady of bourgeois origin, but by marriage (she was married four times) she was connected to a great number of prominent political figures in the pale. Since the accusation of witchcraft brought against her was immediately made the opportunity of imputing "guilt by association" to these family connections, the *bona fides* of the prosecution is not altogether above suspicion. The importance of the political factor does not emerge so clearly in the first hearing, before the Bishop of Ossory, a guileless Franciscan who readily found all parties guilty; but it leaps to the eye when the case was removed into the Irish Parliament, a body representing only the English colony and riddled with that colony's standing feuds. From then on, the issue was treated not as one of fact but as a trial of party strength; this continued to be the case after it had been again removed, into the English Chancery (which had no jurisdiction in sorcery, and which ultimately released Dame Alice).

Myself, I am not prepared to regard such judicial evidence as is a by-product of complex Irish vendettas as "judicial evidence" in any intelligible sense of the term. One would guess that there was some basis for the original charge, but this need mean no more than that Dame Alice or one of her acquaintance had dabbled in the ordinary magical quackery that would be rife in a superstitious age and society. The case establishes little to our purpose beyond the indication it gives of the kind of accusation that was then topical enough to be used as a device of party vilification. Least of all will it establish what some have been most anxious to draw from it, namely the antiquity of the coven; since obviously it was most important to those who were using it for a party smear to drag in other names besides Kyteler. But there was talk of anointing a stick, and of wafers stamped with the Devil's name, and of an attendant imp by the name of Robert Artisson, claimed to be an emissary of the Devil and never brought into court. This is enough to show that many beliefs characteristic of the later panics had already made their appearance in one form or another by this date. The Langton case, of course, points the same way, though less clearly. It is worth giving a little more attention to this date.

In 1324 it was about a hundred years since the Inquisition first grew up and slightly more since the Fourth Lateran Council (1215), which had defined the status of the Devil in Catholic doctrine. Both these events are related to the Albigensian movement of which we shall have to say something more later. The movement had been long stamped out by this time; but a kind of parody of its doctrines was reported by the Inquisitors among the first witches to engage their attention. The first true witch-scares were just now beginning in France. They seem by this time to have aroused very little interest elsewhere; and if one was looking for a notable scandal involving diabolism, it would be most natural to look back sixteen years, to the affair of the Templars in 1308. I do not think it can be maintained that the accusers in the Kyteler case were drawing ideas from that quarter, and the Templar case would intrude rather awkwardly at this point; but we shall have to return to it, and it will be well to keep in mind the other early manifestations of Anti-Sadducism in that generation.

In England, witchcraft cases continued for the rest of the Middle Ages proper to be chiefly conspicuous by their absence from the courts. However, Miss Murray has some interesting things to say about the institution of the Order of the Garter by Edward III later in the fourteenth century. It is a part of her theory that garters were an important item of insignia of officers in the coven. When the King adopted this badge, with its admittedly puzzling motto, *Hony soyt qui mal y pence*, for a select group of companions fixed at twice thirteen, the inference is plain that this was the double Royal Coven of England and Edward (Chaucer's contemporary) an overt Dianist. It will be remembered that, according to the traditional story, Edward took his inspiration from an incident at Court, when the Countess of Shrewsbury's garter slipped to the ground, and the King, seeing her mocked by the bystanders, gallantly bound the garter round his own arm and uttered the celebrated words as a reproof. This, we are told, is ridiculous. Our bluff and hearty ancestors were not so easily embarrassed; but the Countess had indeed reason to lose countenance, for the revelation that she wore garters proved her a heretic; ladies of the true faith used Faith to keep their stockings up. She would have been in danger of burning at the stake, as a Maid of the coven, had not the King given overt proof of his own adherence to the *vecchia religione* and dared anybody to do anything about it. This was surely very commendable frankness. But it is worth noting that the lady can have stood in no danger of burning, for the statute *De Hereticis Comburendis* was only passed under Edward's grandson, Henry IV (it was directed against Wyclif's followers).[12] There are other points

---

[12]Maitland, *Roman Canon Law in the Church of England*, cap. 6, "The Deacon and the Jewess," discusses how far it may have been lawful to burn heretics before 1401, the date of the statute. The same essay contains an intriguing passing mention of a case of sorcery associated with religious fraud.

on which I am not satisfied. In the first place, it is a complete mis-
conception to suppose that prudery was unknown in the Middle
Ages. Fashion was already by this time more daring than it had been,
so that ladies of rank were boldly revealing their foreheads and chins;
but these are a long way from the knee. There is no particular ground
for calling that age franker than ours, beyond the fact that its prudery,
of course, differed in detail. Realistic gusto, as distinct from salacity,
was not a characteristic of its polite literature; it is a peculiarity of
Chaucer and even so of Chaucer in one mood only. The tradition of
courtly love is a tradition of euphemism, of even adultery treated as
something existing on a high spiritual plane. The courtly attitude of
mind did not correspond to the facts; and that discrepancy is everywhere the father of the snigger. The traditional story may be true or
false; it is psychologically true to its period. To wear an article of a
lady's clothing—and preferably a fairly intimate garment—prominently
displayed about one was a well-established custom among the chivalrous classes; it indicated that you were the lady's accepted champion
in case a suitable quarrel should arise. Edward was indeed asking his
courtiers whether they wanted trouble, but only in the standard,
formalized context of etiquette. So, at least, we may as well suppose;
for given a known custom of the time, it offends against the economy
of hypotheses to reinterpret the incident in terms of an unknown
custom.

There is also the point to consider that the Grand Coven of England
was constituted, on this theory, very late in the day; and that it was
constituted very oddly. (The significance of the number thirteen is,
of course, no problem at all; but I shall advert to it later, for the sake
of completeness.) There were to be twenty-six members of the order,
making two covens, one for the King, one for the Prince of Wales.
Every coven, in the Murrayite view, should contain a "Maid," but
these for the greater part of their history have contained no women.
The order did, however, include the Bishop of Winchester, and still
does. Set aside the oddity of a coven containing a bishop, why Winchester? Why not Canterbury? Miss Murray has suggested that the
Archbishop of Canterbury may have[13] stood in a specially close
relationship to the Crown, and she is probably right in this guess of
hers. Of course, the reason was that Bishop Edington was a minister
and close favourite of Edward's; but was it not rash to assume that
all his successors in that see would be pagans? Not all bishops were,
even on Miss Murray's view. Edington himself cast doubts on his

[13]"May have" is the way she tends to put it; see, for example, *Divine King*, p. 88.

Dianism by founding a priory and a handsome chantry for the good
of his soul. Moreover, the official badge of the Order (technically) is
a representation of St. George and the Dragon; and the origin of that
legend may be as pagan as you like, but it will be difficult to link it
to witchcraft.

There is no visible element of paganism in the Order of the Garter;
but actually it would not have been surprising, or significant, if there
had been. For Edward was attempting to revive the purer chivalry of
an imaginary past, of the Arthurian age; and though it is probable
Arthur existed, it is certain that his legend contains a large admixture
of diluted and more or less Christianized pagan myth. If elements of
paganism did reappear in this context, therefore—which they do not—
we should have to deal with an antiquarian revival, not survival. I
mention this because it is the sort of consideration we need to keep
permanently in mind in discussing this subject. I may as well mention
here also that the motto of the order, which I have called "admittedly
puzzling," does not present a *historical* problem; it was all the rage
at the time to adopt riddling and enigmatic devices (like the *Forse che
si, forse che no* of the Gonzaga). Even if the legend does not supply
the true explanation, we need look no further; the age was one that
took delight in deliberate mystification, encouraged by the dying con-
ventions of chivalrous romance.[14] (Another instance sometimes
pointed to as revealing witch-symbolism is the "collar of SS" worn
by the Lord Mayor of London, heralds, and others; this was borrowed
from the Order of the Sword—of the House of Lusignan, not the
German order of this name—whose motto was "Silence." It was
adopted by the Lancastrian party in the Wars of the Roses—anybody
is free to guess why.)

We may, in general, ignore all witchcraft cases, before the scares
but after the first examples, where the whole gravamen was sorcery,
manipulation of the unseen, and not explicitly devil-worship. We can
thus exclude all the few early cases in Britain. All these were either
cases of petty spell-peddling with which the ecclesiastical courts were
adequate to deal and for which penance was deemed sufficient without state intervention, or else political cases. The Church after 1400

[14]The phrase *Hony soyt qui mal y pence* stands at the end of the anonymous
poem, *Sir Gawain and the Green Knight*, which is roughly contemporary in date
with the founding of the order. Since the poem undoubtedly in part derives its
material from Celtic mythology, this might seem to support the idea that the phrase
has pagan connections, except for the facts that Celtic pagans are unlikely to have
spoken French and that the author of *Sir Gawain* was almost certainly also the
author of *Pearl*, a poem of undeniably Christian inspiration.

had the theoretical right to call on the "Secular Arm" to burn a witch, in England as it had had a century or so before elsewhere; but it did not use it. In the violent times of the wars of York and Lancaster, charges of sorcery were laid against great persons, but not often, and still of sorcery alone. It is *petitio principi* to make these cases prove anything we do not otherwise know, for party animosity will clearly suffice to explain them. The fact that a great person was found guilty of a crime in England in the fifteenth century tells one simply nothing about his guilt or innocence. The crime of sorcery was officially believed to exist, and in theory though not usually in practice it was more feared than in earlier ages and carried heavier penalties; this is about all we dare say, and this says nothing about the continuity of paganism or even the prevalence of diabolism.

Literary evidence remains to be considered; also Miss Murray's views on the sacrifice of kings or substitutes. However, we may here consider two of her suggested instances, in which she relies on positive indications of witchcraft and not merely on violent death at an appropriate time. The relevancy of her other examples to our subject is not so obvious that we can spend time on them without a separate discussion of the theory that would hold them relevant.

The first case is that of Joan of Arc. We may leave aside the fact that Miss Murray's account of it contains the usual host of minor errors.[15] The two absolutely basic points remain clear: that the real result of her trial was to establish beyond doubt that she was not a witch, and that even without this it would be absurd to doubt that she was a sincere Christian. There really needs very little discussion of the second point. The first may not seem so evident, but properly considered it is the more striking. Joan was accused of witchcraft, in the sense of sorcery, for the usual reason: political propaganda. Sorcery would be the most gratifying explanation, to the English, of her success against them; and Satanism, carrying with it the inevitable penalty of the stake, would dispose of her more surely and condignly than the alternative charge of heresy. The court that tried her had the strongest of incentives to find her guilty, in the shape of pressure by armed force. It was a strong court, of experts, with the assistance of the University of Paris, the leading theological authority of the day; Joan had even less assistance than the Inquisitorial process admitted, as she was allowed no proctor and her confessor was not present. While the English threatened the judges with one hand, they offered

[15]E.g., Joan did not take her mother's surname, but her father's; she did not "quarter" the lilies of France in her arms; she was never called "Maid of France" in her lifetime, nor "Maid of Orleans" by herself, nor "Maid" at all as an official title.

them every facility with the other; Joan's native Lorraine was in the control of their allies, and they were able to furnish a mass of detailed evidence of her early life. The evidence was gone through at great length with the object of extracting from it a case for finding her a witch; and after all this the court was obliged to abandon the attempt. The greatly reduced list of counts on which she was found guilty turned wholly on heresy. It is true that the sentence as published named her a "sorceress" also, but this was an evasion for propaganda purposes. After her first condemnation, Joan was released from sentence of death on retracting her *errors*, that is, on accepting the assurance of the Church's experts that her "voices" were illusory. Here again, the retractation as published contained matter not included in the version she set her mark to (or at least this is probable), but still they had not forced her to confess herself a witch or they would have been free to burn her, which for their own safety they were anxious to do. The most they could do was to sentence her to life imprisonment for her former obduracy. This did not satisfy the English, who (it is clear) drove her into breaking the terms of her penance, so that she could be represented as a relapsed heretic and burned after all. It is a sorry story, but its effect is (if that was necessary) to clear her of the charge of "Dianism." The question whether she was a heretic could still be argued, except by Roman Catholics, who are now obliged to believe she was not; but nothing emerges more clearly from her whole history than her sincere, and at least would-be Catholic, piety.[16]

There are even other difficulties remaining in making her out what Miss Murray would have her, a "substitute victim" for Charles VII. Charles had not been king for seven years or anything like it and on the Murrayite theory ought not to have needed a substitute. Joan did not go willingly to her death, as a substitute victim should; if she was selected for self-immolation, why on earth did she not admit she was a witch, at any time during the many months of her imprisonment, and so save everybody a great deal of trouble? Instead, she denied all charges, most strenuously and persistently; her recantation was made to *avoid* death; and in any case, her death at the hands of the English, after she had been captured by the Burgundians and nearly saved by the Church, could not have been contrived by the French.

Of all examples Miss Murray has produced of the witch's sacrifice, none is more obviously false than this. But all can be explained more easily on some other hypothesis, as I hope to show.

[16]See Bibliography, s.v. Sackville-West, Pernoud.

If Joan had been the selected victim, presumably those Frenchmen who tried to rescue her, such as Gilles de Rais, were not Dianists or not privy to the secrets of the Grand Coven. But Gilles has to be made out a member of this coven, from the coincidence that he was a companion of Joan and was later condemned to death for sorcery. He is a figure who has attracted many attempts at biography and remains the centre of much speculation. Probably we cannot hope to know the final truth about him, but that does not mean that we are bound to accept the unlikeliest of the guesses. De Rais (or de Retz) was one of the Dauphin's most energetic supporters and became Marshal of France; he was a man of great wealth and power, and widely celebrated for the magnificence of the state he kept. While still in his prime, he retired from Court to his estates in Brittany and lived in a seclusion that became a matter of ugly rumours. In the end these grew into positive and lurid accusations, before the Inquisition, of murdering in repulsive circumstances an incredible number of handsome children, and of resorting to Black Art to restore the fortune he had lavished on his peculiar amusements. To all this, with much gruesome detail, he ultimately confessed, and was executed, together with accomplices, after reconciliation with the Church. Opinion has varied as to whether his confession was sincere and the charges true, or his confession the result of third-degree methods and the charges fabricated by those who coveted his estates. Neither view is altogether easy; but to adopt Miss Murray's suggestion that he was a member of the Royal Coven sacrificed in place of the king his master involves more difficulties still. The crimes he confessed to are fully conceivable as to their nature, if he was a homosexual sadist, and only unconvincing in quantity; it would almost exceed human possibility to be as infamous and on such as scale as Gilles was reputed to be, but the confession rings perfectly true psychologically if the number of small boys involved is accepted as an exaggeration. On the other hand, it may very well be that the charges were inventions; but there is this difficulty in supposing them the work of greed: that Gilles's estate by all accounts *was* severely embarrassed; his fortune was no longer the dazzling prize it would have been before he began his career of crime, and that was the reason alleged for his turning to sorcery. Doubtless there was something to save from the wreck, but if he was to be delated to the Inquisition his heirs had no expectation of succeeding, since his estate would be forfeit, and if the Crown was the culprit and the charges mere fabrications they could have been made against richer men. The Marquis de Sade, who was also accused of sexual offences beyond his physical power to commit, and who was nevertheless a sexual degenerate as his writings show, was jailed without trial, by *lettre de cachet*, at the request of his family to prevent his squandering the estate; but this could not be a motive in Gilles's case owing to the very different procedure adopted. The easy solution is that there was a good deal of substance in the charges, though they were exaggerated by rumour; and that it was only after rumour had got going that the possibility of profit struck anybody. The solution that would bring in the sacrificial cycle would bring in more problems with it. If it was necessary Gilles should die to observe a rite of the witch-cult, but also necessary that the witchcraft side of the question should be camouflaged, why was it not omitted entirely? The murder charge alone would have been enough. If Gilles had to die for the sake of the coven, why did accomplices to his sorceries die with him? The case against the sinister Pregati, the chief of these, was that he had supplied the expert knowledge of sorcery that Gilles lacked; this is perfectly credible, especially as they seem to have gone in for the pseudo-philosophical, learned kind of magic that leads to Black Masses rather than for the kind we are specially concerned with; but it hardly supports the view that Gilles himself had for long previously been a prominent figure in the witch-cult. He also resorted to village wise-women; and again, why should he need to? If the evidence is not a complete fake, it strongly suggests that Gilles was not himself knowledgeable in occult matters; and if it was a complete fake, we cannot deduce from it what it set out to prove—that he was a sorcerer and an apostate.

Neither of these cases is really helpful in the one way we could have hoped; neither of them gives any but the vaguest indications of what was then generally believed about cult-witchcraft. But this is the less necessary because we have most of the information we could require for the period, at least for what was then believed by educated people, from other sources; we have reached the age of the *Malleus Maleficarum*.

Although it is strictly a digression, it will be convenient to consider here rather than later the only other cases offered as examples of Dianic royal sacrifice that will require to be discussed in any detail. Since in neither case was there any specific mention of witchcraft contemporary with the events, their value to the argument for continuity is indirect at best; but it is justifiable to link them to the two former because they have been so linked in many people's minds since Miss Murray first put her views on the subject before the world in

1921. These, which would seem her favourite examples, are William Rufus and Thomas à Becket.

The main reason for suspecting that William Rufus was a Sacred King, doomed to die at the ritual moment by the ritual means, is, of course, that he died violently and the argument is rather dangerously short of actual kings who did so. There are, however, subsidiary reasons; a mystery can undoubtedly be made out of the circumstances of his life and death.

In the first place, there is a mystery about his personal character. William II is an accepted "bad king," but why? Nothing very dreadful seems to be recorded of him, no infamy that could not be paralleled in the lives of rulers who have left a more respected name. It is therefore suggested that he was not a Christian; though indeed, according to Miss Murray, few of his successors were either. Now, here we come up against one of the real difficulties in dealing with monastic chroniclers: the uncertainty of their sources of information. It must be remembered that the chronicler was dependent on what he could pick up; he was not personally in close touch with the great, and, if he recorded nothing but good of a man generally disliked by those who knew him, the explanation is that he did not know him. Most monasteries, indeed, had their contacts; but the impression they give depends on the chance of who their contacts were. It was an age that had yet to see the discovery of public opinion; news was too hard to come by. Political enmity to William could hardly spread beyond the small circle of magnates who knew him well as a man and as an immediate overlord. It would, indeed, normally be expected that some reflection of their views would appear in the scriptorium of some convent where this lord or that was a familiar guest; and this seems to have occurred, for William is described by some as "wicked," without further particulars. The simplest explanation for this vagueness, and the one tentatively held by most historians though it cannot be proved, is that he was a homosexual. This fits in well with what is known of him and would account both for the general hostility he aroused and for the general silence about its cause. It would account for both much better than the idea that he was a pagan. The vice must have been common in that age, when celibacy was regarded as the highest ideal a man could pursue, when his friendships with other men and his loyalty to lord or vassal were his most compulsive emotional ties, and marriage largely a matter of legal convenience. But it could be common without being condoned or willingly mentioned, as we all know. It was probably regarded, then as now, with more disgust than crimes admittedly lower by any logical moral standard. The Devil is worse than any sodomite, but less distasteful to contemplate.

On this supposition, therefore, the mystery can be explained without affecting what I formerly said of the monks' reluctance or lack of reluctance to mention royal depravity. It would go some way to explain the next problem, that of his death. The traditional story, or perhaps we should say the official story, is well known: that he died in a hunting accident in the New Forest when an arrow shot by a companion (Sir Walter Tyrrel) glanced off a tree and struck down the king. Death from this cause is freakishly unlikely, and there are difficulties in accepting this account; but they do not necessitate any reference to Dianus.

It seems clear that the king's accident took nobody by surprise. The body was left where it lay; Tyrrel, according to legend, had his horse's shoes reversed at the nearest forge and left for Normandy with no other delay, while the rest of the Court rushed to Winchester with equal dispatch. Henry Beauclerc, William's younger brother, seized the Treasure and was proclaimed king before the corpse had been recovered and William's death made sure of. He was in a hurry, because the elder brother, Robert Courthose, Duke of Normandy, was living and in a position to contest his right; he cannot have known how lethargic Robert was to prove in the next months. In later legend, the news of William's death spread with miraculous speed, and the incident was surrounded with signs and portents before and after. The body was said to have bled on the ground long after death; which to a Murrayite is clear proof William was a sacrificial victim, though any normal folklore specialist would see in it clear proof of a popular belief that he had been murdered. That he *was* murdered seems fairly plain. Whether some mute inglorious Harmodeus and Aristogeiton were involved or whether the whole affair was merely political in motive is open to speculation, but probably there was a widely ramifying conspiracy of which Henry at least was aware and William himself had received veiled warnings. The tales of marvels may have been a spontaneous popular response to the sudden deed of blood, or manufactured to explain why so many people had acted as if they had expected the calamity. The common people were impressed, and William dead inspired a sympathy they would not have felt for him living; the deeds and thoughts of the great were mostly unknown to them and the king a very remote figure, but the neglected corpse in the wild wood, that Purkess the charcoal-burner dragged to Win-

chester to find out whose it was, caught their imagination and has
ever remained there. It will be seen that the circumstances do nothing
to support the idea of sacrifice. The complete lack of interest at
Court in what had happened to the body is at war with it; and the
popular traditions (about bleeding on the ground after death, about
Tyrrel's flight) point to popular suspicion of foul play, not popular
satisfaction at a good old custom kept up.

Some of this crops up again in the popular attitude to Thomas à
Becket and the stories told about his death. His case, however, presents
no mystery. Saint he may have been; pagan he was not. The case
for making him a sacrifice is that he had been the king's close companion; that he died by violence, unresisting, when apparently fore-
warned; and that no condign punishment fell on the offenders. Even
Miss Murray does not claim that he was not a Christian; she seems
to hold that his office, continuing that of some (utterly hypothetical)
national Archiflamen Dialis, carried with it pagan duties he was, till
the final moment, reluctant to perform. She has not noticed that her
whole ground for supposing him a willing victim at all rests on the
word of a "biassed" monastic chronicler; biassed, in this instance, to
make out Thomas a martyr. Doubtless he was, but not for the sake
of Dianus.

It is not as if the series of events leading up to the crime was not
well known. The "sacrifice" theory has to ignore completely Becket's
quarrel with Henry; its nature, its causes, and its results. Why, if
either of them was a pagan, should they have quarrelled over Church
matters at all? Why should the question of who was to control the
national church have been the biggest issue in politics unless the
national church was an immensely powerful institution? The theory
must ignore the whole history of this conflict and Becket's exile; to
make Becket a suitable substitute for Henry, it must try to maintain
that they were not enemies. That the cult of Becket after his death
was both enormously popular and specifically Christian is too obvious
to require elaboration. But perhaps the greatest difficulty of all is the
fact that Becket's death did Henry not good, but harm. It was a political setback from which he never fully recovered, and he, not the
actual assassins, had to take the blame for it.

It may also be asked: were there not better substitutes to be found?
Henry had a son, of the same name, who was crowned in his lifetime; there you have a king-substitute for certain, whether or not
he was a substitute victim. His coronation was not recognized by
Becket; was this because he was jealous of a rival for the honour of

immolation? But Becket at the time was not close to the throne; even on Miss Murray's theory, an actual relative would have been a better substitute, and few who have given the Plantagenet family any attention can doubt that Henry would have cheerfully offered up his wife or one of his sons. I may perhaps give vent to a personal prejudice and say that had he sacrificed Richard Coeur de Lion it would actually have been of some tangible benefit to the country.[17]

None of the suggested cases of human sacrifice in the Middle Ages supplies a better explanation than we already have for any problem. On the contrary, the theory creates a horde of new problems. Unless we had to believe that such sacrifices occurred, and therefore had to look for instances of their occurring, there would be no reason at all to regard any of the assassinations cited by Miss Murray as anything other than ordinary assassinations. I shall shortly consider whether there is any reason for us to believe this; but it is, I think, already clear that these "sacrifices" are useless for the purpose of establishing the antiquity of the witch-cult, and to maintain that they do so is sheer *petitio principi*; the antiquity of a sacrificial rite must be established before we can be required to accept these examples as sacrifices, since in themselves there is nothing to suggest it. We must also now disentangle the question of human sacrifice, which is not well authenticated as a practice of witches, from those ceremonies that are reasonably well authenticated. The Sabbat need not be linked to any custom of royal sacrifice at all. Still, if we admit this, we have to admit one rather awkward corollary: that if we should find reason to suppose that the witch-cult in most of its aspects was a late invention, we should not then have disposed of the sacrifice theory—though this is not very likely, for if the surviving paganism of the Middle Ages was not witchcraft, what was it? There are very few other pegs on which to hang a belief that paganism survived, beyond the actual age of conversion, at all.

It is now a problem which to tackle first: the question whether the regular sacrifice of a divine king was a part of witchcraft (or at least an element of pre-Christian religion in the areas concerned) or the question how old the witch-cult was when it emerged as a cause of scandal and hysteria. It was my original intention to take the second of these first; but as it is not probable that a final answer to it can be found, whereas the question of sacrifice does strike me as more hopeful, perhaps we had better take them in the order in which I have here placed them. However, in that case, we must re-

[17]See Poole, R. L. (q.v., Bibliography) for Rufus and Becket.

phrase the former. We have to consider: is there any ground for supposing that the pre-Christian religion of England or any Western European nation involved the regular sacrifice of kings? And is there anything to link human sacrifice, and a seven-year cycle governing it, with the witch-cult? And did sacrifices of the first kind occur in the Middle Ages? And lastly, was the mediaeval witch-cult under the patronage of a Court and aristocracy that was, for most of the relevant period, crypto-pagan? If we can answer an unequivocal "No" to any one of these questions, we shall be entitled to isolate the argument, as regards sacrifice, from the argument as regards the antiquity of the cult as an institution having a history, which as I have suggested is something other than the antiquity of any given element that helped to compose it. If, on the other hand, we can answer an unequivocal "Yes" to all, this does not compel us to believe that the cult, considered as an institution, is older than Christianity in Western Europe; for the same caution applies; it may have grown up later and taken on this sacrificial element from the paganism out of which it sprang. In that case, we should be able to say with fair confidence that the cult was more pagan than it was anything else; but we should still not have decided how old it was or how it came into being.

CHAPTER FIVE

Divinity That Doth Hedge

IT WILL COME as no shock, to anyone who has read so far, to learn that I personally believe the whole human-sacrifice theory of the Murrayites is nonsense from beginning to end. There may be some who would like to hear my reasons for this view.

In no single instance of all those put forward by Miss Murray is there not an alternative and a better explanation of the facts. The reader can, I think, afford to take this as established; if he cares to do so, he may go through *The Divine King in England* applying Occam's razor (the principle of economy of hypotheses) to each case. There is, in each case, a complete explanation on other lines, into which the determined Murrayite has to force an additional and unnecessary element of pagan ritual. The only possible exceptions are the very early instances about which we know so little that they supply no indication one way or the other. Without something more solid to corroborate them, these hardly amount to proof, and if they could be made to prove the custom they would not prove its continuance. The very slight factor of credulity and bigotry in the reporting can only be counted *against* theories involving sorcery or paganism, not for them, as soon as one asks oneself in what direction a given biassed writer is biassed, as one always should.

But, it may be said, granted each individual case could be otherwise explained, we must give full weight to the effect of the body of cases, taken as a whole. The reader may again be interested in ploughing through the whole lot and seeing how much of a common element really emerges; and he may like to be told on what ground the group of instances selected is held to form a class apart from other violent deaths. Or he may take it from me that there is *no* common element (violent death of a prominent person itself excepted), and the selection is merely arbitrary. There is *no* pattern that runs through these cases; the mode of death varies enormously (even poison is claimed as a proper method of sacrifice, and in another place we are told that the victim should bleed); the rank or office of the victim, the sex and age, whether he was in or out of favour, all vary as they ought not to vary. Even according to Miss Murray's claims, the "cycle" could be calculated in two different ways and the sacrificial season was any date in any of four months of the year. As anthropology, it does not begin to make sense.

But (we may be told) at least there *was* the cycle; at least one can trace a series of sudden deaths, among persons close to the king in one sense or another, that fall into a cycle of seven years. Actually, one cannot. The "cycle" has been established not only by switching at need from calculations based on the king's age to calculations based on regnal years and back again, but also on miscalculation and plain errors of date.[1] Neither of the two cycles will bear examination. This is as well, for if ever a theory needed shaving by Occam it is this theory of two concurrent cycles *both* determining the time when the king or his surrogate was to die.

There are other small difficulties, but perhaps I have said enough. It is, however, a point of some interest that sudden deaths of kings, in England and elsewhere, are not, in fact, specially numerous in the Middle Ages. When the occupational hazards of kingship and of all feudal lordship are taken into account, it is apparent that what we have to explain is not the number of kings who met violent ends but the number that did not. Here also, of course, "sacred kingship" could be brought in, but not sacrificial kingship; more the Biblical conception of the "Lord's Anointed." This would not of itself point to or from paganism; an idea that the king's person was inviolable could plainly be Christian, and while there is every reason to believe it was held it was obviously not held universally.

It is not, of course, necessary in real history or in real human life that an idea should be universally accepted without question in order for it to exercise an important effect. Nor is it necessary for a religious system to be or have once been universal in order for it to be counted as a religious system. Failure to allow for this, and a consequent pre-disposition to make out their theories universally valid, are faults not

[1]This was exhaustively pointed out by reviewers of *The Divine King*, notably Mr. H. Trevor-Roper in the *Sunday Times*; the point is so well established that it would be fruitless to go further into it.

only in Miss Murray but in the whole post-Frazer school to which she belongs. Frazer himself gives the impression of having believed, if he was not prepared to claim, that his myth of a dying divine king would be found universally, or almost so, at a certain level of primitive culture. His followers, as followers will, went far beyond him. It should be remembered that Frazer's predecessors had had a penchant for the universal, world-wide explanation valid for all mythological systems; the dying king simply replaced the solar myth. The penchant remains popular though not with anthropologists, so that Frazer remains the most recent scholar of eminence in the field to have catered, unwittingly, to the need of the non-specialist for a portmanteau theory. More recently, the idea that all the world's myths can be explained along the same lines has gained a new lease of life because it appears to agree with the psychological theories of C. G. Jung. (In fact, however, it does not; if all myths sprang direct from the collective unconscious, then Jung's theories would require that men and women in the same culture should entertain different myths, which clearly they do not.)

Frazer's works still carry conviction because they seem to lay bare a substratum of identical beliefs near the roots of every cult, a paganism truly catholic and truly œcumenical. This is attractive to men of our century, both because poets have long been telling us how admirable it is to be pagan, and because the fashionable smattering of psychology predisposes us to accept these assurances. One would have thought that even a fashionable smattering of anthropology, by now, would be enough to raise doubts whether everything is really so simple, but in spite of Malinowsky, Meade, and Benedict, such fantastics as Robert Graves flourish like green bay trees.

If Frazer had always been safe in assuming that his examples were examples of the same thing (and the chief criticism of his method is that he assumed this too readily), he was not entitled to speak, and he himself did not, for the cultures that had not supplied him with evidence. Surveying mankind from China to Peru, we find in both China and Peru that there had formerly been a sacred king of immense authority hedged in by intricate ceremonial taboos. So far so good. But in neither does it appear that the king was bound to die young to renew the strength of the god he represented; neither sovereign had his life bound up with the fortunes of a plant, or seems to have been identified with a crop whose annual cycle of growth and death was ritually mimicked or mythologically interpreted. This is only one example out of hundreds that might be adduced, where *part* of Frazer's divine-king cult clearly existed and other important elements as clearly did not. His less discreet disciples would be ready to assert that the missing parts must at some time have decayed.

We may allow the school of Frazer to deduce Hercules from his foot, but not an army of giants from the parings of Hercules' toenails. Even if the arguments of *The Golden Bough* are valid for the regions that supplied the evidence (which may be disputed) they could not, without new evidence, be extended to other regions. That like causes at a given level of culture everywhere produce like effects sounds reasonable, but fails to take account of the infinite variety of humankind; and we cannot assume it occurs.

All this has to be said, because there is still a widespread disposition among non-specialists to believe that Frazer's main thesis can be taken as proved, and that moreover it is universally applicable so that in any society, if you dig down far enough, you will find a religious system of the kind he described. This impression, more than any positive reasoning, is the strength of Murrayism; and this impression must be dismissed as an error.

I have said something of the little we know concerning the religious systems of the Celts and Teutons in Britain. I was then speaking more of gods than of sacrifices, but the two subjects are probably inseparable when what one is discussing is genuinely a religion. Everybody has heard how the Druids burned their victims in wicker baskets, whereas no one has heard of human sacrifice in the German forests; but it hardly matters at the moment, seeing it is possible for human sacrifice not to be the sacrifice of a king, and indeed it usually has not been in the examples we know of positively.[2] Did either the ancient Britons or their Teutonic contemporaries kill their kings? If we accept the suggestions of Caesar and Tacitus, they cannot have done so as a general rule, for the institution of kingship was not universally found among either people. This raises an interesting little marginal note on Miss Murray's view of English history. She constantly speaks of England as if it had been, back into dim antiquity, a single nation with a king and a high priest and probably a Grand Coven as well. In fact, however, there is no reason to suppose that anything even roughly corresponding to modern England formed a single monarchy till the ninth century A.D. The *first* kings of all England were crowned according to a Christian rite; the *first* national high priests were Archbishops of Canterbury.

[2]Consider, for example, the appallingly bloodthirsty religion of the Aztecs.

If space would permit, we could go much further than this. Not only were there several kingdoms in the island in the age of conversion, but they were recent kingdoms. Kingship itself is an institution capable of growth. In Roman Britain kings were naturally rare, and so they were according to Tacitus in the German forest. Kingship is not universal in primitive society today; and it seems probable that, though kingship of a kind was universal both among Britons and among Anglo-Saxons in the age of invasions, it was not universally ancient. Moreover, general acceptance was won for the sacred claims of monarchy largely through the propaganda of the Christian Church. It was under Christian influence primarily, and secondarily under the influence of Imperial Rome, that the Western European peoples came to hold that high idea of the office of a king that we tend to assume everybody held until very modern times. At this and at every stage of our enquiry it is essential to recall how deeply Christian ideas—the ideas, perhaps, of a crude kind of Christianity—permeated the mind of mediaeval society.

We cannot exclude the possibility that either or both the British and English ethnic religions may have involved human sacrifice, and conceivably though not probably sacrifice of kings.[3] It would, however, be very hard to believe that such rites, if they survived in any form, were not transformed, and reinterpreted almost out of existence, when the country as a whole became officially Christian and with it, in all probability, whatever pagan customs were kept on. To a people whose *knowledge* of religion was mainly derived from the Church, whatever their practices may have been, the idea of sacrifice must have been permeated by whatever of sacrifice was to be found in Christian tradition and popular Biblical homiletics. Most references to sacrifice in the Scriptures concern offerings of animals, a practice certainly familiar to the Angles and Saxons; but the likeliest references in mediaeval preaching are to the Passion of Christ and its various Old Testament "types," especially the offering up of Isaac by Abraham. This last is splendid authority for the substitution of an animal. But suppose the crucifixion was taken as the archetypal human sacrifice. According to Mr. Robert Graves crucifixion (which undoubtedly originated as a sacrificial rite before it was resorted to as a punishment) was the established means of death of the Celtic divine king. Woden, when he sacrificed himself to himself, hung on

[3]It is true that Schramm, in his *History of the English Coronation* (otherwise invaluable), asserts (p. 4) that the sacrifice of kings for their people was "not unknown" in northern Europe, but he adduces no specific instance.

a tree. The sacred mistletoe of the Druids hung on a tree, the same tree, the oak; and this is the "Golden Bough" itself, the king-god's external soul, according to Frazer. The oak, by the same authority, is associated with Dianus. It may be added that another accepted Old Testament "type" of the Atonement was Moses' displaying of a brazen serpent on a cross; and the ambivalence of the serpent symbol in Christianity is familiar to all.

Hence, a priori, one would have said that the divine king in England (or indeed throughout Western Europe) ought to be crucified. It would be easy to build up, conjecturally, a pre-Christian rite of this kind; Mr. Graves has actually done so. And even without this, such a means of death would be suggested by a very slight degree of Christian syncretism, as examples from West Africa go to show. The considerations that would urge the Dianists to adopt such a practice, if they did not already have it, must have been so forcible that if they did not crucify their victims, there ought to be some special reason why they did not. It cannot have been prudential, for the cult of a crucified king would be particularly easy to camouflage. It might be hostility to any influence from the alien Church, but all religions suffer such influences and find it easy enough to persuade themselves that it has not occurred, that the borrowing was the other way.

Whether crucifixion ought to have been the method or not, however, there must have been a proper method. On the analogy of the Bible and of most other religious systems, if we reject crucifixion we should expect to find fire and a knife to be the usual elements. They are not usual among the examples put forward, for in them no pattern is to be found. But consider fire alone. Traditionally, the Druids are supposed to have employed it. It was later (though not in England) the usual punishment for witches. It may perhaps have been the custom of witches periodically to surrender one of their number voluntarily to the flames of the Secular Arm, and to have construed this as a sacrifice. (This sounds improbable, but it would not be altogether unlike the practice of the Thugs in India.[4]) But that leaves the gap to be got over, besides divorcing sacrifice to Dianus from royalty. If this was ever an idea in the witches' minds (I am not pre-

---

[4]Who strangled their victims in honour of Kali, and had no objection to being hanged themselves. The British authorities, flagrantly disregarding the religious susceptibilities of the Thugs, discouraged the cult by shooting, not hanging, the members who fell into their hands.

pared to exclude the possibility that it may have been), then it was at most a custom of the fourteenth century or later that looked back to a hint in older legends for its inspiration.

There is still the question of the seven-year cycle to be disposed of. Such a cycle, as I have briefly indicated, has no part to play in English history at large, but it may still have something to do with the witch-cult; it may have existed, even if we are satisfied that kings were not killed at its bidding. It does not correspond to any cycle in nature, which for a primitive religion must be a disadvantage; nor does it even reconcile two natural cycles on which a primitive calendar could be based, such as the solar, lunar, menstrual, or sidereal. It does, indeed, reconcile the 365-day year with the seven-day week, if you ignore leap-year, but this is a very slight achievement and leaves the seven-day week to be explained. But I doubt if this is really a problem. As is well known, the number seven is thought of as a number of mysterious power in several religious systems and also, for example, by the Pythagoreans among superstitious philosophers; poetically, "seven years" stands for "a long time." Miss Murray gives unconscious tribute to the power of the number seven when, in a book whose main subject is the effect of this "cycle," she speaks of seven—in contrast to thirteen—as a number specially sacred to *Christians*.[5] But indeed her whole theory of the cycle is a tribute to this power. In her first work on the subject there is no mention of a seven-year period; she is open to conviction on how long the cycle may have taken. The precise figure creeps in later, apparently quite unnoticed, unchallenged, and unexamined. We need look no further than the recesses of Miss Murray's unconscious for the seven-year cycle.

But she did not invent the *cycle*; she only presumed the figure seven. The idea that witches periodically owed the Devil a victim—at intervals running into years—is to be found in other writers, though it is a very elusive belief. I do not think it occurs prominently in any Anti-Sadducee material of the age of repression, and it would hardly help if it did, for such a custom would be automatically associated by such writers with the Faustian compact and probably derived from some version of the Faust legend. Human sacrifice does occur in many accounts as one of the horrific accompaniments of the Black Mass, but this again is hard to fit in with witchcraft; in this case the victim is most often pictured as a baby, sacrificed, of course, whenever occasion demanded and not at long, fixed intervals; and the origins

[5]*Divine King*, p. 188.

of this superstition almost certainly are to be sought in quite another direction than the religious traditions of the witch-cult.[6]

John Buchan believed in the cycle; he was a Scotsman; and Miss Murray in *The Witch-Cult in Western Europe* concentrated largely on Scotland as the richest source of detailed information. I am inclined to suspect that Scots folklore can supply the clue; but that it is a clue that leads, not to witches, but to *fairies*.

Now, of course, fairies have been believed in pretty much as widely as witches; and they are and long have been closely associated ideas, so that there is plenty of philological evidence to link them—they get spoken of in the same context. The Murrayites have treated fairy beliefs as part of their problem, and Miss Murray herself devotes a chapter of the *Witch-Cult* to the connection. But it does not follow that they really are connected in origin; or that witches, in all senses, are connected other than in popular parlance with fairies, in all senses. For "fairy" is another difficult word. For example, there is an absolute and fundamental contrast between the "fairy" who is an individual mischievous inhabitant of our own world, though himself supernatural and perhaps unseen, like Puck, and the "fairies" who live their own secretive lives in their own marvellous country under the hillside, who have their own king and queen and their own customs, who may help or harm the "mortals" who may happen to come in contact with them and periodically may make forays into human territory but do not ordinarily belong there. If the two kinds of fairy get confused in folklore, which does happen, that is plain confusion and nothing more; essentially the two beliefs are quite distinct. Shakespeare, merely drawing on rustic superstition for decorations to *A Midsummer Night's Dream*, made Puck a subject of Oberon and Titania; Rudyard Kipling, taking the whole thing far more seriously, felt the necessity to make Puck explain why he was not like the common run of fairies. The real explanation he ought to have given, of course, is that "fairy" is a vague approximation, a word to describe that which ultimately cannot be described because it is only vaguely imagined and corresponds to nothing in the phenomenal world; the name cannot be more finite than the thing named. This difficulty over words is a further reason for viewing with suspicion

[6] Of course, such stories are largely the concoctions of horror-journalism; if they took their inspiration from any existing belief, it was probably the stories of ritual murder spread against the Jews (e.g. the legend of St. William of Norwich). Ritual murder, though not of children, is also an habitual accusation against Freemasons; like sexual orgies, the slaughter of babies is a standard atrocity story likely to crop up in any context.

any argument turning on the use of two indefinable terms together that would have us believe witches and fairies were real persons in real contact with one another and sharing a common tradition not shared by those who thus lumped them together in language.

The kind of fairy who appears to have given us the sacrificial cycle is of the second kind indicated above. The legend of Thomas of Erchildoune is perhaps the most familiar instance of the way in which such a rite—and even the seven-year term—is associated with the customs of Elfhame in Scottish legend. Indeed, it is the only example I know of that may not be very modern. It is quite likely that all other stories may have been based upon it, for there is no more fatal error one can make in considering folk-tales than to suppose that they must each have an independent origin in fathomless antiquity. Or perhaps there is one worse error: to suppose that a tale whose origin *might* be explained in terms of an ancient custom known to have existed elsewhere is evidence that the same custom once existed in the area where the tale was taken down. Both suppositions could be a danger to our present purpose; both reveal a profound misunderstanding of the conditions in which folk-tales evolve and which determine their popularity and chances of survival, and both are quite common among educated people. It may be that a story will make more appeal to an uneducated audience if it is rooted in beliefs they actually hold; but one should never lay stress on the *former* religion of a region as a factor determining the psychological attitudes of its more backward inhabitants. If a myth or a legend has been forgotten it has been forgotten, and no retelling of it has a prescriptive right to popularity; the social and economic conditions of a community are just as likely to determine what kind of story it will enjoy. Indeed, these will help to determine it, religion or no religion.

The reader will shortly realize why I drag all this in; for the moment, we must consider these fairies of ours a little more closely. According to theories which have enjoyed a wide vogue since the late nineteenth century, and of which the *Zeitgeist* must by now be rather tired, we are to look for the surviving remnant of a displaced population whenever we hear tell of the "Little People." When Celts drove out Picts, and Angles and Saxons later drove out Celts, some few of the original inhabitants would linger on in hidden communities in the woods, or underground. They would survive by secretiveness, and so gain a reputation for invisibility; this they would owe partly to their green camouflage clothing. They would be smaller of stature than their supplanters, and hence gain the name of "Little

People." Having been of a higher culture, they would retain many special arts in which their skill would impress their neighbours as magical. Towards these neighbours they would be shy and suspicious, but not always hostile; on occasion they would intermarry, on other occasions they would trade, though generally in secret. Their closely guarded skills, mysterious movements, and frequent but unacknowledged commerce with the village-dwellers would create the legend of the fairies' helpfulness to favoured mortals. Gradually with intermarriage, they became merged in the common stock, and later still the children of mixed unions forgot the secret crafts and stubborn pagan myths of the older people. But long before that time they had made allies of the witches, who were either their converts or their own nearest kin, the product of the earlier mixed marriages; witchcraft was their religion and their legacy to the invaders.

Now, all this is very fine and large, but it is very far from specific. When and where did these aboriginal communities survive, unconquered, unabsorbed, even undiscovered? It is hard to believe that they survived till Domesday Book in England. When did they finally become absorbed? Who, exactly, were they? How, when they had been driven to a fugitive existence in holes and corners, did they preserve industrial skills superior to those of village and town? Their green clothing must have been dyed with woad; where did they grow it, and how on earth could they conceal the evidence of an industry based on that material? And how much nearer are we to an explanation of those heroes who spent years at the Elf-queen's court, lost to all knowledge of men but riding abroad at their ease in Elfhame?

We may as well begin by disentangling the two kinds of fairy I mentioned before. I am prepared to pass over the question whether we should also distinguish a pixy from a brownie and so forth. The essential distinction is between the fairy who bears an individual name and is closely associated with humankind, who is mischievous or helpful but *interested* in men and constantly in and out of cottage kitchens, and the fairy who bears a generic name and is neither particularly benevolent nor particularly malign but *different*. I suggest it is easier to suppose that there are here two traditions sometimes found mingled; this does not offend the economy of hypotheses, because we have already more synonyms for "fairy" than we know what to do with, implying independent origins for some beliefs, and because some fairy beliefs are not compatible with others.

The geographical distribution of the various folklore elements is of prime importance. In England generally, and in parts of southern Scotland, the fairy is primarily Puck, Robin Goodfellow, Aiken Drum;

a domestic spirit who belongs to the haunts of men, who generally is without companions of his own kind, and who is always named in the singular. He has all the appearance of a demoted minor god of hearth or field, a *daemon*. The smaller deities of the Britons, as I have suggested, were probably not anthropomorphized to any considerable extent before Roman times, but we are now speaking of much later; the Roman period itself supplies three centuries in which such a change might be wrought, even if we had to suppose these godlings were not brought over from the shores of Schleswig-Holstein. Here would be a "pagan survival" indeed, but what an unimpressive one! All the helpfulness, nearly all the commerce with men, much of the skill, and even the invisibility of the fairies belong to these household genii, rather than to the fairies of Elfhame, the pygmy revellers under the hill, who live in their magically protected lands much the same life as men of the outer world, though on the whole more enjoyably.

Two things are worthy of note about the latter tradition: it is much more firmly rooted in Celtic soil, and some of the stories are astonishingly recent. Some that are told in Ireland claim to be hearsay at only one remove. There are fiddlers whose fathers taught them tunes they heard played at the fairies' dances (they sound exactly like ordinary Irish jigs). The Irish as a nation are not celebrated either for literal accuracy or for the sense of time, but we are only concerned with the fact that such stories can be seriously repeated. This man's father saw them, that man's grandmother was one, the other man had a pair of shoes mended by one. All this is contemporary. It does not refer to any dwarf Picts. In a country where proving things out of the census returns is more than usually a popular pastime, we can be even more sure than we should be of Britain that there are no dwarf Picts unaccounted for.

Picts may have been little men, but they cannot have been much shorter than Welshmen or Lowland Scots. These are shorter than the other British peoples, but they are not Lilliputian. If the fairies had that reputation in Wales and the Lowlands, it is likely they were so small as to be positively invisible, and, in fact, not there. The point to note is that it is *not* the conquering nations, but the conquered, who have produced most of the legends. There remains, I admit, Scotland. The Scots invaded from the west, and may have driven the Picts eastward into the forests that then grew there.[7] The Picts *were*

---

[7]Before the general adoption of the coultered plough (which is not before the Dark Ages), invaders commonly took to themselves the land we should regard as least fertile, driving the people they supplanted into the heavy soils which they did not know how to cultivate.

a small race, the Scots a tall one; and though we know that in fact
the two managed to live side by side quite openly, it is possible that
refugees took to the woods, and later when the Lowlanders colonized
from the south and east they came in fleeting contact and avoided one
another thereafter. This would be acceptable enough, if we were
prepared to throw overboard any theory of the fairies' superior crafts-
manship. And of course the Picts (who had already been Christianized from Roman Britain) may have reconstructed their old kingdom,
creating legends of the Queen of Elfhame and her court, and reverted
to their pagan religion, giving rise to stories of the seven-year cycle
of sacrifice as a custom of the fairies. They are reputed to have been
matrilinear and to have copulated in public, both of which details
are jam for Mr. Robert Graves.

Well, it is possible. I would not like to dismiss it out of hand, and
neither would I like to ground an argument on it. Consider what we
are told about fairies. Much of it is not true. How ready are we to
believe that whatever in legend *could* be true, *must* be? The fairies,
in Lowland Scotland as elsewhere, possess powers that cannot be
explained on the "fugitive race" theory. There is a tendency for fairy
gold to turn into dead leaves. You could say the same, poetically,
about Dryads; and, not long ago, German professors would have
insisted that this is a reference to autumn. Fairies are sometimes able
to create an illusion of summer warmth or indoor luxury in the wet
November woods, like Keats's Belle Dame Sans Merci; but more
generally the realm of Elfhame is a whole world like our own but
(to outward seeming) more favoured, existing all the time alongside
the common world and divided from it by some invisible frontier. In
any case, the things said about it belong to daydream; and if this is
merely the product of ignorant gossip about elusive savages, where
are we to draw the limits of ignorance? Were the simple crofters such
good anthropologists, and such poor observers otherwise, that they
penetrated at once to the point of the fairies' religion and got everything else wrong?

It seems clear that we need not presume any factual basis at all for
Elfhame. I do not, of course, mean that none of the fairy legends
can have had a basis in fact; but the consideration just mentioned
requires that we should rest no deductions about a possible shred of
original reality upon the fairy legends as they have come down to us.
For these we need to seek, in any case, for alternative explanations.
They are not hard to come by. Fairies, when represented as another
and more fortunate nation, a kingdom not of this world without being

tiresomely *above* it, are likely to be a product of escapist fantasy; hence, the work of Celtic poets after Saxon invasions, or of the wretched inhabitants of the bleak Lowlands, who were not oppressed by foreigners, but who lived on the margin of subsistence in a cold, hard, hungry world, huddled in their squalid little burghs for fear of wild clansmen, and comforting themselves with dreams of a happier life attainable within a day's journey and without the rigours of sainthood. Ballad-mongers and story-tellers catered for this inarticulate desire and told of it as if it was a fact; Elfhame was a kingdom of the kind of Cockayne or Rock Candy Mountain, the Jerusalem of the underprivileged, the land where everything was easy. I am inclined to believe that there was some existing tradition to draw on, some dim memory that was not quite the Hesperides but more of the old Gaelic paradise or limbo of the dead; for there is just perceptibly a touch of the authentic uncanny about the Scots faëry to separate it from these other clownish Utopias, though this may be no more than the trail of semantic associations across the mind. In any case, the more genuinely it derived from legend, the less it can have done from fact; it is precisely the element of unreality, the enchanted realm that is not really there, or where everything is other than it seems, that gives body and staying power to the "Rhyme of True Thomas" and its related legends.

This of course helps answer one possible objection, that fairies were *feared*. I do not think they can have been much feared by those who actually created the stories, for these cannot have ultimately believed, believed with their whole hearts, or they would have been free to invent nothing. To those who really believed, fairies would always be uncanny; as powerful supernatural allies of the grown-ups, they may have been used to quell tiresome children and so got a bad name, while midwives and gossips not expert in anthropology spread rumours of changelings. But the most circumstantial accounts of fairies are concerned to emphasize the pleasures they enjoy and the peculiar advantages of their country. Of course, there are drawbacks; the fairies, for example, are not Christian. They are conceived as having no religion at all, really, and indeed it is rather necessary they should have none, for it is essential to Elfhame as an escapists' paradise, a place of rest, that it should be neutral in the cruel wars of heaven and hell. Probably the fairies have no souls, though according to some (such as Maurice Hewlett) they could acquire one in certain circumstances. The mortal who went among them ran the danger of losing his. They were nonetheless not mortal in the ordinary sense;

syncretists since the Dark Ages have supposed they were minor angels involved in Lucifer's fall, conditionally pardoned but bound eternally to Middle Earth. And there was that question of sacrifice. Some who were seduced into that other world found after a time that that shadow hung over it, and fled. Nothing is ever made explicit about the shocking custom; perhaps, as they were not Christians, their tribute of blood was owing to Satan, but that is a mere matter of words. The essential point was that the hero should flee, and return to his own country, and the point of that is obvious. The story-teller had got him into the land of the Lotophagoi, and he had to bring him back again somehow; otherwise there was no ending to the story and nothing to vouch for its authenticity. If the hero went away and never came back, how did anybody know what happened to him?

This may seem a tame explanation; but we ought not to shirk it for that. Not all folk-tales are impregnated with wild poetry or deep symbolic meaning, though this may have been in the minds of some who have worked over them to improve them as anyone is always entitled to do. Besides, the literary device is not really so thin and unmeaning as it may look at first sight. The requirement is that the hero, dallying with illusion in a suspended state between Good and Evil, should suddenly be presented with the unavoidable choice between the faith of his baptism and utter renunciation of it, and that is a theme quite worthy of serious literature and a requirement that this plot-device meets. The thing had been done more crudely.

It was done more crudely in the earliest example of this class of story that I know of, from twelfth-century Wales. This was recorded by Giraldus Cambrensis in his *Itinerary*; it was told as fact, the elf-friend in this instance being a man well known to Gerald's informant (who was a bishop). The region was one recently subdued by the Marcher lords, whereas it has left absolutely no evidence of having been occupied at any time by Picts, and so it fits well with what I have already said. These fairies lived the usual gay life underground, and are explicitly said to have had *no* religion; their guest was expelled for trying to steal their gold to give to his mother.[8]

---

[8]Giraldus Cambrensis, *Itinerary through Wales*, cap. 8. I cannot leave Giraldus without mentioning another detail he supplies which may perhaps be significant. Under his own archdeaconry of Brecon, he speaks (cap. 2) of the miraculous reputation of the chapel of St. Alneda or Elynid. This was a place of pilgrimage for the country about; the pilgrims *danced round the church*, and went into a trance in which they performed various convulsions, construed as a pantomime of their previous acts of Sabbath-breaking (even then, apparently, the gravest sin known to the Welsh). Afterwards they were carried into the church and eventually revived, and

I do not know if Thomas of Erchildoune had read Giraldus Cambrensis, and there is no reason to doubt such stories were already current in Scotland. But this example does help to indicate which details may have been Thomas's improvements on his original. He introduces the person of the Queen, the danger of sacrifice, and the gift of truth-telling he came away with. If they were his invention, they are undoubtedly improvements and such as a literary man working over folklore material might produce; the story is tied up more neatly and made to contain a love-interest. Suppose Thomas or some other rhymer was responsible for the sacrificial cycle, that is, for grafting it on to fairy legend; need we look further for the source of the idea itself? Should we have to assume that the belief, to be introduced into a folk-tale, must have previously existed in the same body of folklore? Thomas of Erchildoune was an educated member of the laird class, so it is hardly necessary; but if it was, it would not be necessary to confine enquiry to such Scots folklore as derived from no known source outside Scotland and therefore could be presumed indigenous. There are other possible sources that would have been available to an illiterate Lallans Maker. Thus, the people might believe that their own ancestors had made human sacrifices in the old days because priests with a very vague idea of paganism might have told them so. This is of the order of the things that happen; compare the misconceptions that a modern Scotsman would entertain about the religion of *his* ancestors, Roman Catholicism, bearing in mind that such misconceptions today are much easier to check. Why should the people at large have been more knowledgeable in the Middle Ages than they are today about the religious beliefs and practices of their forefathers?

They would in any case have heard of human sacrifice among the pagan. It supplies part of the theme for the legend of St. George, which was widely popular throughout all Christian countries in the Middle Ages. This example is so clear that we hardly need mention parallels in the lives of other martyrs, nor go into the question of preaching in the Middle Ages or the sources of non-Biblical stories drawn on by preachers. Many such stories that the people would hear and folk-tale narrators work over were doubtless pagan originally, the story of St. George among them; but we know that the Church was

---

were deemed absolved. This very curious account, much earlier than any description of a witch's ring-dance, does look like a pre-Christian or extra-Christian tradition, though actually the nearest parallel to these phenomena is afforded by the revival meeting, or the Jansenist convulsions in eighteenth-century France.

an agency by which they were spread, and we need not postulate imaginary other agencies.

It is therefore conceivable that a custom of periodic human sacrifice was ascribed to witches by mere mental association with fairies, and that it had previously been ascribed to fairies, considered as non-Christian neighbours of the world of men exempted from its hardships, for purely literary causes; and that the whole corpus of fairy literature, thought it may have drawn on Celtic tradition or preserved a reminiscence of it, may have grown up and enjoyed popularity for social rather than religious reasons. I would emphasize again that the fairies are, to say the least of it, poor allies in a Holy War; they are not so much hostile as indifferent towards the Church.

> I am no the Quene of Heaven, True Thomas,
> I never held my heid sae hie,

can hardly be taken as a claim to rival divinity.

This impression is confirmed if we consider how this whole topic is treated in English literature of the age of witch-persecutions. Fairies, it is immediately obvious, were to Shakespeare's age what they are to ours, a pretty product of rural simplicity. Queen Mab may once have been a Celtic goddess of terrible aspect; we know her as the gossamer creation of Mercutio's speech. In *A Midsummer Night's Dream* fairies are introduced as they might be in a modern ballet; indeed there is more serious folklore, not less, in *Swan Lake* or *Giselle*. Spenser uses his fairy knights (who were inspired by legendary *human* figures like Roland or Arthur) as pegs to hang allegory on rather in the spirit of Tolkien. By the time of the "Cavalier" poets, when witch hysteria was mounting to a crescendo, fairies had sunk to the nadir of their importance. In the "Farewell Rewards and Fairies" of Bishop Corbet they are a joke.

It is clear from this last example that to talk as if you believed in fairies as a phenomenon of the recent past and as religious dissidents, and regretted their passing, was perfectly safe in the reign of James I, as any such light-hearted attitude towards witches would not have been. The two were still regularly linked in the popular mind, as they are today; the mental association was as natural then as now, except to a fanatical witch-hunter. The preachers and pamphleteers who agitated for greater severity did not dwell on the connection. They may not have believed in it; and whatever they were capable of believing, they must have despaired of ever hanging a fairy.

I am not at the moment concerned with the hysteria, except in so far as it may throw light on the origins of beliefs that were to be fastened on the figure of the witch in the imagination. As regards human sacrifice, we might expect to find it talked of among the rites of the Sabbat, but in fact the goat-god seems usually to have been content without it. We should expect to find, and we do find, that the seventeenth century can furnish instances where it is supposed to have occurred, not at Sabbats on a blasted heath but at the private, indoor Black Masses of a more urban and book-learned kind of magician. There is only too much reason to suppose that babies were sacrificed to the Devil in the Paris of Louis XIV; kings, on the other hand, plainly were not. A regular traffic in spells and horrifying rituals—the kind of thing you need an unfrocked priest for—came under the notice of Louis's police; but nothing is known of it that would link it with a genuine native tradition, either of sorcery or of superstitions about sorcerers.[9] (This sort of thing was then believed—probably with little foundation—to be common in Italy; but Italy at that time was often held to be the home of all depravities. In any case, the Black Mass is typically the superstition of a more or less educated society, and it would take some education to stage it convincingly.)

I asked four question at the end of the last chapter. They were: is there any ground for supposing that the pre-Christian religion of England or any Western European nation involved the regular sacrifice of kings? Is there anything to link human sacrifice, and a seven-year cycle governing it, with the witch-cult? Did sacrifices of the first kind occur in the Middle Ages? Lastly, was the mediaeval witch-cult under the patronage of a Court and aristocracy that was, for most of the relevant period, crypto-pagan?

I think I have suggested reasons why we should answer "No" to all these but the last. As regards the first, I would emphasize that what we are called on to grant or deny is that there are *grounds for supposing* the custom suggested did exist; not that it did exist in fact. I would also emphasize that it would not be enough that ideas of human sacrifice, but not of the sacrifice of kings, should have formed a part of those religions; for other kinds of human sacrifice are possible and seem to be more common. It would also not be enough to show that such ideas could be deduced from myth; for many religions, including the Christian, have myths of sacrifice but not the custom. Unless we have some pretty positive indication of the custom's having existed

[9]See, e.g., Rhodes, *Satanic Mass*, Pt. III, *passim*.

recently in the Age of Conversion, to postulate its survival is an addition to our problem and dares the razor. Once we read mediaeval history without a predisposition to find human sacrifice at the bottom of every political assassination, I think it is safe to say that we shall not find it there. The motive that should impel us to such a predisposition is largely abolished if we do not feel a need to establish that where you have witchcraft, there you have the sacrificial cycle, and therefore if you have witchcraft at Court, then you have the sacrificial cycle at Court.

But look where this leads us. If that last point is valid, and evidence for the periodic immolation of kings really immaterial, then we are no nearer solving our remaining question; our three "No's" may help make a "Yes." We are not entitled, on the basis of the argument so far, to deny that witchcraft rather than Christianity may have been the real religion of the feudal aristocracy and the intimate circles of kings.

I have indeed denied that it was "the real religion of England in the Middle Ages" in any sense that would exclude the predominance of Christianity in intellectual leadership and in the country at large; and I am ready to say with entire confidence that the contrary view is based on mere ignorance. As to intellectual leadership, it was Christian from the first moment that one can employ such a phrase, and owed its leadership to its Christianity. The Church preserved all the learning that survived the Dark Ages, even pagan learning and legend; every clerk would have some vague knowledge of the Augustans as part of his grounding in Latin, though his might often be the classical scholarship of Partridge in *Tom Jones*. Certainly some churchmen found those studies more attractive than any matter of breviary, and startling evidence of "paganism" might be drawn from the literary products of the Age of Faith. But the Diana they invoked to light them to a lady's window was a danger to discipline, not to the Faith; such paganism was a problem of internal good order in the clerical estate. The Church had its rebels; but that is nothing to our immediate purpose.

It is difficult, indeed it is impossible, to believe that kings and great magnates, or even the run of bonnet lairds of the feudal classes, did not support Christianity. Some were saints; and in these cases we know a good deal about their private lives. We know less about lesser men, but it remains clear that certain kinds of piety were respectable and taken for granted. King John was a benefactor to monks; indeed he was an unusually lavish one, though most kings either founded abbeys or favoured those their ancestors had founded. Often we know what houses prayed for them after their death; and that is to know very little compared with our knowledge of Alfred or Edward the Confessor, Charlemagne or Louis the Pious or Louis the Ninth. Not only kings but the greater local magnates, and sometimes the most bloodthirsty of them, were not only benefactors to the Church but connoisseurs of new fashions in piety. There were saints, not all of them warriors, and devotions, not all of them easy, that made a special appeal to the nobleman. The Orders of the Temple and Hospital, of which the first was afterwards to gain so dark a reputation, began as attempts to find room for the knight in the most rigid kind of monastic life, and there must have been knights who demanded such admittance. Indeed, the Crusades as a whole demonstrate how, by the eleventh century, feudalism itself had become Christianized; and of course they also demonstrate that the official religion of Western Europe was something more than a lukewarm pretence. The things that Christianity drove men to do in the Middle Ages may be worthy of praise or blame, but Christianity was capable of driving men.

It was not perhaps a Christianity that would look very familiar today. If feudalism had become Christian, Christianity had in a sense become feudal, and there was little enough of the Sermon on the Mount in it. The gradual changes that are perceptible in the predominant lay attitudes to religious matters, and their possible correlation with changes in social attitudes, form a fascinating study but one far beyond my capacity, and it will in any case not be necessary to do more than glance at it here. Suffice it to say that the Catholic faith in the Middle Ages (that is to say, in England from the eighth or ninth centuries onwards and in other countries from other times but in all the Latin West from about 1000 A.D.) received the full and active support of the leaders of society, and in many instances it is clear that the grandee's object in supporting it was to save his own soul, not to secure a temporal ally. I am afraid this is too large a question to be more than asserted here; anyone who does not wish to accept it has the option of studying the works of profounder scholars than I, but there is certainly no informed controversy on the point.

It is, however, obvious that conversion, whether of Court or of People, did not occur suddenly at a given moment; pagan survivals there must have been and were, but we must make it clear what we mean by this. We have to distinguish at least three kinds of "surviving paganism": the conservatism of those who were unconvinced by the missionaries and consciously hostile; the May-games and such like that were still held, though officially their pagan purpose no longer existed, and which in the absence of the first kind of conservatism would survive only as usage, not as religious usage; and the customs, such as those of the Yule feast, that were officially Christian though for those who happened to know it they had once been pagan.

Conversion was gradual, not only in the sense that first one man and then another was converted, but in that a man or a nation that had accepted baptism advanced to full and conscious Christianity by stages. The work of explaining and specifying Christianity to a people already Christian in allegiance can be traced through the legal codes of the Angles and Saxons from Ine to Canute; but perhaps a clearer and more accessible instance, though much simplified, is to be found in the Saga of Burnt Njal. The Icelanders, being divided between Christian and pagan parties, submitted the question to arbitration, and as a result agreed, as a body, to become Christian. Having decided this, they next asked what Christians were required to do, and adopted laws to enforce outward conformity. Later, these were tightened up and secret as well as open paganism was forbidden. This is probably more or less what occurred in many places; though conditions in Iceland were peculiar by reason of the looseness of its political structure. Elsewhere the function of making these decisions and enforcing them fell not on a popular assembly but on a king.

I have said a certain amount about kingship among the pagan peoples that swept in on the Western Empire in the fifth century. It is time to say a little concerning the development of the institution, because, although the true place for such a discussion would be a book on an altogether different subject, our subject has been treated in such a way as to make some picture of mediaeval society as a whole, and mediaeval monarchy in particular, a necessary piece of spadework. I must warn the reader that while so far I have not, to the best of my belief, stepped outside the limits of what is common ground to those with the equipment to judge, I here begin to intrude personal opinions, and it is by no means certain that all would approve my presentation of the period.

The Teuton invaders (to adopt a useful but unfashionable word) had had kings of a kind, but set little store by the institution. Fate and the Law were above gods and kings, and a brave man could defy all four of them, though not safely. But in the conditions of the invasion the ruler of divine blood had taken on a new practical importance as leader of the war-band, a position only he could normally fill because only he could hope to command free men. The personal tie between the leader and his chosen companions was then the highest bond of obligation known; formalized as vassalage it became the basis of social organization in the new settlements. The kings of the new barbarian kingdoms that were set up within the former boundaries of the Empire were first and foremost captains of the sworn war-band or shield-ring, and their nobles were their most trusted warriors. But from the first there were other influences at work to mould the institutions of these new monarchies. The most magnificent king their world knew of had been the Roman Emperor; and still the greatest ruler of Europe was the Emperor at Constantinople. When the barbarians carved up the Western provinces, they were perfectly well aware of what they were inheriting. Many had first been admitted within the *limes* as subject allies of Rome; in France, Spain, and Italy the basic population was still Roman and retained its Roman church and laws. Remoter savages from the far north roved the Mediterranean as pirates or served the Eastern Emperor as mercenaries ("Varangians"); they were familiar figures in the streets of Byzantium, the "Micklegarth" of the sagas.

The Roman example was thus present to the eyes of the invaders; and it was probably from Rome that they acquired the concept of the king as law-giver. It was certainly this example they were following when their kings took to wearing crowns and surrounding themselves with the quasi-priestly apparatus of royalty, purple and fine linen, as when they issued coinage stamped with their effigies.

With the acceptance of Christianity the process of assimilation to the Roman model was accelerated and inspiration drawn also from more narrowly ecclesiastical sources.[10] The Mediaeval Church changed its mind about monarchy, and the secular state generally, more than once. If one closely examines our own Coronation Service a number of strata, so to speak, can be detected; and in the High, the classic Middle Ages, the time of knights-errant and troubadours and that kind of thing, the Church by and large was away out on the left wing. In the Dark Ages, however, the Church took a higher view of secular government, and of kings in particular, than at any time before or since. The reason is obvious: the king was the Church's best possible ally.

In the Dark Ages the Church both favoured, and relied on the favour of, royal authority. By the rite of coronation as it developed in this age, the king became the "Lord's Anointed" in something more

[10]However profound or superficial we suppose the conversion to have been, bishops were thereafter the closest counsellors of kings.

than a figure of speech; by conversion he was Constantine, by unction he was also David. In other words, the Church was reinterpreting the kingship of the Northern barbarians in the light of the monarchy it knew, idealized. The king thus gained enormous new dignity, wider responsibilities, and the advantage of skilled advice. In the modern sense, there scarcely was any "state" before the conversion in such countries as England, so profound was the effect of Christianity on the office of a king.

However, the large ideas of royalty that kings and priests now came to hold were too large to fit the facts; kings acquired a new taste for making laws without always enjoying the means to enforce them. The rise of feudalism, as part of the transition from the Dark to the Early Middle Ages, is a subject too vast to detain us; suffice it to say that it marked a temporary ascendancy of brute realism, and that as one aspect of this the powers of government were delegated to, or assumed by, the local military boss in such large measure that the king generally became little more than the biggest competitor in the business. A little more he always was; he enjoyed, and the new military caste did not enjoy, the advantage of a sacred office conferred by the Church, and in time this proved important enough for kings to recover all and more than all that they had lost.

The feudal nobility were never looked on in quite the same religious light. But that is not to say they were pagans. They now became the usual benefactors of monastic houses, the useful allies of ecclesiastical reformers; and gradually the Church became reconciled to the power of the baronage. As it had consecrated kingship and given it a religious purpose, so now it consecrated knighthood. The knight was originally no more than the mounted soldier; he was a man of account because his equipment was expensive and his value in war great, but morally he was, often enough, a mere mobsman and cut-throat. He was therefore a problem for the Church, but as a delinquent, not as a dissident. The Crusades, almost spontaneously, solved the problem; there was a place even for the lawless tough in the Christian commonwealth. He suddenly found himself a respectable member of society; soon his profession was looked on with reverence and gathered about it a myth. The effect on the knight, of course, was that he began to model himself on his flattering portrait. Knighthood became a semi-religious order, a continent-wide club for the Christian warrior. Ceremony came later; but from the twelfth century, in German vernacular poetry, the ideal and emotional significance of the *Schwertleite* is already prominent.

In the same age the knightly class, the nobility considered as a single order, was acquiring a code of manners. Besides the ideal picture of the chevalier there was becoming defined the ideal picture of the courtier. They are rather like those cut-out figures sold for children, which can be dressed in a variety of paper costumes; for the good courtier is merely the good knight in his times of relaxation. He wears softer, gayer, less practical clothes, and devotes himself to softer, gayer, and less useful pursuits, especially courtly love. This figure, unlike the other, was never given an explicitly Christian purpose; it was not necessary, since the man under the clothes was baptized and his life-work had a religious sanction. When he relaxed, he could be allowed to relax from specific piety also. It is clear from the contemporary literature of Court and courtliness that the gentleman is expected to be a good Catholic but this is the least Catholic side of him. Erotic literature at moments seems to make the lady herself an object of devotion, and the whole duty of a paramour, the service expected by Cupid, is to some extent a parody of Christian devotion and to some extent dabbles in a kind of literary paganism. It is streets away from real paganism; it plays with what is nearly blasphemy for the thrill that blasphemy can only supply when what is blasphemed is really and seriously believed in. I dwell on this kind of point because it is essential to bear in mind the sense in which a particular element of "paganism" in the Middle Ages is pagan.[11]

Courtly love, and mediaeval love-literature when produced by spoilt priests, are pagan only in the undergraduate sense. This is worth emphasizing, because there seems to be a disposition in some quarters to see in them the Mother-Goddess resuming her sway. The new knightly respect for women (only for *some* women; and not shared by the spoilt clerks who use the most pagan language) is not altogether easy to explain. It has been called a product of the cult of the Virgin; it has been called a permeation of high society by the old paganism; it has been called both, the cult of the Virgin being itself a revival of Mother-Goddess worship. (There are other and better explanations, though none that can claim to be final; but they do not bear on our subject.[12]) None of these suggestions can be tested, and none of them supply a complete answer to any problem; but we may as well see how fitted they are to carry conviction.

[11] The known element of Arabic influence on the traditions of courtly love does not affect the argument, since this influence was derived from Arabic poetry and philosophy, but not religion; and was, indeed, as incompatible with strict Islam as with strict Christianity. For this whole subject see Denomy, *The Heresy of Courtly Love.*

[12] See, e.g., Lewis, *The Allegory of Love*, cap. 1.

The cult of the Virgin rose to popularity at about the same time as the new attitude to women becomes perceptible (from about 1100). Both had earlier existed in the Greek Orthodox world. It is easy to believe that they were connected as products of the same root causes; impossible to allow that they were related as cause and effect. "Mariolatry" was popular in society as a whole, though it was of course specially marked among the pious; *Frauendienst* was almost confined to the aristocracy, and was specially marked among the rather impious. It is obvious the Virgin had many worshippers who were not moved to take a particularly high view of Woman generally, because this seems to have been the case with the mass of the laity and almost all monks.

I have already mentioned the main objection to the Mother-Goddess theory in this connection: that when *Frauendienst* starts to take on a non-Christian tinge the rival set up against Christ is not Aphrodite, or any other mythological figure at all, but the individual human woman; and it may be added that she herself is not commonly represented as hostile to the Church; personal piety was one of the socially correct graces in women, and none but Christian piety was contemplated. In the literature of the period the names of goddesses are fairly frequent, as they were in the eighteenth century, and for the same purpose: ornamental allegory. As for the Mother-Goddess, no cult focussed on Woman at all was ever less matristic; the *medons paramours* as *mother* is to be found only in the works of Maurice Hewlett.

It is scarcely worth bothering to enquire, when this is said, whether the root of *Frauendienst* could be the worship of a Great Mother reinterpreted as Mary-worship. But is the cult of the Virgin itself so to be explained? In a sense, I think we can exclude such a view; but only in a sense. We know too much about its rise to popularity to believe the promoters of the movement had any sneaking sympathy with the heathen. I am speaking, however, only of the West, not of the Eastern origins. It is fairly likely that many saints of the Greek Church are naturalized Olympians in origin, though I do not myself believe the cult of the Panhagia is to be included in that class. The cult of the Virgin was introduced into Western Europe by Christians and for Christians, and the Latin world before the twelfth century managed to get along somehow without any mother-goddess. To some of the followers of Jung this must seem hard to believe, but the fact is clear.

(The Jungian view of the mother archetype may of course help to explain the popularity of the cult of the Virgin, once it had become established. Nor need we be surprised to find that the cult shows *parallels* with pagan worship.[13])

The natural course of my present narrative would next bring me to speak of the first mediaeval heresies and especially of the Albigensians. I propose however to withdraw them for separate consideration; the more willingly, because they were none of them, in themselves, movements of central and dominant importance in the history of their age.

Of this history I shall find room for only one more development here. The "nation" and the "national interest" are abstractions; and men in the Middle Ages did not find it easy to think in abstractions. Indeed, this only gradually became possible to them. Theologians had to employ abstract terms, but even to a theologian an abstraction could hardly remain abstract and still be thought of as really existing. To be fully apprehended it must have an objective correlative, or be expressed in some visible symbol. "Sin" in the Dark Ages was thought of in the same terms as *crime*, as a matter of positive wrongful acts; a proud man is one who is visibly vainglorious. Knightly "honour" is indistinguishable from reputation, good fame; reason is essentially argument; liberty, a legally enforcible right; law indistinguishable from custom, and both law and custom something to be bodied forth in public symbolic acts. Catholicism, with its sacraments and incarnate God and resurrection of the body, was peculiarly suited to such an age, and anything like gnosticism profoundly out of sympathy with it, though gnosticism did inspire some few heretics and Catholicism bred the Nominalist controversy. It was the Church, and symbolism borrowed from the Church as a didactic technique, that taught mediaeval man to apprehend the reality he could not touch or see.

A man had a country and a king; he had hardly a nation. What sense of collectivity there was, beyond individual obligations of man to particular man, was almost without emotive force. It was only gradually, under stress and aided by the symbolical habit, that a sense of group-cohesion, of common interest in certain shared purposes and rights, grew up on the modest scale of such bodies as the gilds. The merchants of a town, having a common cause against its lord and against other towns, would band together in a brotherhood that gave visible proof of its existence in ceremonies, feasts, and acts of corporate worship; the members would be formally sworn to participate, and all would be as formal as it could be made, for there was no instinctive sense of class- or group-solidarity; it had to be created. The same kind of process was taking place throughout society in the twelfth and

[13]See Neumann, Erich (q.v., Bibliography).

thirteenth centuries; as it affected the privileged part of society, it produced in time a sense of cohesion and common interest among the whole baronage or the whole *sacerdotium* of a kingdom, where the king was strong enough to be felt as a menace. To take England as an example, this process is complete, as far as the aristocracy is concerned, by the middle thirteenth century; and so, from that time on, you have conscious political action supported by the baronage as a body, and you have political propaganda, measures and movements and talk of the national interest or the Community of the Kingdom.

This becomes a permanency, because it achieves formal, symbolical expression, in the various Parliaments and Assemblies of Estates that grew up in most countries about this time. These were specially solemn meetings of the king's Court, but they were also occasions of calling together, in the conduct of public business, the whole nation in symbolic form; men qualified to speak for every interest that went to make up the national interest. It therefore came to include, besides feudal magnates and prelates, representatives of the petty nobility and of the merchants, though naturally not of the unfree peasantry whose "interest," like their whole lives, was confined to the manor and did not exist on the national scale. Many factors went to the making of such institutions; but once made, they had this in common, that they provided a visible expression for the idea of a nation and in them, for the first time, the king was truly king of the nation. It would be a grave error to look on this development only as an early triumph of Whig principles; the king derived from it a new dignity and a new sphere of authority. He could, in practice, dare to do things with its aid that he could not have done before: consciously legislate in the modern sense, and raise higher taxes. But also he could now appear more visibly royal. The occasions of Parliament or States-General or Cortes were the occasions when he put on his most sumptuous regalia and held court for the most varied and distinguished body of subjects that ever foregathered; when he took weighty counsel in the sight of all his noble barons, and holy bishops, and trusty-and-well-beloved citizens of his free towns. It was then that the size and wealth and assembled talent of the kingdom could be seen, and its history and liberties and good customs, its admirable past and promising future, spoken of and remembered. From this age, patriotism in the modern sense was possible; from this time on, but not before, kings as such might be regarded as holding an office that carried responsibilities not to God alone nor to particular men alone but to the nation. Moreover, from now on (for some centuries) the king really dominates politics as he never did before. Kings may be weak or strong, but they are bound to be important. They may be pious or wicked, but they have political as well as moral obligations. In this age the idea of the royal victim might have grown up, because in this age the idea of a king dying for the people would have made sense.

Before I close this chapter, candour compels me to admit that I have not suggested a final answer to my fourth question, whether witchcraft was patronized at Court by crypto-pagan rulers. I think, however, any competent mediaevalist would agree that magic prob- ably, and in the form of witchcraft very possibly, was surreptitiously employed by some in all classes; and perhaps specially by politicians about Court, including kings and their favourites, because they had obvious need of its assistance. On the other hand, they were not, therefore, pagan, because in that age there was nothing contrary to the Faith in *belief* in witchcraft, and employing it was plain sin, like fornication, in which a Christian could of course indulge and remain a Christian though not a good one. We can be perfectly confident that the nobility and people at large in every kingdom of Latin Christen- dom were actually Christian in intention in the High and Late Middle Ages; to deny it is to fly in the face of the evidence. But common sense and the evidence of course equally forbid us to suppose that these people were, consistently and always, Christians in achievement and in the highest sense.

༄

A Hunt for a Huntress

༄༄

.... Nevertheless, it should not be omitted that some wicked women, won over to Satan's side (*retro post Satanam conversae*) and beguiled by deceits and hallucinations of devils, believe and profess that they ride out on beasts by night with Diana the goddess of the Heathen and a numberless multitude of women, and cover great distances in the silence of night, and on particular nights (*certis noctibus*) are summoned to this service. But would that they only perished in their faithlessness, and did not drag down many with them into the same unfaith! For a numberless multitude, beguiled by this false opinion, hold it to be true, and . . . revert to the error of the Heathen, when they suppose there is any divinity or spirit of power save the One God. Wherefore priests must preach to the people . . . with all urgency, that they may understand that this is altogether false and that such illusions are bred in faithless minds not by the Holy but by the Evil Spirit. . . . Satan . . . when he gets possession of some worthless gossip's wits (*mentem cujuscumque mulierculae*) . . . leads astray the mind he holds captive, deluding it in dreams; and this faithless mind supposes that things experienced only in the imagination happened to the body, not to the spirit. . . .

THUS (WITH A good deal of verbiage I omit) Regino, Abbot of Prüm, writing about 900. The passage occurs in the course of what was perhaps meant to be a lengthy footnote to his collection of canons relating to sorcery, though it may also be itself a canon, the act of some council otherwise forgotten. Owing to a fusion of chapter-headings in Regino's work, which may not have been unintentional, it was read by most later canonists as an act of the Council of Ancyra (314) which it certainly was not. Somebody, perhaps in the first instance Burchard of Worms, about 1020, added to "Diana" the conjectural emendation "vel Herodiade"[1]; Gratian in the next century incorporated this in the text, and on Gratian's high authority the "Canon Episcopi," as it came to be known, was generally accepted for the rest of the Middle Ages. Latterly, with the rise of Anti-Sadducism, it became inconvenient, as it did not seem to square with contemporary opinion on the Sabbat; Kramer and Sprenger were put to the trouble of explaining it away. Doubts began to be cast on it in the following century, by the Jesuit witch-hunter Delrio. In the seventeenth century Etienne de Baluze suggested on stylistic grounds that it was perhaps a fragment of a lost Carolingian Capitulary (he was able to prove without difficulty that it was not a canon of Ancyra). This suggestion was adopted by Migne and has been repeated by nearly every subsequent commentator, some going so far as to re-christen it the "Capitulum Episcopi." Kittredge, in our own day, stated as a fact that the Canon was earlier than Regino, but probably he did so inadvertently. Nobody has yet discovered an earlier source. In the manuscript notes published after his death, Professor H. C. Lea suggested tentatively that Regino may have written the Canon himself.[2]

The debate will doubtless continue unless an earlier origin of the text can be found. Nobody nowadays, however, expects a very much earlier origin to come to light. It is fair to assume that the hypothetical council was held, or hypothetical capitulary issued, close to Regino both in time and place. I propose therefore as the simplest course to treat Regino as the author, with the caveat "or a near contemporary" understood.

It was hard that the Anti-Sadducees should blame the Canon for not agreeing with their beliefs about Walpurgisnacht; for there is reason to suspect that these beliefs are actually in part derived from it. Certainly they, and everyone else, have always assumed without question that it was to the Sabbat that the Canon referred, which is not immediately obvious from the text; and both they and the Murray-ites have relied utterly upon it to establish the Sabbat's antiquity.

But does it really refer to the Sabbat? And if it does, are the Murray-ites correct in supposing that it supports the "Dianist" interpretation;

[1]Not only MSS of Burchard but Burchard's own usage varied, and in his *Decretum*, XIX, cap. 5 he paraphrases the canon twice over—articles 70 and 90—and in the former refers to the lady as "Hulda" (cf. p. 111).

[2]Migne PL cxxxii: Regino of Prüm, *De Disciplinis Ecclesiasticis Libri II*, cap. 364; cf. in the same volume notes to the same by Etienne de Baluze. Lea, *Materials*, p. 170ff; Kittredge, *Witchcraft in Old and New England*, p. 244, where he also argues that the Canon did *not* refer to witches.

does this evidence help establish the continuity of paganism? The author certainly considered that these women were slipping back into pagan errors, and he may have thought they were witches; he does not apply to them any Latin word having this sense, but this is rather the suggestion of the chapter taken as a whole. What he is describing is not very close either to the later idea of the Sabbat or to an act of pagan worship, at least as he describes it. As proof of the survival of anything but a popular belief it is all exceedingly thin, and Regino's suggestion is that the belief is both pure delusion and not *consciously* pagan; it is something a Christian congregation had better be warned not to believe. This of course fits in very well with the conditions of Germany in the ninth century, when the conversion of most of the country was fairly recent history; elimination of this superstition would be a step in that consolidation of conversion I spoke of in the last chapter. To admit that pagan beliefs were not yet quite dead in this region and age is to concede nothing to the Murrayites, for it has never been disputed, and never taken to prove that the conversion of Germany and the West generally was therefore always incomplete. It tells us nothing whatsoever about the survival of pagan beliefs in the High Middle Ages, nor does it tell us that full-fledged paganism survived even into Regino's day. Full-fledged paganism is obviously not what he is talking about, but insufficient Christianity.

Let us consider the name "Diana." Did the Germans in their heathen days worship Diana? Of course they did not, knowingly and under that name, though I suppose we should allow a shadow of credit to that assumption so dear to the hearts of comparative religionists of the Graves type that they *must* have done so, without knowing it. This would not make a German churchman of the late Carolingian epoch use the name. But he wanted a Latin name for a mythological personage, because he was writing in Latin; and his earliest grammar-studies would have given him a working knowledge of the Olympian Pantheon as it appears in literature of the Augustan age. So we are to suppose that the leader of the phantom cavalcade was a female, probably though not certainly worshipped as a goddess by the local populace before conversion (for the author may have been mistaken on such a point), and who had certain attributes in common with the *literary* figure of Diana which were enough to distinguish her from other Graeco-Roman deities.

The literary associations of the goddess Diana would be to an educated man of the ninth century what they are to an educated man of the twentieth: with the moon, with hunting, and with chastity.

We need not presume all these were present; in the context, hunting or the moon (or both) are clearly the more probable. This Diana is the leader of a mounted meinie of women; they were mounted, perhaps, on beasts other than horses, but apart from the goddess's own presence, and the suggestion that a preternatural distance was covered on these occasions, there seems to have been nothing contrary to nature in their progress. There is no mention of any other activity of theirs, or any act of worship more than is implied in being obedient to a leader thought of as divine. We may perhaps take the "wicked women" involved to have been witches of the hagwife variety who claimed acquaintance with this "Diana" to get themselves credit, and of course the cavalcade may have had many nefarious purposes, for it is not stated where they rode or why. But to make the Canon refer to witchcraft at all we have to read into it rather more than it says; and even so there is no visible link as yet with the witches who danced their ring-dances in honour of the Horned God.

Certainly, if one was to lie on the psychiatrist's couch and let one's mind wander over the associations called up by the Canon *Episcopi*, one might very well arrive at the Sabbat. One might think, "Diana—moon—horns—Devil," or "women riding out by night with Diana—pagan women riding by moonlight—servants of the moon-goddess riding to a secret rendezvous—witches carried through the air on moonlight nights to the Sabbat," or "Diana—Actaeon—horned man and naked women—Sabbat." But a train of mental associations is not a proof; and the thread is really rather tenuous. The common element is not great between a nocturnal cavalcade of women, led by a goddess, to a place and for a purpose unstated, which is a delusion and does not in fact occur, and a real ceremony of worship of a male being, equally nocturnal, but not confined to women, in which riding in a large company is not a necessary part though *supernatural* transportation (not necessarily on any beast) perhaps may be. However, the train of associations—indeed many possible trains—do exist; so that it is on the cards the belief in the Sabbat might develop out of the belief that is here condemned.

The Canon can only be taken to show that the belief in this "riding with Diana," or with *somebody*, existed in about the ninth century in Germany. It can even be narrowed further: some beings rode with some Being; the latter was female, immortal, and (in the eyes of churchmen) non-existent; the former were female, and may or may not have been mortal. Some who held the belief supposed, on the evidence of their dreams, that they had taken part in the ride. Their spreading of pagan errors, with a possible motive of vainglory, may have been the extent of the "wickedness" imputed to them; they are represented as honestly deceived, and the chapter can be so read as to single them out, by contrast, from sorcerers. These women did not actually ride out; very possibly the original legend had not asserted that real women did so. The Canon's psychological interpretation is perfectly credible; given the legend, it is not in the least unlikely that it would affect the details of dreams of rapid and easy travel (which are a common class of dreams), or that such dreams would be assimilated to the legend on waking. Primitive and uneducated people frequently do fail to distinguish between dream and actuality. The claim that particular women had taken part in the legendary nocturnal rout could easily arise in just the manner the canonist suggested, even though the original legend had been concerned wholly with inhabitants of another world. (When I say "original," I mean of course "in the stage immediately previous to that in which the ecclesiastics became aware of it," in late pagan times, which is as far back as it concerns us to look.) It may have originated in some ceremony, but it must in that case have lost its factual basis and survived only as a popular belief. We cannot suppose that any such rite then continued to be performed, for if it did, that and not the old wives' tale it gave rise to would be what Regino would inveigh against.

What, then, was the legend? We know a good deal about the beliefs of the Germans in the period before Christianity took a sure hold, but not quite enough to answer this question for certain. What we can say is that stories of a "phantom hunt," which look promising, were widespread in the Northern world, though the hunter is usually a man in legend as in real life, and in Germany (in the relatively modern period when folklore came to be studied) was usually Wotan. This last is not an insuperable obstacle. There is also, very closely related to these stories, the cavalcade of the *dead*, which is a recurrent theme in folklore over a wider area including the Celtic countries. I have already suggested that in them it developed usually into the fairy revels. Before the Church had spread the idea of rewards and punishments after death, it could have almost any significance, and afterwards it could develop in several different directions. The departed spirits might be on their way to the shades, or back to some kind of reincarnation; they might be out for a holiday, or in attendance on a god about his business. They might, in particular, be out hunting, for where the legend of the "Wilde Jagd" existed it is clear that it was regularly associated with the cavalcade of the dead. In the case under discussion, one of these last would seem to be the likeliest interpretation.

In Germany the leader of this rout might well be a Walküre, a female "chooser of the slain." She was certainly a woman; tradition preserves the names Holda, or Perchta, or both, and Holda can be identified with Nerthus, the German Earth-Mother, which looks hopeful. (We cannot of course be sure that the names were not attached to the legend in relatively modern times.) In France and England we hear of Herlechin, of Herla, of Herne the Hunter, whose legends make it abundantly plain that they are Lords of the Dead.[3] The alliteration with "Herodias" leaps to the eye; and probably it is not the only alliteration involved. In countries of Teutonic speech it is reasonable to guess that a male leader of the rout was described as "Heretoch," "Herzog," or a cognate formation: the Leader of the Host. Names that alliterated with this may have been independently coined in several places, and one of these may have been known to the glossator who supplied "vel Herodiade," but who took it on Regino's authority that the leader was really female. "Vel" is indeterminate between "and" and "or"; later ages were to imagine several female leaders, and to concoct a legend that made this Herodias the daughter of Diana. Of many alternative names the one that showed the most staying power at least in literary references was Dame Habonde, Abonde, or Abundia, whose first known appearance was in a poetic paraphrase of the Canon in twelfth-century France (the continuation of the *Roman de la Rose*, by Jean de Meung). This name puzzled the clerks, as well it might, for it seems to have no natural roots in France. "Epiphania" was one not-very-confident gloss, and "Abundantia" another; the second of these was a classical goddess of sorts, a minor figure of the Roman Emperor-cult, but an unexpected one in this context. Another bare possibility is that if the legend was German in provenance "Abonde" might derive from "Abend," evening. "Lady of Evening" would be a perfectly reasonable description of Diana, who would have little enough in common with Holda, the Earth-Mother, or a euhemeran personification of Plenty.

Regino's evidence is the first we have of this nocturnal rout. It is clearly not the only source of all later stories, for it speaks of a caval-

---

[3]Herne and his companions are to be found in most standard works on folklore; Lea supplies some more obscure examples and the subject is touched on in Murray, *God of the Witches*. Familiar as it is, however, I know of no one who has commented upon the alliteration.

For the continental examples see Bächtold-Stäubli, *Handwörterbuch*, s.v. "Abundia."

cade exclusively of women and fails to mention whether they are living or dead. Since those stories which are explicit on this point, make out the leader to be male, and give him a name alliterating on "Her-," cannot derive from Regino, the earliest of them must derive independently from folk-tradition in another but related region. But every subsequent *literary* appearance of the goddess and her female meinie could derive from Regino and cannot be taken as evidence for the popular beliefs of the region and age that produced it; and those that do not derive directly from the Canon could derive from earlier literary uses of it. This is obvious; what is not so obvious is that actual popular beliefs could derive from this source also, in countries out of reach of the original legend, and could be profoundly influenced by the learned glosses even in the area that supplied Regino with his information.

The Canon *Episcopi* was accepted into all major canon-law collections; and it deals with instructions to preachers. It had authority outside Germany; it laid a certain obligation on bishops and their clergy; it is most likely that bishops and their clergy sometimes fulfilled this obligation, and in doing so brought to the knowledge of their congregations precisely the superstition they were concerned to root out. Often enough the preachers may have got the whole thing rather garbled. The parish priest would not have a Gratian of his own to consult; he would remember, perhaps with advantages, the verbal instructions given him by bishop or archdeacon. In these circumstances it is easy to see how Diana might come to ride farther afield. The more simple-minded the priest, the more ready he would be to suppose Diana a real devil instead of a false goddess, and the "illusion" spoken of, the glamour or unholy fascination she was able to cast over the minds of the unwary. The train of associations I spoke of earlier might begin in his mind, or in those of his hearers, and the condemned opinion be confused with any existing belief, or true knowledge come to that, that happened to supply a point of coincidence.

(Thus, to anticipate, Albigensians and Waldensians were not good Catholics, and they met, in time of persecution, by night; so probably it was they who rode with Diana, and supernatural flight of women to their assemblies did, indeed, come to be reported.)

Passing from mouth to mouth, and growing in the telling, the story took on new elements, by confusion with other stories, by mere exaggeration and impromptu embroidery, and conceivably also by the influence of actual dreams. In some way or another, the "riding" of the original became, almost universally, construed as flight through the air; and the women, very reasonably when it had been forgotten (if this was the case) that they were supposed to be dead, were identified as witches. In almost all literary versions from Jean de Meung's continuation of the *Roman de la Rose* to Heine's *Atta Troll*, Diana drops out and Dame Abonde or Herodias, or both, lead the rout; it is reasonable to suppose that this also occurred in the popular versions. It is reasonable to suppose that preaching based on the Canon *Episcopi* was instrumental in building up the picture of the witch-cult that would be entertained by the unlearned in the early mediaeval centuries. There is, however, direct evidence only for the picture entertained by the learned. Here there is a small confusion to be overcome. Many writers in the Middle Ages mention the foolish opinions of the ignorant vulgar regarding witches but unfortunately when they do so they are merely paraphrasing the Canon *Episcopi* and not telling us anything about the actual beliefs of their unlearned contemporaries. Jean de Meung for example takes the Canon as his authority, not only for what was true or untrue about witches (he clearly makes the identification) but for what other people, less educated than himself, believed about witches. He is not to be taken as an original authority for the folklore tradition. So far as we directly know, the transfer of Regino's legend to witches, the importation of an element of supernatural flight, and the ascribing of the legend thus distorted to the ignorant masses, may be wholly an aberration of the learned; the people may never have believed what the educated had read that they believed.

However, the legend grew, whether among the learned or the unlearned; and Herodias, rather than Diana, was usually spoken of as the goddess of the witches. I am myself convinced by the reasons I have already put forward to suppose that this name was attached to her on account of the coincidence of sound. It was, of course, borrowed from the Bible; the name is Greek and would not otherwise be known to the Folk nor yet to the canonists of that epoch. Was it perhaps borrowed for any other reason? Did the Biblical figure of Herodias suggest a logical analogy with our huntress? It does not at first sight seem very likely; but even if it did not possess any analogous significance to start with, the probability is that it came to acquire one, and that those who believed witches worshipped Herodias revised their idea of witchcraft in the light of that belief, if their idea of witchcraft was not the source of the belief.

Herodias, the reader will remember, was the sister-in-law and later the wife, contrary to Mosaic law, of Herod the Tetrarch; and it was her daughter who so pleased Herod with her dancing that she secured the death of John the Baptist as a reward, Herodias having a grudge against him. In modern adaptations of the story, the daughter is supposed to have had her own reasons for demanding John's execution; this is a literary invention of the nineteenth century, and so is the name "Salome" by which she is known. In the Bible she is not named; and this seems to have made possible, even in the nineteenth century, some confusion between her and her mother.[4] If it was possible then, it was much more possible in the early Middle Ages, when hardly any of the laity were in a position to consult the text. And if a confusion between Herodias and her daughter was reasonably easy, a confusion between the two Herods was much more so; I imagine the reader will find, if he thinks about it, that the name "Herod" brings a composite picture to his mind, of the king who ordered the massacre of the Innocents in Bethlehem and the tetrarch who, besides having John the Baptist beheaded, played a minor role in the Passion of Christ and subsequently in persecuting the Apostles. It is most improbable that the average worshipper in the Middle Ages ever got them disentangled. The elder Herod certainly was a popular villain of the Mystery Plays in the latter part of the period, and both Herods would recur in much the same kind of context in the stories—of the Nativity and the Passion—that the ordinary church-goer would be most often told. "Herod" (possibly both of them, though the authority is for the younger) was also held up as an object-lesson on account of his salutary and repulsive death; and in the early Middle Ages though hardly in the later John the Baptist was a popular saint.[5] All these considerations would help to make Herodias, with the convenient accident of her name, a colourable female villain for the New Testament if one was required. It would be easier to choose a male villain, but it may be noted in this connection that the writers of the Gospels and Acts are not so consistently hostile to any other villain, except Judas Iscariot, as they are to the two Herods; and even Judas would be excused by a persistent, though always heretical, opinion that would make him the accredited agent of the Atonement, authorized by Christ's words, "That thou doest, do quickly."

Would the name "Herodias" suggest anything more specific than general hostility to the holy? It would presumably also suggest dancing

[4]E.g., Heine, *Atta Troll*, where it is not clear whether the mother or the daughter is referred to. Legend requires Herodias, but Heine's description would fit the conventional Salome better, and was indeed a main source of part of the convention. (The name "Salome" was supplied by an ambiguous reference in Josephus, which may be to another person.)

[5]Going by church-dedications, outside Italy. In Italy, where dedications to John the Baptist are not evidential (on account of the custom of building separate baptisteries), iconography indicates that he retained his popularity without a break or decline.

—anti-Christian and lascivious dancing. As I have said, the mediaeval Church looked with disfavour on dancing as such; priests must often have warned their congregations against it, and if they wanted a Biblical example Herodias and her daughter supplied the only suitable one. Thus, if some ceremony that involved dancing as a major element was practised in secret and recognized as anti-Christian, Herodias would be a very appropriate patron for it. If it existed, but was not recognized as anti-Christian (or only so recognized by fanatical moralists) this is less likely but not impossible. Suppose that the young people of the village stole out by night to dance when the priest had told them not to—which is not hard to suppose—the priest, if he suffered from the worst inconveniences of celibacy, might easily lay all the blame on the girls and assume, not necessarily correctly but in the spirit of most of the propaganda, that the dances led to sexual irregularities; he might easily stigmatize the offenders as daughters, or servants, of Herodias for simply dancing, and if he got really worked up he might warn the people of the danger of heathenry arising when women went out at night, as when they rode with Diana, Herodias, and Dame Abunda; and so on. This would involve a slight lapse of memory but no more.[6]

The whole trend of the argument from the character of Herodias, so far, has led us back to the Sabbat. We might as well give "paganism" its head for the moment, and call to mind the circumstances in which mediaeval peasants would learn most that they knew about the Herodian dynasty. In the later Middle Ages, as I have said, the Mystery Plays would be a principal vehicle; whether something less formal on the same lines preceded these is not a question I feel capable of discussing, but at least we can be sure that the occasion in the year when the infamy of the *elder* Herod would be made most of, by whatever medium, would be the same throughout the period, namely the Holy Innocents' Day, December 28. This of course falls within the old Yule or Saturnalia feast that was Christianized as Christmas; and actually it is well known that the feast of the Innocents was allowed to perpetuate far more of the old Saturnalia than the Nativity itself. It was the great day of the Lord of Misrule, and was the excuse for horseplay and a general relaxation of social discipline under cover of which pagan usages might indeed survive

[6]Actually, the most usual charge against dancing is that the attitudes of the dance mock, by parody, the Passion of Christ; a curious, and one would say highly specialized objection. But the whole subject cannot be considered in isolation from the attitude of moralists to laughter, gay clothes, football, and almost every other surrender to the play instinct (on which, see Coulton, *Five Centuries of Religion*, vol. I, appendix 23, *passim*).

uncondemned, though at the cost of losing all religious status in burlesque. Yule of course was a festival of the winter solstice; those who observed it would naturally observe the summer solstice also, and this was represented in the Church calendar by St. John the Baptist's day, June 24.[7] So people who, when pagan, had observed a solar year and still kept up the old occasions of solemnity with a new interpretation (and this applies to most if not all the area we are concerned with) would hear, on these occasions, a good deal about "Herod." (The decollation of John the Baptist is actually commemorated on August 29, but as this is less of a feast, ecclesiastical and secular, than Midsummer, the story is just as likely to have been told on either date.) Suppose the simple rustics, taking in the Baptist's honour one of the rare holidays an agricultural population can hope for in the summer, should dance on that long evening. Imagine the fulminations from the rood-loft at Mass next morning, if the parish happened to be unlucky in its priest! Can it be doubted that the name of Herodias would be held up to execration, and all her various misdeeds dwelt upon?

The relatively pious, learned and unlearned alike (for when I say "learned" I do not mean necessarily "intelligent") could thus easily come to think of Herodias as the chief villainess of the Bible and she-adversary of the Faith, and as a promoter of lascivious dancing and consequently fornication, *and* as the mysterious leader of the witch-cavalcade—in which you, of course, were too intelligent to believe, but in which it was well known that witches believed because canon law and the best literary authority and the parish priest all said so. This clearly brings us much closer to the Sabbat; but it will only work for the name "Herodias," hardly for Diana or Abunda. The name "Herodias," even if the original name was something similar, can only have been applied to the goddess from outside, by Christians or at least in the light of Christian tradition, because there is no other possible source for it; but this plainly is not the case with the other two, of which "Abunda" at least was as commonly employed. Herodias *would* be the chief she-villain of the Bible story to men of that age, because all the other possible villains of female sex—Jezebel and so forth—occur in parts of the Bible with which the people at large did not become familiar till translations became generally available at the Reformation; she would readily be associated with dancing, and she was identified with Regino's Diana from as early as the eleventh century. Diana indeed fades out thereafter; but what of

[7]On account of Luke 1:36.

"Abunda"? The appearance of this name, in France shortly before the first outbreaks of witch-hunting there, is about the only corroboration of Regino that cannot derive from him, that points to the existence of the belief he records as a genuine popular belief in the Middle Ages proper and long after the age of conversion. The name, so far as we know, carries no other mental association than with the nocturnal rout; if it was habitually employed in that connection, then the link between the rout and the Sabbat must be very tenuous, for Abunda never came to be associated with the latter and *both* must have been living legends in France about the beginning of the fourteenth century.[8]

It is not, therefore, completely satisfactory to explain the picture that evolved of witch-assemblies as a confusion arising out of the Canon *Episcopi*. Among minor difficulties I may mention the question of the calendar: all this line of argument has been pointing towards a paganism, real or imaginary, governed by the solar year or possibly by the solar and lunar combined. But popular tradition throughout Western Europe is unanimous in regarding Walpurgisnacht and Hallowe'en as the high holidays of witchcraft; these are not governed by the moon nor do they bear any relation to solstice or equinox, though of course as they are exactly six months apart (April 30 and October 31) their rhythm is ultimately that of the solar year.

Up to the beginning of the age of witch-trials, all evidence of what witches did or believed is of course wholly from outsiders, from those who professed not to share these practices and beliefs. This obviously is a disadvantage, but one we must put up with. The unreliability of ecclesiastical writers concerning the religious systems of backsliders and heretics need hardly be stressed; but unfortunately we have now to consider an instance of it in any case. Our immediate

---

[8]Lea, *Materials*, p. 203f.

Of course there remains a possibility that "Habonde" derives ultimately from *abundare* and that the lady began as a Gaulish goddess of plenty. In that case we should rather expect to find Abunda, Diana, and Herodias *together*, for the Gaulish goddess involved was one of a trinity. This is enticing, but obviously far-fetched. In fact we do *not* find all three together (though in Classical, or at least euhemerized myth, Diana herself is triune and a mediaeval ecclesiastic could know it, e.g. from Marcianus Capella). "Habonde" is a verb form, and not Celtic; and there is still the question why this one goddess should survive when all others are forgotten. Even if "Abunda" derives in some way from some ancient deity native to the soil, there would be no reason to suppose she had retained her old attributes; the survival of the mere name among people ignorant of the worship formerly paid it is possible (and in the German parallels undoubtedly occurred), but it would cast little light on the nature of "Abunda" at the time of her new emergence—and the name would continue to baffle.

problem is to find or guess where the Herodian rout was to lead and what ultimately became of its Queen. Assuming it belongs to the same set of ideas as the Sabbat, what is the connection? And assuming the leader was the witches' god, how did this god come to change sex? One of our few positive clues leads us to the heresies of the twelfth and thirteenth centuries.

The Waldensian heresy, and the Cathar or Albigensian, are only within the margin of our subject, and we cannot delay to treat them here in detail, except to mention that the Cathars were dualists.[9] They are brought within the margin by that same fatal attraction of the Unknown which gives Magic its power over the mind. To many who have speculated along the line we are pursuing, these two heresies have been more unknown than they need be, and therefore seemed more magical than they were. Unfortunately this stricture must apply to some Inquisitors and contemporary Christian writers. For the present I will ask the reader to believe that the history of these sects though poorly documented is not so mysterious as to be called occult.

In the early thirteenth century the Church and its allied governments undertook the extermination of Catharism; and it seems likely that they were fairly soon successful. The Waldenses, who were never so alarming to the orthodox mind, were already fugitives from the law; they still survive in small numbers in the Italian Alps, but the Cathari have long been extinct. We do not know how long; the sect must for a time have preserved its identity under cover, as the Waldenses were able to do, in this period, in the cities of southern France and northern Italy. As they were both more or less conspiratorial groups of dissidents, they came to be confounded together, and for propaganda purposes it was assumed that their secret gatherings were occasions of moral depravity. Nothing, of course, is less likely; but this is the sort of thing that is always said when unpopular people, Jews for example or Freemasons, are known to perform rituals in secret. One or the other sect seems to have tried to revive the *agape* or love-feast of the early Church, from which Orthodox liturgy and Catholic Mass are ultimately derived; they seem at all events to have attached importance to a common meal that was much more like a meal than the ordinary Eucharist, and to this they may have added the "kiss of peace." As the propagandists had it, they met in secret to feast and then put the lights out, whereupon the most awful goings-on ensued, Nameless Orgies in fact. This seems to be the standard invention of prurience in the face of secrecy, when stimulated by

[9] See appendix B for a fuller account.

odium theologicum, and as such we can afford to dismiss it, at least so far as the central tradition of either sect was concerned. But it is of course possible that these, like so many heretical movements, may have proliferated in eccentric splinter groups, and among such it would not be surprising to find some very ambiguous demonstrations of "perfection."

It is also conceivable—it has been suggested—that the Cathars, or some of them, held it a part of their superiority to their fellow-men to worship, not the Power of Good, but an ultimate principle of the universe, a *primum mobile,* considered as above Good and Evil; or that they held it a matter open to choice whether one adored the good or evil half of their dualism. Actually, few dualists are as dualistic as all that, and it is abundantly clear that the Cathars in general were not, that their condemnation of Evil was no less total because of the large powers they supposed it to possess. But of course their attitude towards the Devil, while less diplomatic than that (say) of the Yezidi of Iraq or the modern Zoroastrian "anthroposophists," would make it easier for others to regard him as a fit object of worship. Moreover, it would be possible for sincere Albigensians to turn to Satan in times of misfortune, if, seeing the evident success and hostility to themselves of the Lord of This World, they took the Christians' Adversary to be in fact the God of Good. In any case, something like satanism could be colourably imputed to the Cathars, and the propaganda-drive against them if it did nothing else to interest us did give the *idea* of devil-worship an airing.

At any rate, we are left, beyond reasonable doubt, with a strong impression in the minds of the new-forged Inquisition that what they had most rigorously to fight was a single ramifying secret society under many names—Waldenses, Albigenses, Patarenes[10] or a dozen others—which held the Devil in higher honour than was permitted to Christians and which practised, probably, abominable and lascivious rites at its secret assemblies. None of this need have been true, though we are not exactly qualified to deny it. Inquisitors found it harder

[10]The "Patarene" heresy offers a neat example of the kind of confusion that might arise. In Milan in the eleventh century there arose a party of discontented democrats. Though essentially a political, not a religious party, they supported the reforming Papacy (Hildebrandine) both against the Emperor and against the entrenched rights of the local clergy, who were not amenable to papal control. They were known, in contempt, as "Patareni" (rag-pickers). They were really forerunners of the Guelph party, but locally they were remembered as plebeian anti-clericals, and "Patarene" came to be applied to any religious dissident. The descriptions given of them seem to fit the Waldenses; it is highly unlikely that there ever was a distinct Patarene heresy.

to distinguish the tenets of the Waldensians proper when "Waldensianism," already confused with Catharism, became a convenient label for all sorts of religious eccentricity. It was simpler, intellectually, to lump all popular heresies together as "Waldensianism"; and as this had already been condemned, it was more convenient legally.

This was an advantage, for at this time the Inquisition had material to keep it busy in many places quite remote from the original centre in the South of France. Even the Franciscan Order gave trouble, with the apocalyptic speculations of the "Fraticelli"; the other-worldliness of monasticism as a whole had always some affinities with Catharism, and the suppression of the first popular heresies had removed a symptom without attacking the roots of the disease. From this time on, long before the Reformation, the Church was never wholly free from the competition of short-lived enthusiastic sects. There is no special need to suppose that these have any direct part in the ancestry of sects that arose later and demonstrated some of the same eccentricities; for the vagaries of ignorant revivalism seem to be much of a piece in any age. Shakers and Holy Rollers in modern America, Doukhobors and Skolptzy of Russia, Muggletonians and Anabaptists and Fifth Monarchy Men show many of the same characteristics, it would seem quite independently. In every age, an imminent expectation of the Second Coming has induced men to throw off family ties and sometimes also their clothes, to abandon the practice of marrying and paying taxes, and take to the wilderness there to dance and sing to the imagined piping of the Holy Ghost. "Brethren of the Spirit" in the fifteenth century, Adamites in the seventeenth, Doukhobors and Holy Rollers in the twentieth have practised nudity in the attempt to reurn to Eden and live as the angels. Circumcellions, Flagellants, the Penitentes who still survive in parts of the old Spanish colonial empire, and the Klysty of Russia have relied on a savage asceticism rather than on faith, works or sacraments. Both these extravagances involve a denial of the flesh but are held by their enemies to promote sexual licence. It may, I think, be allowed that an attempt to achieve an angelic superiority to the flesh is apt to bring about this ironic result; therefore we may allow that it may have occurred among the Cathars. I would, however, urge that a Cathar origin is not the only explanation for a Cathar reminiscence in other heresies, since heresies continually show parallels where there is no derivation.

The Inquisition is hardly to be blamed if, in an age when the popular heresies were just beginning to be disturbing, Waldensians became the nigger in the Dominicans' woodpile. But if they were at the bottom of every little local rebellion against the Faith, including those that occurred at a great distance from their known refuges, how did they manage it? Perhaps a confession gave them the key to the mystery, or perhaps a shrewd Inquisitor worked out a theory that later interrogation of suspects confirmed; the explanation of course was that Satan assisted them, and in particular provided them with the means of supernatural flight.[11]

The reader has perhaps begun to wonder how long it would be before we returned to Diana and Herodias. Actually, all we have done is to catch up with the field; the mistress is still to seek. But evidence of a kind is forthcoming that in Italy at a much later period followers of the *vecchia religione* accepted a myth that linked Diana with Herodias ("Aradia") and which ascribed to their cult customs recognizably of a kind with those imputed to the Waldensians in the days of their submergence.[12] Evidence of another kind exists from the Middle Ages, and from shortly before the beginnings of the witch-scare, to link Waldensianism with supernatural flight and with sexual promiscuity in the minds of ecclesiastics whose direct knowledge of the sect's assemblies does not seem to have been great. There is also literary testimony from this period[13] for a tendency to turn the Canon *Episcopi* inside out, accepting the nocturnal rout of Diana's serving women as supernatural indeed, but (possibly) a fact. If it was supernatural but did occur, and if it was no miracle of the saints, then no special link with witches needs to be established; those who enjoyed such a privilege, extended either by Diana or by the mysterious idol those dreadful Waldenses secretly worshipped, were "witches" in the ordinary connotation of the word.

Thus we have a number of elements that went to make the Sabbat, not combined in one synthesis, but linked to each other and present in the minds of the more or less educated, by the end of the thirteenth century. I must admit that a mental connection, at this date, between Diana and the Waldenses is merely inferential; but it existed later, and it becomes easy to believe when we recall that popular preaching, in which the new orders of friars busily engaged, was much commoner than it had been; and it is virtually certain a preacher of low education, trying to rouse a congregation with less, would sometimes call any dangerous set of heretics "heathen," "sorcerers," and "idolaters."

---

[11]Lea, *Materials*, p. 203 f.   [12]See cap. 10.
[13]E.g., Gervaise of Tilbury, quoted Lea, *Materials*, p. 173. See also *ibid.*, p. 90, for the beginnings of dissatisfaction with the *subjective* interpretation of the Devil's powers.

By the end of the thirteenth century, the characteristics of angels and devils had been much clarified by the theologians, and generally in a sense opposed to the rationalism that had been favoured by Regino of Prüm. This was the first great age of the universities; Paris, the home of the new theology, was thronged with the ragged scramblers for learning as a step to preferment, with the bishops and archdeacons of the future and with the tonsured misfits who were to fill their jails. As instruction was almost wholly verbal and often passed on from memory to those who could not squeeze into overcrowded lecture-schools, and as the majority of those who matriculated failed to stay the course, we ought not to assume that the clergy of the thirteenth century were as a body markedly more learned than their predecessors; it is only safe to say that some tincture of more or less digested education became much commoner than before. This may well have been enough to defeat a healthy scepticism without always setting up a trained critical faculty in its place. If the Thomists were prepared to affirm the notional possibility of the powers and activities ascribed to Satan in popular belief or what they took to be so, many must have assumed that these things were proved as facts. If the Devil, under the Permission, might take bodily form, if he could aid and abet lascivious women to deceive their husbands, then who could doubt that he would take advantage of a Permission that must have been so agreeable to one of his temperament? For Satan is now about to elbow Diana off the stage, everywhere, it would seem, except in gallant Italy.

As one would expect of a fiend from the Pit, his thrusting aside of his poor pagan forerunner was abrupt and without finesse. We simply cease to hear of Diana, and hear of Satan instead. We can assign to the change as a convenient if arbitrary date the Jubilee year, 1300. It is a turning-point of respectable antecedents; Dante stood then *Nel mezzo del camin di nostra vita*. The curious may search the so-varied population of the *Inferno* for those who can shed light on our problem; they will not find them.

This was also the year when Lovetot brought his lurid accusations against Walter Langton; and to this case we must now briefly return. I hope I have given the reader reason to believe, with me, that, scoundrel as Walter Langton was, he was on this occasion calumniated. Moreover, the documents tell us less than we are told in some modern accounts of the case. It remains significant that Langton stood accused of paying homage to the Devil by kissing him from behind, *et eum osculavit a tergo*. However false the story, something must have suggested it; Lovetot is not likely to have invented this detail of infernal etiquette.

The Devil, in the surviving records, is not described as having taken animal form; but presumably if no form was specified he was thought of as taking the shape he ordinarily wore in plastic art, that is, of a chimerical monster, more or less half-man, half-goat. *A tergo* might mean that Langton kissed him on the back of the neck, but this would seem to be meaningless; almost certainly the phrase was meant to convey that the kiss was on the hindquarters. The essence of this homage was thus already considered to be that it was obscene; and given the mediaeval view of the Devil this is intrinsically likely. The tragic and august Satan of Milton and later writers was not then the common conception; devils in the mediaeval imagination are normally grotesque spirits of indecent mockery. We are entitled to guess from this evidence what we are not entitled to say that it says, namely that Langton was supposed to have kissed the fundament of Satan in the form, more or less, of an animal.

Now, this is almost exactly what had been said of the Albigensians.[14] Crucial for its wording is the description of their assemblies given in the mid-thirteenth century by William of Auvergne, Archbishop of Paris: "Lucifer is permitted to appear to his worshippers in the form of a black cat or of a goat, and to require kisses from them, in two forms—one repulsive—under the tail of the cat—the other horrifying—on the mouth of the goat."[15] Here, it seems to me, popular etymology has been at work on *Cathar* and *Bougre*. "Cathari catum sub cauda osculant"; "Les bougres baisent un bouc sur la bouche." The correspondence in the puns (which at a pinch would work in either language) seems too close to be accidental; though as etymology both are, of course, bad guesses, and the root of the idea may have been taken over from some quite other set of horror-stories. Conflated, the two supply the later belief. That Cathars and cats were related in the popular mind does seem to be plain; and of course cats, like goats, are linked in the popular mind with witchcraft also, though the connection does not bulk large in learned accounts.[16]

[14]E.g., Bull *Vox in Roma*, 1233.
[15]William of Paris, *De Legibus*, cap. 26, quoted Lea, *Materials*, p. 202.
[16]This passage may be allowed to stand as originally written, in order that the reader may judge whether the explanation is intrinsically probable. I only learned since that the hypothesis can be further supported. In a passage of his *Contra Haereticos* (I, cap. 63), surprisingly vitriolic for so chaste an author, Alain de Lille, a good generation before William, glosses "Cathar" in precisely this way, as derived from the obscene worship of a cat. It will be noted that between the two accounts,

However, the idea of accusing a secretive sect of broadly this kind of abomination is much older. In one form or another, it has attached to the Jews in many ages; the Romans chose to believe that their worship was in some way disgraceful, and the secrecy that surrounded the Holy of Holies and what went on there (a secrecy quite unlike that of a normal mystery cult of that age; the Jews themselves, even the kohanim, were forbidden to witness it) was imposed for this reason. The Romans also claimed that the Christian god was really a donkey; and in later ages the Jews were certainly represented as humiliating themselves before a goat.[17]

In this case we are probably justified in assuming continuity, for the Jews have continued to be secretive and unpopular; and together with frequent scare-stories about ritual murder (such as have been raised in modern times against Freemasons) they supplied a much-needed ground for hating the Jews. Righteous hatred is a cherished emotional outlet for the mob in all ages; Anti-Semitism is not easy to square with the Bible, and has to be rationalized somehow. It is worth noting, in connection with the accusations against Langton, that the Jews had been expelled from England ten years previously. On that occasion, it is reasonable to suppose that every available calumny was given an airing; and with the Jews gone, England went in sore need of a "substitute victim."[18]

Transference of accusations from one enemy to another, where both are hated or feared for the same underlying psychological causes though not ostensibly for the same reasons, is always easy. Conversely, it cannot be expected to occur where the reasons are apparently the same but their subconscious impacts differ. Thus, racial prejudice may operate against Jews and Negroes, but fear of the Negro has, fear of the Jew has not, a sexual root; so Jews are not lynched on suspicion of rape, and Negroes are not supposed to control the world's commerce by a malign international conspiracy. On the other hand, Masons and in some countries Roman Catholics are looked on, to a lesser degree, in much the same light, as surreptitious monopolists of

---

the goat has crept in and the etymological explanation has dropped out. E. Amann, however (*Dict. de Théol. Catholique*, s.v. "Luciferiens") claims that this piece of primitive onomastic is to be found in later writers also.

[17]Sometimes, more reasonably, the Jews are supposed to have adored a pig; both versions are familiar in the long history of German Jew-baiting. I must admit it is pure inference (based on graffiti) that the Romans held comparable beliefs regarding the Christians.

[18]The Jews had indeed filled hardly any other role in English society just previous to the expulsion; they served as a cover for Christian usurers but their own financial power had greatly declined.

jobs and power. Accusations of practising a secret degraded religion seem to go together with accusations of excessive and malignant power, when it is necessary to lay the blame for the world's troubles on somebody. Even the capitalist lackeys who for their own sinister ends poisoned the wells in the Ukraine to procure famine—exactly the kind of thing witches were accused of—were also heretics and backsliders from the faith of true Marxism. Poisoning wells was also a charge against Jews, as was sorcery. Such charges are easily made when a scapegoat is needed; and a scapegoat may serve two purposes. He may satisfy an inarticulate desire for vengeance against Fate or the Government, with luck diverting vengeance from where it properly belongs; or he may be made to carry away absolutely fabricated guilt in order to get him out of the way.

The latter seems to have been the whole motive of Philip the Fair of France in instituting the proceedings that ended in the dissolution of the Order of Knights Templars. This took place in 1308, a generation after the effort to maintain a Christian garrison in Palestine had collapsed, and much longer since the original *raison d'être* of the order had ceased to be its main function. Its wealth in the Levant and its international contacts had made it a principal agent in financing the Crusades, and it remained an organization of great financial power. It was in fact a banking house, the greatest in the Christian world, even exceeding the Knights Hospitallers whose history had pursued a similar course. In France, where royal policy under St. Louis had been largely concentrated on the Crusade, the Temple had actually taken over the financial administration of the kingdom and become, so to speak, corporate treasurer. It was immensely wealthy, and probably reputed more wealthy than it was. As against most West-European organizations in this field, it had good access to the "hard-currency area," that is, the Arab and Byzantine world of the gold standard, while most of the West still used more or less adulterated silver.[19]

The assets of the Temple were therefore a matter of great interest to their largest client, Philip the Fair. He had embarked on a foreign policy far beyond his means. He had tampered with the coinage, and so sparked the nearest thing the Middle Ages knew to a panic on the exchanges. He owed money everywhere, but specially to the Templars; and as he was in their hands anyway, any money he could raise for his

[19]The most accessible modern account of the Templars that is free from superstition is G. A. Campbell, *The Knights Templars.* Delaville le Roulx was perhaps the most painstaking of many historians of the order. The account of the process leading to the dissolution, by Michelet, is respectable but superseded by G. Lizerand (ed.), *Le Dossier de l'affaire des Templiers.*

own purposes was in danger of going to pay them.[20] This was the moment for Philip to play his trump card: his control of the papacy. Philip lived in an age when the conception of kingship favoured by kings was not universally shared, and the conflict of ambition and feudal limitations was constantly driving Philip and his fellow-monarchs to very questionable expedients. It was a golden age for the shyster lawyer and the hired bully, though it can also be regarded as the dawn of the picturesque, the "romantic" Middle Ages. Philip had already used a combination of force and diplomacy to secure the election of a subservient French pope and the removal of the Holy See to Avignon, under his paternal eye. He now made the most extreme use of his opportunities. In 1308 the French court brought a series of startling accusations against the Templars. Torture confirmed their truth, and a few star witnesses were sent to Avignon to confess. The pope, with some reluctance, consented to dissolve the order. Its property, in theory forfeit to the Church, was everywhere seized by the secular government, though outside France most of it was ultimately returned to pious uses. Those knights who did not die on the scaffold or during interrogation were imprisoned by twos and threes in the custody of bishops. Two kings only—of Portugal and of Cyprus —refused to have any hand in the sordid business, and there the knights remained for some time at liberty, protesting their innocence. Some who had confessed were so impenitent as to withdraw their confessions, and it is clear that the world at large was not altogether convinced; but no further inquiry was thought necessary. In that year the Order of the Temple disappeared from history; since when it has, unfortunately, entered the realm of fiction.

The principal charges against the Templars were: of sodomy; of confessing and administering penance to each other, not being in holy orders; of making omissions from the Canon of the Mass; of denying the divinity of Christ, and defiling the Cross; and of paying obscene homage to a devil in animal form, whom they called "Baphomet." It seems that these can be separated into two groups: sexual perversion and crypto-Mohammedanism. The first was probably true of many; the second was at least a natural suspicion. Philip had something to go on. He must have set spies on the order, and concocted the detailed accusations on the basis of their reports.

Sexual perversion is, of course, a normal and permanent danger in any community cut off from the usual sexual outlets; it is known in

[20]Grunzweig, A., "Les Incidences Internationales des Mutations Monetaires de Philippe le Bel," article in Le Moyen Age (Brussels), vol. 59 (1953).

every boarding school, barrack, and prison. It is specially likely in a community such as the Templars, men sworn to celibacy who had been chosen for, but were not leading, a strenuous military life and who were enabled by their corporate wealth to live in fair comfort. It must be accepted that homosexuality in particular was part of the unacknowledged background both of mediaeval monasticism and of knighthood. This need not have weakened the spiritual force of these institutions, any more than it does that of School or Regiment. It was, as in these, an absolutely unavowed but crucial problem that everybody secretly knew about. Algolagnia—sadomasochism—is also very probable under a monastic rule. It is highly probable that the order did contain a pervert clique that indulged in paederasty, mutual flagellation, and a little *recherché* sacrilege; and that the order as a whole helplessly tolerated it from a fear of washing dirty linen in public. This again is a permanent tendency in celibate institutions, reflected in the exaggerated and mealy-mouthed horror with which an "example" of, allegedly, unique infamy will sometimes be made. Philip, if he had any experience, must have known that he could not hope to incriminate the whole order on this ground alone; all such institutions are permanently organized to rebut just this charge.

The imputation, however, could usefully be confused with one that fell naturally on the Templars as a body. There could be no doubt what charge was most suitable. They had long been blamed for every misfortune that befell the Kingdom of Jerusalem, up to the final loss of Acre (which they had in fact most gallantly defended). Zealous crusaders new to Palestine had been shocked to see the permanent garrisons "gone native," and the Templars in particular were widely suspected of being "soft on" Islam. There was a certain amount of substance in this; at least, the Templars had had private relations with Arab states, and the Franks of Outremer had come to a kind of neighbourly understanding with their enemies while their cousins in the West still entertained a picture of the Mohammedan religion built up out of ignorance and war propaganda. Even without Philip the Fair, a suspicion of Moslem sympathies would probably have been fastened on the Templars, and the idea of dissolving the order, or of merging it with the Hospital under stricter discipline, had already been aired.[21]

That these ideas were exploited in 1308 is made almost certain by the name "Baphomet" applied to the Templars' beastly god. Many suggestions have been made as to the mystic meaning of this word;

[21]Runciman, *History of the Crusades*, III, p. 432.

the easy answer is that it had not got one, but was suggested by, or intended to suggest, "Mohammed"—a word of very variable pronunciation. The easy explanation, when it actually explains, is to be preferred. I am prepared to believe that some degenerates in the Templar camp invented the name and paid mock-religious honours to an idol so described; I am not prepared to believe that "Baphomet" sounds like "Mahomet" by coincidence.

The charge was not made explicit; but that was not the business of Philip's lawyers. It was for the Church to define precisely what crime the Templars had committed; Philip's concern was to build up a strong impression of deep depravity unmasked, and thus justify his own high-handed actions. He may well have meant to supply evidence that could point towards Albigensianism or Islam equally and according to the pope's choice; Albigensianism has been read into it by some modern writers.[22] There is no need to discuss the denial of Christ, and so forth, at length; even if we accepted such charges as true, they would tell us nothing.

The Templars, under torture, admitted all that was required of them; those who confessed to the blackest charges, of desecrating the Cross especially, mostly claimed that they had so sinned under duress and in terror of their lives. Later, many claimed that their confessions also were made under duress and in terror of their lives. The process at Avignon was conducted without the use of torture, but only a select few were examined. Doubtless those who obstinately denied the charges did so in terror of their lives also; it is a two-edged argument. The exact truth cannot be known; but we can at least deny categorically what some have wished to maintain, that those witnesses who so constantly protested that they had acted against their convictions under the stimulus of fear are to be regarded as martyrs to one faith or another. Perhaps some may have worshipped Allah or Baphomet; but they had little faith in him.

The point is sometimes made that few of them actually died, and a mystery hangs over the rest, who must have escaped and preserved their special abominations, perhaps under cover of Freemasonry (which did not yet exist). This is a misapprehension; we do know what happened to the remainder; they were sentenced to do penance under episcopal supervision and distributed to ecclesiastical prisons. Some may have escaped, but there is no reason to suppose they were able to re-create their society in any form. They are nowadays often supposed to have possessed occult secrets and to have practised sor-

[22]E.g., Rhodes, *Satanic Mass*, cap. 2; Gardner, *Witchcraft Today*, cap. 6.

cery, but this was not even included in the wild charges against them and there are no grounds for it. Their attraction for the Masons lies largely in the accident of their name, and in the Masons' own hostility to the Roman church, and their reputation as occultists is the product of deliberate mystification in recent centuries. Nothing of the kind was put about at the time, and it would have been a useful smear. Another point is made that their insignia indicates a system of symbolism common to some modern sorcerers. This could obviously be because the moderns had imitated it; and as their habits and badges were prescribed for them by papal authority, this is the only possible explanation.[23]

I hope I have now said enough of the Templars; they have a place in every discussion of our subject and must be attended to, but I think they need no more detain us. We have at least managed to bring together in time most of the separate elements that went to make the Sabbat as the Inquisition conceived it, as the Inquisition now began to investigate it. We have, moreover, assembled them more or less in one place, or one region: from the Holy Office's new headquarters at Avignon eastward across the Alps, by this time the refuge of the Waldensians, and about as far north and west to take in Lyon and Albi. We have seen several ingredients of the later stories ready to fuse in the region where witch-hysteria was to come to a head, not far from the birth-places of Kramer and Sprenger. We have lost sight of the moon-goddess; but perhaps she, or at least her attendant maids, may yet reappear.

[23]Gardner, *Witchcraft Today*, p. 76.

CHAPTER SEVEN

༒

What Song the Syrens Sang

༒༒

FOR THE PURPOSES of the last chapter, I have been working on the assumption that the beliefs generally held about witchcraft in the age of persecution, including some of those held by witches, originated outside witchcraft in historical times, and became transferred to, or adopted by, the cult by a syncretic process we have still to consider. It is, however, time, if we are to preserve a balanced mind on this problem, to give the opposite view its head; and I shall now consider the cult as a possible pagan survival, at least for much of the present chapter. That is to say, I shall now discuss how far, and in what sense, it can reasonably be explained as a pagan survival. For "syncretism" is of course a double-edged argument. If we deny, as monstrously improbable, the suggestion that the craft in its last days was uncontaminated by recent and Christian influences, we are still not entitled to assert that it was wholly a product of such influences; and I do not think such an assertion would strike anybody as fully reasonable unless they were prepared to suppose that the cult never existed outside the bigoted minds of superstitious judges.

In justice to Miss Murray it is necessary to state that her first work on this subject, *The Witch-Cult in Western Europe*, gave due credit to these considerations. But the vagaries into which the Murrayite school were to stray were already foreshadowed in this highly significant passage: "The witch-cult being a survival of an ancient religion, many of the beliefs and rites *of these early religions* are to be found in it. Of these the principal are. . . ."[1] The italics are mine. The "early religions" referred to continue to baffle me; but the rites and beliefs were those commonly supposed, in 1921, to be standard features of any religion at a certain stage of culture. The quoted passage con-

[1] Murray, *Witch-Cult*, p. 161.

cludes: ". . . the principal are: the voluntary substitute, the temporary transference of power to the substitute, and the self-devotion to death." The words occur in a section on sacrifice, and had they occurred elsewhere a different set of principal rites and beliefs might have been named; "relating to sacrifice" should perhaps be understood. Even so, I should like to be informed of *one* "early religion" of which this much is objectively known. Miss Murray's position was that which Frazer was even then labouring to prove; it had not, and it has not, been proved yet.[2]

Unlike Miss Murray, we are not entitled to presume the former existence of a standard dying-god cult, nor that it was the most serious rival to Christianity in the Age of Conversion, nor that the witch-cult, if it perpetuated any pagan system, must have perpetuated that one. We may, I think, assume that it preserved some elements of pre-Christian worship, for this is intrinsically more likely than not; but let us be clear what we mean when we say such a thing.

When a pagan god ceases to be worshipped as god, he may survive as a folklore figure or as a swear-word. This is one kind of pagan survival, and a god who was named in magical incantations in a society which, as a whole, had learned to make a distinction between religion and magic would be surviving in something like this sense. The god who is still worshipped by religious conservatives, after society as a whole and officially has abandoned him, of course survives in quite another sense, but not, where the competitors are an ethnic and a "higher" religion, in a sense so different from the former as at first sight it might appear. For nothing ever survives a revolution, intended to overthrow it, quite unchanged by that experience. A pagan religion, as ordinarily understood, is the product of the community that follows it, built into the fabric of its life, and in a sense it *must* be a "state religion" in order to survive; it is simply the totality of cult observances pursued in that society, and therefore may absorb any number of syncretic elements without the necessity of reconciling them in a coherent body of doctrine, but by the same token it is only the fact that everybody follows it that holds it together. In an organized and elaborate pagan system, the principal rites will naturally be those that are important to society as a whole, rites for example of harvest or war; birth, marriage, and death are minor religious occasions and the

---

[2]The standard edition of *The Golden Bough* appeared in the same year; but its thesis had already appeared, notably in *Baldur the Beautiful* in 1914. No work of Frazer's occurs in the *Witch-Cult's* bibliography, but I presume an anthropologist of that age knew of the theories of the then acknowledged head of the profession.

concern of rather junior gods (or a minor concern of great gods).
When the great gods have lost their public worship, how shall we say
that the "religion" has survived?

When a pagan system ceases to be officially sanctioned the pagan
gods cease to be the same kind of gods; or at least there will be a
reshuffle in the Pantheon and the small everyday divinities will
emerge as the strongest. But in another way also they are bound to
suffer change: the people, obstinate pagans included, are bound to get
new ideas about gods from the supplanting religion. There would be a
tendency for a god who had been morally neutral to be thrust over to
the side of immorality by the introduction of a specifically *good* god;
but this might or might not affect the conservatives immediately. It
would be a change first felt by the new believers. The opposite, of
course, can occur when paganism attempts a counter-reformation, as
in the brief resistance of Julian the Apostate; paganism may transform
itself into a rival "higher" religion, but even if—which I think has
never occurred—it should succeed in such an effort, it will survive
only by ceasing to be itself.

Thus, if Woden and company lived on at all, they must have
undergone what anthropologists have called "detribalizing" or "acculturation," and Professor Toynbee would call "assimilation to the
Internal Proletariate"—the experience of the savage who drifts to the
city and puts on trousers. As we should expect, one frequent result of
this process is loss of social status; the god may be reduced, like
Welland-Smith, to a condition of servitude to man's minor needs. Or,
again as in the world of human culture-contact, it may drive the god
into the criminal classes, or at least deprive him of an intelligible
purpose in life and give him the option of avoiding slavery by becoming a buffoon.[3]

The transition would of course come easier to the lower orders
among the old gods, who probably would be the least anthropomorphized, and also those whose worship had always been more magical
than religious. Of course, this points to a survival of the yokel godlings
among the witches. But it does not point to the so concrete, so vividly
anthropomorphic god they are supposed to have worshipped. By the
very late date when the persecutions began, even they must have
become familiar with the distinction everywhere else accepted between
magic and religion; and this is what the accounts of trials suggest if

[3]For a survey of work on this subject see Herskovits, M.J., *Acculturation: The
Study of Culture-Contact.*

they suggest anything to the purpose. The witches by their arts could command the aid of spirits, but their "devil" commanded *them*.

This last point indeed is one of the reasons for taking the witch-cult seriously, for suspecting at least a grain of truth in tales of the Sabbat; for this picture of the goat-god as a tyrannous master could hardly have grown out of the same set of sheer misapprehensions that produced the legend of the Faustian compact. But then where does the goat-god come from? As I indicated before, there are difficulties in finding room for him in Celtic Britain, whose Druids had developed a fairly sophisticated animism with no known or probable element of anthropomorphism, a cult that was not adapted to, but swamped by the religious concepts—polytheistic and fully anthropomorphic—of the Roman invaders. Celtic and Roman Gaul is a different matter; there indeed the native gods, like the native art, could and did grow easily enough to fit a broadly Hellenistic pattern, and in the process powerful cults of hybrid gods might arise. There was Cernunnos the Horned; and there were also goddess-triads who might easily be identified, rightly or wrongly, with Diana.[4] As it is much easier to suppose a French origin than a British origin for the witch-cult if the incidence of the panic is any indication, the existence of such cults must be taken into account. But Christianity also was earlier and easier established in Gaul, and its adoption would still have its predictable effect on the popular attitude towards the elder gods.

We know that many Celtic cults died out without trace, at some stage of the process of conversion. We can guess that many godlings were demoted to pixy status, and that others were vaguely remembered for a time as mere names. Those that survived in any physical form survived in human form or then acquired it, for not only was that the strongest tendency of Roman syncretism, but by the time that our problem becomes visibly a part of folklore all Western Europe had long since come under a yet stronger Hellenistic and anthropomorphizing influence than the Roman Empire in the shape of the Roman Church. I suppose I need not elaborate the point that the God of the Christians is more absolutely human than any other god; I suppose I need only mention the cults of saints. The debt of Christian iconography to Hellenism is perhaps less generally recognized. The Christian conception of an angel, ignoring the Bible entirely, has been borrowed from the classical winged "fury," "victory," and so forth, not

[4]Cf. p. 117, note 8. And see Burchardt, J., *Age of Constantine the Great*, cap. 5 (p. 124f. in American edition, Doubleday, Anchor).

to mention the purely Renaissance adaptation of the Eros as a "cherub." The halo of the saint is found, at Pompeii for example, adorning the heads of gods and heroes very far from any ideal of Christian sanctity. The Devil is usually imagined along the lines of Pan and the satyrs, though here again the borrowing has been more direct and obvious since the Renaissance than it was formerly. (Earlier versions may have been influenced by the Egyptian Goat of Mendes; for Christianity was certainly in contact, at its first beginnings, with Alexandrian syncretism.) Christ in the catacombs appears generally either as Aesculapius or as the Good Shepherd, modelled upon the shepherds, good, bad or indifferent, who might play their oaken pipes on the walls of any villa, if not actually in Arcady; a literary, not a realistic conception. The Cross itself has an earlier history as a religious symbol; this has little enough to do with anthropomorphism, but may help to show the extent to which the missionaries who converted the Germanic peoples had in their own minds a conception of religion much nearer to that of classical antiquity than their catechumens had ever entertained; much more "pagan" as most people would understand the word.

Thus, to those who did not immediately get the hang of Christianity, the lesson to be learned from it concerning the nature of the gods would be much what the Romans had tried to teach. The introduction of Christianity would strengthen the anthropomorphizing tendency in paganism. Thus, a cult which up to that moment had not worshipped a man-god might then begin to do so; a totem-society whose rites had concentrated on a beast might worship the beast, become half-man, if the new iconography offered them an example of such half-men; a witch-doctor who had formerly on occasion impersonated a beast for magical purposes might now impersonate a god with the same attributes. A man who used to dance in skins and a horned head-dress would suddenly come to realize that he had been taking the form of the powerful Satan, whom the new priests were so afraid of; whom therefore he ignorantly worshipped, him declared they unto him.

The goat-men of old Greece, whose songs and dances in honour of the vine may have given us the first tragedies, had certainly their like in the prehistoric West. Probably tales of horned and cloven-footed godlings did not suggest, but were suggested by their mummers' costume. In the West, in the Dark Ages, many influences may have combined to make a new legend. Satyr and faun, reinterpreted by the Church as lamia and cacodaemon, were introduced by new names but in much their old guise to peoples who, at a much earlier period and perhaps still, knew the original on which these portraits were drawn, but did not know, any more than the priests, which was portrait and which was original. Medicine men in skins and masks with branching horns, and perhaps with an artificial phallus, dance on the painted walls of caves in France. Their "devilishness" is fairly striking; and cave-paintings also supply female figures startlingly close to the familiar nursery idea of the witch.

It is easy to conceive how a sorcerers' society whose leader had been accustomed to assume the disguise of a beast might become, under the influence of the general conversion, a secret sect worshipping a god half-man, half-animal, identifiable with the Church's Satan, and adoring the leader as the god's manifestation. Such a development need have been no more than a clarification of ideas already latent in the rites though not consciously present to the mind of the ordinary initiate. For myself, I think this much more likely than that a separate religion on the lines of the witch-cult existed fully formed in ancient Gaul. (The Romano-Celtic syncretic god Cernunnos I take to have been a *parallel* development, not part of the ancestry of our "Dianus"; as his worship and his appearance must have been assimilated to the Roman standard, this I think saves some explaining away of improbabilities.)

All this is very promising; but the Devil's promises are to be received with caution. Suppose we accept that the magical rites of whoever painted those caves were taken over by the Gauls, and, if they did not get transmuted into a religion at any earlier date, rose to that rank under the stimulus of the first Christian opposition. Suppose that these rites had been practised by people below the Gaulish Druids in the social scale, and for that reason they were equipped to survive the overthrow, first of the Druids, then of the hollow transplanted paganism of the early Empire. Or perhaps the cult was in a better position to protect itself during the invasions and the conversion because it had always been a secret society. Can anyone suggest a reason why what was evidently, in origin, a hunting cult should be specially plebeian, specially strong centuries after hunting had lost most of its economic importance, specially a cult of women, or specially secret?

The shaman, in his first appearance in cave-painting, is evidently disguised as a deer. It presents no great problem that he should later adopt the form of a goat, for the degree of realism is not likely to have been always very great; but it does present a problem that a being ultimately derived from a deer-spirit should be privileged to survive as a god when all other gods were forgotten. Bran and Rigantona and their kind survived as human heroes in folk-tales, if they were ever anything else. Puck and his kind were believed in as supernatural creatures but not worshipped. If those who danced round the maypole did so in honour of a god, they did not know it. The most determined believers in the survival of pagan worship will not go so far as to claim that more than one god survived, or at most two, a male and a female, in different local traditions of witchcraft. What special advantage had our "Dianus"? If it was simply the fact of being already the witch-god, how did a witch-god come to have these attributes? There are many possible answers to such questions; but I will suggest, as one not often considered, that perhaps one of the reasons why Dianus was better fitted to compete with the God of the Christians was that he had been designed or discovered with that competition in mind.

Of course, it is not impossible to believe that witchcraft, being a very ancient cult and probably the most ancient of all, dates back to times when men's chief reliance was on hunting and therefore was in fact primarily a hunting cult in origin. No other detail known or suspected about it, apart from the genius's costume, will fit in with this view, but this perhaps need not trouble us; we only have to suppose it possible for the cult entirely to change its inner nature while clinging to scraps of tradition in outward form. This sort of thing constantly occurs, and perhaps would be specially apt to occur among unlearned devotees of the occult.

Miss Murray has suggested[5] that the main witch-festivals were related to breeding seasons of animals. Her argument is highly unconvincing on this point; and actually, of course, Walpurgis and Hallowe'en are not at all closely related to any natural cycle at all. They are, empirically and very vaguely, related to climate, dividing the year into spring-summer and autumn-winter; and if their dates did not establish this, the traditions (quite independent of witch-beliefs) surrounding them would. Probably at first they were variable, and later became fixed, quite arbitrarily, in terms of a twelve-month calendar, being placed respectively on the eves of the first predictably pleasant and the first predictably beastly month in northern Europe. A calendar so primitive might point to anything, including hunting, for hunting techniques vary in cold and warm weather; the life of all animals including man is profoundly affected by these changes, and probably welcome of the one, dread of the other are so natural as to be instinctive and not to require any economic explanation.

[5]Witch-Cult, pp. 130, 178.

Still, the argument from the witch-calendar points this way at least, that it reinforces the view that the first origins of *organized* witch-craft were older than scientific calendars, and probably older than agriculture and the known pagan religions. If the witch-cult wor-shipped a corn-god, this was already syncretism, and a connection with a hunting god, one would say, is just as likely. But in fact the witches of the Celtic West must have taken on every god of the Celtic Pan-theon, for sorcerers are generally free from bigotry in such matters.

I suggest that a dancing costume appropriate for the purposes of sympathetic magic at a time when society relied principally on hunt-ing or, a little later, on herds became traditional among the medicine-men or shamans who were to the humble in Celtiberian territory what Druids were to the great. (It is, I may say, guesswork that such a class of person existed, and of course I am passing over at least one intermediate stage of culture, that which produced the megalithic monuments of Britain.) These exercised most influence in the least Celtic part of the community, the submerged aboriginal proletariat, if there was one. This was also the class least touched by Roman influence later, not so much because it was conservative in spirit or remote in habitat, though it may have tended to be both, but because it was poor and stupid; and to this, the shamans themselves would naturally be exceptions. Gradually, the Hellenizing tendency of the invader's culture, or Christian-syncretic anthropomorphism derived in part from the same source, had the effect of converting the doctor-ghost-animal into a more or less human god and the priest (still at least half magician) who at times personified him. The god was there-fore, in a sense, both very old and very new; given credit by ancient observance, but in all the essentials of divinity newly self-promoted as a response to the challenge of new and more compulsive religious ideas. "Dianus," if we may still call him so, was perhaps the creation of some anonymous reforming genius among warlocks in the last days of paganism. This kind of thing happens; parallels could be found among the Plains Indians in the nineteenth century. It is, however, much more likely that any such change in attitude was gradual, unconscious, and unbeholden to any single prophet or even class of prophets.

The witches, though, were in closer contact with the missions than the Plains Indians; and they must have been interested in what they were able to learn. In particular, they would learn that the new priests knew all about their god and had a healthy respect for his importance.

True, in the Dark Ages the mental picture of Satan had hardly been standardized in the form we know; he appears in the hagiography of the period as a Protean creature, ever changing his shape in the cause of deception, and his most constant characteristic was lechery. This is probably why the iconographic devil is, or in a franker age was, a chimaeric clown with a gigantic privy member; it may also help to explain his bewildering variety of spare faces. Change of appearance and phallic prowess would reasonably be part of the horned god's reputation, and would help to establish that, while all the old gods were of course devils in a certain sense, he was *the* Devil. This identification would become clearer as the manner of representing the Devil became more fixed; it may, of course, itself have assisted this process, but we should have to class this as an unnecessary and complicating hypothesis in view of the known other influences at work. Once the identification was made (I am speaking of Satan misinterpreted by the witches at least as much as Dianus-Cernunnos misinterpreted by the Church), then it supplies a strong reason why this god should retain his power when other survivors decayed.

As any proof of identity with the actual Dianus is quite impossible, I think it will not cause confusion if we adopt this name, understanding inverted commas, to mean "the male witch-god as seen from the witches' point of view." The names quoted as applied to him in seventeenth-century accounts are too various and too obviously local for our convenience. This need not prejudice the question, still to be discussed, of his relationship to a possible Diana, since we can adopt other names for her, and anyway the caveat has been entered.

In all the later trial evidence from northwest Europe the god is male. In Italy, however, and in England, there is some highly dubious evidence for a goddess, with or without god, as the centre of the witch-cult in times *more recent* than the persecutions. Some theorists, notably Mr. Robert Graves, would wish to make us expect that the principal deity of such a cult should be in reality, or in origin, feminine; and though we have seen that the Diana of the Canon *Episcopi* has a slighter and less certain connection with witchcraft than might at first sight appear, we have not absolutely disposed of her. The modern evidence, for what it is worth, points to Diana and indeed names her (in both instances); but it smells so strongly of the lamp that this is not, I think, an important consideration.[6] Still, there is this much to point to a female deity, that the witch in the popular mind is

[6] See cap. 10.

normally a woman; the great majority of the victims in the panic times were women, though where a whole coven was unearthed it often included men also. At least we may say that if the mediaeval populace knew anything very precise about the cult it was, specially if not exclusively, a cult of women, for this is common form in popular tradition all over Europe.

I find it very hard to believe that the witches' organization perpetuated an organization that had existed in the pagan past. I will accept, quite readily, that a cult having a special power to attract women may have survived among those women of the peasantry who are the most resistant to change of all social classes anywhere. Its organization, and its independence of a more general paganism that had ceased to exist, were, must surely have been, products of the first taste of repression. I should expect to find the need for caution producing in many different places an internal discipline of the same general character but differing in detail; I should not expect to find the ramifying and uniform coven-structure, and I do not think we should find it if we could go back to the Dark Ages and look. We should probably find (presuming we should know where to look) a number of unrelated local groups each confined to as many as could be trusted, and with strict limitations on the recruitment of new members. If there was a witch-master, he would make the rules; if there were many in different places they would act with only the vaguest knowledge of what their confrères were up to.

I said, "a cult having a special power to attract women," and I suppose one thinks first of some kind of fertility rite. (Men are just as interested in fertility, but women are themselves capable of it, which makes them, usually, the proper people to perform such rites.) But if the practice of some kinds of sorcery, no matter what kinds, was confined to women in the relevant culture and time—as is probable and as it certainly was later—then the "cult" in question could be witchcraft *simpliciter*. Witches may have been united, in origin, by nothing but the professional tie; an organization for some special form of worship may have developed from this, and perhaps later than the official acceptance of Christianity. Everything else that marked the "cult" (supposing we knew what *did* mark it) could be accretion, accidental borrowing or the invention of some controlling shaman who rose from time to time to dominate a group; though in this case the "accretions" must at some stage have included a kind of confederacy and pooling of experience between several leaders, either spontaneously or at the bidding of some reforming genius. All this I shall consider later, and hope to make it a little more convincing than perhaps it looks at present.

Witchcraft is presumed by Miss Murray to have been, at first, principally a fertility cult, and we still share so many of the assumptions fashionable in 1921 that this is still the natural conclusion to jump to. It is, however, necessary to look for some indications of it; there is no rule of comparative religion whereby all religions are presumed to be mainly concerned with the crops until the contrary is proved, though a hasty reader of, say, the *Encyclopaedia Britannica* might get that impression. As we have seen, the witches are more likely to have been interested in animal husbandry to start with, though that is still a question of fertility, and presumably they would turn over to arable when society at large did so; but did they? the hints we can pick up do not in fact point that way very forcibly; indeed, they furnish some new difficulties, though these are hardly insuperable. The powers, in later ages, most often ascribed to witches not only by Inquisitors and judges but by simple villagers, their neighbours, seem the very last we should expect of the promoters of fertility: blighting cattle, setting familiars to milk cows dry, raising storms, procuring abortions, and so forth. When a midwife was a witch (and probably most of them were; in a superstitious community they would need to be experts on charms), she was believed to be able to procure a painless delivery at the price of the death of the child. Theologians were much occupied by the power of sorceresses to make a man impotent, especially to "ligature" him towards particular women, and otherwise prevent the use of marriage.[7] The great mass of authorities concurred that the copulation of witch and incubus-devil, at the Sabbat or elsewhere, was normally sterile.[8] The dates of the chief witch-festivals, which were also popular festivals among non-witches, are not at all closely related to the agricultural year, but they would be quite logical occasions for rites of *human* fertility; the associations of May Day are mainly erotic (or were, before Organized Labour annexed it) and those of Hallowe'en are with death. But what did the witches do on these occasions, to promote fertility, more than other people? Certainly, in the opinion of their neighbours, they did not do

[7]Though Lea gives a great deal of attention to "ligature," its connection with witchcraft as distinct from other forms of sorcery is not obvious; it would, however, be a convenience for the witch who desired to attend the Sabbat without her husband's knowledge, if she could temporarily kill his desire for her.

[8]*Malleus*, Pt. I, Question 3; and see Qq. 3–11 for this whole aspect of the subject. The whole of Pt. I of the *Malleus* is remarkable for its prurience.

as much; their magic seems to have been regarded, predominantly, as
hostile to life and growth. It is hardly worth urging on the other side
that it was also thought to encourage and facilitate lechery.

It is, I think, dubious whether we ought to lay much stress on the
malignity of witches at this point; if they could curse, then doubtless
in the opinion of laymen though not of theologians they could bless
also, and their power to blight animal life, including human, may
perhaps be taken to imply a power to fecundate it. I am more impressed
by the sterility of the witches' intercourse and their skill in poisons
and abortifacients; these are well-attested beliefs never, I think, repu-
diated by witches, and they are not easy to square with a cult whose
primary purpose was the encouraging of fertility, though poison, I
will admit, is probably irrelevant to the present argument.

There is, in fact, nothing to show that the witch was more active
in promoting fertility, in any form, than her neighbours, and some
reason to fear that her interest was all the other way. Is it conceivable?
Could you have a characteristically female, and probably orgiastic
cult that was *not* primarily a fertility cult? It sounds, to me, highly
improbable; but this feeling I think is mere fashion and not to be
trusted. We must regard with extreme circumspection any hypothesis
which has become a standard solution in our own day, if we are
going to dismiss as mere bigotry and parrot-talk the fashionable demonology of the Renaissance.

But suppose you were to paint a picture of the Sabbat, as it was
described in the persecuting ages, and show it, not to someone reared
on psycho-analysis and post-Georgian poets and neo-phallic novelists,
but to a Roman or a Greek. Could he mistake it for a picture of something else, something in his experience? Almost certainly he would
take it for a Bacchanalia, or a festival of similar nature. Wild dancing
by frenzied women, and possibly also men, probably naked or nearly
so, led by a figure of partly human, partly goat-like characteristics,
possibly with the addition of an actual goat or a phallic emblem,
would not seem to any observer in classical times at all difficult to
interpret. The dancers are clearly Bacchantes or Maenads, and they
are honouring the god who sends their frenzy, in delivering themselves to the rule of the divine afflatus present in the fermented
grape or the leaves of ivy. They may also be celebrating harvest or
vintage; but they are not, mainly, promoting the success of the next
harvest or the next vintage. Nakedness, orgiastic dances, phallic
worship are not in this connection directly magical in intention; they
are merely concomitants of the general throwing-off of restraints, the

abandonment to ecstasy, which is the proper service of the god who sends the ecstasy. They are his servants, inspired by him, submerging their individual wills in the inspiration. The inspiration is, of course, deliberately induced, but it is still accepted as divine, indeed as being a means of direct, immediate communion with the divine nature.

This is very often the way in which intoxication or the narcotic effect of drugs is construed by primitive peoples when they first discover these effects. Again, the American Indians supply instances; and Mr. Aldous Huxley has recently become an advocate for drugs as a means to mystic experience.[9] The trance condition, the suspension of ordinary judgement, is common to drunkenness and to mysticism, and the savage is hardly to be blamed if he regards with religious awe the means that bring him by the quickest and easiest way to the Cloud of Unknowing. Ceremonies in honour of drunkenness could of course only survive on some other pretext when drunkenness had developed into a quite secular adjunct of ordinary social intercourse; though it is worth noting that among the Greeks this process was hardly complete until late Hellenistic times, as their libations and the extreme adulteration of wine at their tables show. Among the Romans, on the other hand, the induced ecstasy of Dionysiac festivals does not seem to have been held in the degree of reverence it commanded from, say, Euripides.

Bacchantes drank; Maenads chewed ivy; Mr. Huxley takes mescalin, as the Aztecs did before him; probably the Delphic sybil employed similar devices; sulphur springs attracted oracles to their fumes; primitive men all over the world have valued liquor or tobacco or some befuddling herb as a source of inspiration from on high. Our witches had their ointments.

The formula of the "flying ointment," which was of course a strict secret, seems to have varied; the sixteenth-century sceptic Wier collected several.[10] It is intrinsically probable that most who manufactured it did not possess any clear understanding of what they were about, but proceeded empirically and analogically in the usual manner of primitive pharmacy. Ingredients that would have had a strong effect, taken internally, but almost none in an ointment, would be hopefully included, and others, bat's blood and so forth, for their symbolic value. When any formula came to light, it is probable that those who reported it have been tempted, on occasion, to make it more lurid, more what one expects from the witch's cauldron. We cannot, for several reasons, be sure of the basic constituents; but the

[9]Huxley, *Doors of Perception*.　　　　[10]Cf. p. 41, note 3.

impression emerges fairly strongly from the indications we have that the more effective unguents consisted essentially of a solution of aconite or belladonna, or sometimes both, on a fat or oil base, whose exact composition was immaterial. (Some mention is to be found of the fat of unborn children and so forth; but the most convincing suggestion is that the magical ingredients were made up into a wash separately, and the oil added later by the individual witch to suit her skin, which is sensible.) It might include other herbal toxins, or herbs intended to supply a scent, or merely thrown in for the sake of analogy; it seems to have been darkened with ordinary soot, and I suppose this would make an effective camouflage if used in sufficient quantity. The most important elements, however, are the toxic. Either belladonna or aconite would probably produce a numbed, floating, dizzy sensation of irresponsibility and divorce from the earth, though aconite would be rather the more apt; both would promote the hammering of the heart and so convey excitement; and probably this excitation would have an aphrodisiac effect, which is specially the reputation of belladonna. Ultimately, they would make the anointed subject reel and stagger and lose control of the faculties, much as excess of liquor will do. The effect of course would vary with the quantity employed and with the natural dampness of the skin; it would be greatly reduced, at least outwardly, if both belladonna and aconite were used together, for they are antagonistic. I suspect that quite often the drug failed to work; but of course other factors—exertion and collective excitement—would assist it. The effect of alcohol is greatly increased by a contributory willingness to get drunk on the part of the drinker, and doubtless the ecstasy of the Sabbat was assisted by an exercise of faith. Still, the faith involved would be faith in the ointment as much as faith in the god.

I suggest, then, that this is what specially distinguished the witches from other pagans in the days when paganism was a force. They were the rout or menie, predominantly female as in the classical parallels, who celebrated on great occasions of the year the spiritual energy released by the use of certain herbal drugs. They were familiars of those—probably the horned shamans—who inherited the discovery, and possessed the secret knowledge of herbs, of those herbs that were sacrosanct because deadly. Aconite and belladonna, which gave them ecstasy and the illusion of supernatural energy, which released them temporarily from the bonds of nature, were death to the uninitiate. (A little of either will kill you, taken internally.) They were the favoured of the imperious gods of madness, or rather perhaps they were temporarily holy because temporarily mad. Thus far, such a cult would be religious rather than magical, but its religious ideas could remain infinitely vague for an infinitely long period, all else being equal, since its essence was no kind of dogma but the direct communion with the Absolute, the immediate experience, that those who had the secret of the ointments had the power to bestow.

At what time the discovery was made we cannot guess; nor, therefore, in terms of what stage of religious development it must have been construed. Indeed, the devotee in his or her rapt state of beatitude must have been freed from "religious development" along with all other limitations of earth-bound temporality. There were, however, other people in the world besides witches; to them, probably, the ecstasy appeared first, in animistic terms, as the evidence of the friendly relations of the ecstatics with the spirits of certain plants, hostile to other men. Later, these maenads would be seen as special vessels of the grace of the gods, or their disguised leader and master himself a god of respectable power. Those who did not themselves experience the mystic exaltation would still regard it with awe, with the awe generally felt by the ignorant savage for what he does not understand; for ignorance superb in the seat of judgement would seem to be a product of civilization.

The secret would of course have been a trade secret, the trade being in poisons and aphrodisiacs; it would, I judge, have belonged at first to the medicine-man but have been shared, to some extent, with his junior colleagues, the wise-women who were also herbalists and probably midwives. I doubt (from the paucity of evidence as to the formula) whether the method of concocting the unguents was ever common knowledge to the witch community, but a busy witch-master would need assistants at least in culling his simples. Often, no doubt, it was a woman who preserved the recipe; sometimes, in some places, the recipe was probably lost and had to be reconstructed by rule of thumb. But into all this we need not go; it is not a ground of dispute that the ointment formulae existed, that they varied, that they were secret, and that they were drugs.

An important part of their action as such would be the illusion they could convey of more than human, or more than ordinary, bodily force and vigour. This is normally the case, so far as regards sexual potency, with all aphrodisiacs, and so far as regards resistance to fatigue, with all stimulants. The first, in fact, merely excite, and the second merely deaden the usual physiological danger-signals; but in our own day this is very seldom recognized. This effect would enable the witches to dance untiringly, and to hold their assemblies naked in the open air on nights not always warm. It would carry to their minds a strong assurance of their god's power. In other minds also it may, long before the transition period of which I speak, have bred a similar conviction.

Many savage peoples have shocked many missionaries by the frankly erotic character of their ceremonies and dances. Many anthropologists have pointed out that they do not, on these occasions, merely indulge in licence; their orgiastic rituals are a religious duty or a magical necessity. It has been suggested by some that they may sometimes also be a practical social necessity. Savages, it has been pointed out, are not specially lascivious; indeed, typically they are a great deal more chaste than civilized man, chaste it may be to near the point of frigidity. Those who practise what appears to be an unbridled sexual orgy may be the least lascivious of all; it may be that they require the most intense stimulation simply to accomplish the sexual act. Remarks that have been made about orgiastic rites in ancient and prehistoric worship must be read with this hypothesis in mind; if it is true, it greatly increases the uncertainty that surrounds the interpretation of such ceremonies. Primitive people who subsisted on a low diet in our northern climate may well have needed such customs, if anybody did; and, we may add, the Scots especially. The Picts had the reputation of copulating in public, and dances, to us, luridly obscene may well have survived in that part of the world after dying out elsewhere.[11] The May-games may have been of such a kind in their earliest beginnings, a communal effort, in countries whose climate imposed something like a rutting season, to replenish the human race; a rite only as magical, or as religious, as anything to do with sex is automatically.

Both May eve and November eve would be reasonable times enough to take thought for the next generation; at Walpurgis under the direct and propitious influence of the season, at Hallowe'en as a counter to the power of the dead, or of Death personified. This latter however would be an occasion when orgiastic rites, for whatever purpose, would come easier to those who had access to a stimulant; witches would make a better showing than the general public.

I am not, however, inclined to give much credence to any theory that turns on an assumption of orgies in a former age. People are suspiciously ready to make such an assumption without asking for evidence, and actually such orgies are very poorly attested. A general

[11]This could be the explanation of the scandal at Inverkeithing; cf. p. 64, note 7.

sense of relaxation, a holiday spirit awakened by the awakening year, will account for everything in the May-games that is pointed to as a relic of priapic worship; and after all, we know from experience the gladness of spring's return; we do not need to search for reasons why our forefathers welcomed it. The maypole, I may add, is almost certainly not a phallic emblem, though I suspect it has habitually been so described; it seems, on the basis at least of Frazer's numerous examples, to have been normally a King of the Trees, honoured mainly for sheer joy of the new green leaves. Worshipping trees, like celebrating spring, is in northern Europe almost an instinct, almost unnecessary to explain. This is not perhaps so easy to appreciate now that timber is an industry and afforestation a science, now that our copses are so tidy; but who is there who has never felt the old numinous horror, a little breath of aboriginal panic, alone in the depths of a wild wood? The Druids, priests, men of the Oak, were those animists so spiritually minded that they could stand it; any normal Brython, I feel, would have welcomed a thoroughly anthropomorphic Dryad with profound relief.

But I digress. The witches, it seems to me, were not followers of a particular god except by development and almost accidentally. They were herbalists, preserving certain professional secrets not necessarily or probably known to all of them equally, among which the most important from the religious point of view was the art of using certain poisonous herbs to compound a drug whose effect was to induce a state of ecstasy valued for its own sake. Their transports when under its influence were largely erotic and their rituals partly phallic, because that was the effect of the drug; any other explanation was thought up later. The leaders of their profession were witch-doctors, typically male, whose traditions went back in some sense, ultimately, to the magic rituals of an aboriginal population submerged but not annihilated by the waves of invasion that culminated in the Celtic, the Roman, and the Germanic. Under the influence of an anthropomorphism quite foreign to the ideas of this peasant proletariat, introduced in two stages by Roman Empire and Roman Church, the divinity at first immanent in the ecstasy itself was personified in the witch-doctor as leader of the dance, or rather in his image; but by an ambiguity that was to last as long as the cult itself, divine honours were transferred back and forth between the witch-doctor as a personification of the god and the god as a kind of Platonic Idea of the witch-doctor, an archetypal beast-ghost-dancer. Groups organized by and around such ambivalent man-gods continued, in several places separately, through the Dark Ages and beyond, to give corporate solidarity to a strong, close-knit but necessarily unpopular profession. This, I imagine, was the posture of affairs up to about a century before the witch-cult began to be taken as a serious menace by the Church; that is, up to about the time of the Lateran Council of 1215.

We may, however, admit certain other possibilities. Indeed, we had better do so, for any attempt to explain the witch-cult, its form and its tenacity, wholly in terms of drug-addiction, construed as divine inspiration, will fail. I shall only claim for it that it was, beyond serious doubt, a factor. The ointments were employed; we are not entitled to say that they were invariably employed. We cannot say that they were known to all covens or constantly in use in those that knew of them. In any case, their use would only create a habit, an addiction (which would often be a convenient thing to presume), if they were used at Esbats as well as the infrequent Sabbats; and the Esbat cannot be older than the organized group, and in its Sabbat-like aspects was probably much younger. To Miss Murray, who adopted the term, the Esbat was essentially a meeting for collective acts of sorcery, rather than for worship. This sets up a distinction which probably did not exist for the earliest witches, and I doubt if any ordinary group had regular group-rituals to perform that could safely be classified as magical and not religious; their very regularity would tend to push them over that obscure, though real and fundamental, border-line. The very fact of having regular meetings at less than seasonal intervals I should judge to be a syncretic borrowing; the nearer the Esbat grew to the Sabbat, the more closely the practice of the cult approximated to that of the Church, with its perpetual sequence of Masses, and also (which was probably the point) the more effective became the control of the witch-master, the more essentially theocratic his priestly function. Frequent regular meetings of a small circle would tend to make him more of a priest if less of a god, which without necessarily reducing his power would show a further step in modernization, a development we can hardly ascribe to the first days.

In some places a witch-group may easily have grown up among the women of a conquered race, who when their foreign husbands worshipped strange gods, Thor or Jehovah or what not, preserved the ways of their own people, of the humble people that is to say, as best they could without any kind of professional priestly guidance. They would worship the small gods they had been used to worship while greater folk celebrated official and public sacrifices; they would pass on to their daughters the charms that women needed whatever god might rule; and perhaps when they met together they would imitate as much as they could of the rites that could no longer be openly performed, the outward aspect of the rites that is to say, without any clear understanding of what they had originally meant. They could dance the proper dances; probably they did not know what name to use in their invocations, for this (we may guess, it would normally be the case) had always been a secret guarded from their ears. So they would be ready enough to learn from any who could teach them, whom it was that they worshipped; the parish priest might say (when as obedient wives they followed their husbands to church) that their dances profanely honoured the idol Herodias; or a warlock or initiate from a better instructed group might whisper a name that must remain as obscure to us as that Achilles assumed when he hid himself among women.

When people talk about "continuity" in history or anthropology, they are apt to mean "breach of continuity." That is to say, it is only claimed where it is obviously not complete. Some aspects of the witch-rituals probably existed before the national conversions, and some of these were probably part of the traditions of the people as a whole, who were not therefore witches. It is even conceivable that something like the later organization already existed. But the conversions wrought a change of profound importance; this is plain, even if, as is just possible, the cult had already been a clandestine organization for anti-social purposes under the ban of Druids, emperors, and kings. Just how it began, how old it was when the change overtook it, or what it was like before the change, must remain matter for pure speculation; all I can do is balance guess against guess, and the reader may perhaps prefer to do that for himself. But I will claim that the possibilities I have allowed to be probable really are more probable than others. If it is asked which, of several origins hinted at in previous pages, I actually believe in, I can reply that though I do not think it is my business to prefer any theory, I fortunately believe in all of them. The origins of the cult were, it is reasonably safe to say, diverse, and every element that was ever added to it had a previous history of some kind. There may have been, at one time, or at all times, several independent witch-cults who borrowed from one another whatever in the other they found out about and found attractive; and these may have developed along different lines from a common starting point or grown up into roughly analogous forms for quite different causes.

I have spoken of Occam's razor; and am I not multiplying factors in the problem, or at least multiplying hypothetical witch-cults? I do not think so; I am attempting, in fact, not to multiply but to divide, to reduce a complex problem to a number of simple problems. I suggest that to presume the cult was essentially uniform and internally coherent, so that all its practices must have co-existed in one group and must be fitted into a system, and to presume one origin and therefore a very complex origin for all its aspects, are really to think into the question, gratuitously, complexities that need not be there in Nature; and it is such excrescences that Occam's razor was forged to shave.

Thus, for example, we shall get ourselves in an unnecessary tangle if we assume that the witch-dances which have been described were generally known to all covens; that they all originated as witch-rituals and therefore whoever else also danced them must have derived them from that source; and that they each had a magic significance and therefore each a *different* magic significance. If, as is commonly suggested, the association of witches with broomsticks derives from a dance in which they used such sticks as hobby-horses, we are free to put absolutely any interpretation on such a dance that seems to fit it, since we do not have to fit it into any one theory of origins. It would be rather difficult to fit it into a fertility-rite system. I hasten to add that it fits hardly any better into a prehistoric hunting cult, since before the days of stirrups hunting was generally done on foot; and broadly the same applies to war, but war or something like it is probably the answer. While the men of the community were away on some expedition that required hard riding, the women may have encouraged them, by sympathetic magic, by energetically imitating what they were supposed to be doing—all the women, and preferably not fuddled with drugs. Later, such a ceremony might petrify into custom, and be reinterpreted, its original purpose forgotten. We are never wise in assuming that witches fully knew what they were about, in all its implications. The same rite could, however, be followed for purposes of malefic spell-casting at a distance; the coven might charm their victim into their cast circle, by any of the usual straightforward methods (by name, effigy or emanation), and then constructively hunt and slay his fictitious presence. And, of course, both these may well be equally the true explanation, and could be combined in more than one way; in any of a dozen ways it may have come about that witches in some countries if not all were supposed to make magic use of hobby-horses, and the easiest folklore explanation would always be that they actually rode on them. But we had better leave the subject before speculation passes right over the narrow bound that divides it from a parlour-game.

Before we leave the subject of the very ancient vestiges and survivals in the cult as it became known to the Renaissance period, I must emphasize one further complicating factor, and perhaps the most dangerous of all. This is the tendency of the members themselves to ascribe great antiquity to their practices, either from ignorance or in the interests of mystification. I think we can assume that most ordinary witches would be nearly without any knowledge of how their society came into being, and would show the common human tendency to treat as immemorial what one does not personally remember. The lack of historical sense in humanity at large, and the rapidity with which an innovation becomes accepted as a permanent part of life are astounding, but they are matters of everyday observation. But far beyond any vagueness we have to fear the misrepresentations of the magi, the tendency of the sincere occultist crank and settled habit of the charlatan to claim an immense antiquity for his esoteric doctrines. I am suggesting that the witches may have been themselves sometimes the dupes of such *facticiosi* as Aleister Crowley in our own day, or his precursor Eliphas Levi; that some of the more learned witch-masters have introduced into cult-practices, here and there, deceptive evidence to support their claims to represent a tradition of immense age, and that pretty well all who have ever had the task of inculcating magical doctrines into novices have claimed to represent such a tradition. Few indeed have been those with the audacity to stand forth as the inventor of a spell, a charm, an invocation; few have felt so self-reliant as to admit that they taught themselves what they knew of hidden truths. Formal, Faustian sorcery by the individual magus in his study has always been led astray by forged *grimoires*, concocted ancient traditions and spurious claims to private sources of spiritual information. Would-be necromancers, like Levi and Crowley, have written books, in which this calculated mystification and wordy philosophic Brummagem-ware is plain to see for what it is, and even has something of the pathos of the infinitely ambitious and infinitely bogus. The less literate kind of country spellbinding does not derive from this grotesque affectation, and witches in the ordinary way would have little in common with the Romanticism of the would-be Kabbalists. But something of the same kind of influence must have been felt by the more ambitious leaders. To dabble in sorcery at all is to make a very imperious kind of demand on the universe; no one who felt any personal ambition in that society (and those who rose in it must generally have felt some) can have been entirely satisfied with the powers he was aware of in himself, or not felt the obstinate, irrational conviction that somewhere there was a secret doctrine to be learned, a master spell to be broken, which was the real key to omnipotence; and if indeed it was not to be found, it must be invented. In every group of sorcerers there must have been a readiness to hear, and a disposition to believe those who could colourably present themselves as learned in all the magics, as the real adepts; or to incorporate in the rites, trusting in its authentic immemorial age, any useful improvement that a literate charlatan might be able to suggest.

I do not think we need rate the average intelligence of the initiates so high as to make this impossible; I am not suggesting that it occurred commonly; but in the years that have passed since the date I mentioned a short while back, of 1215, and even in the years between that and the first persecutions, there has been time for it to happen more than once in more than one place, even supposing it to be very rare. At least it is a factor not to be excluded, and one whose only effect must be to spread confusion. In the following chapter I shall consider how well an explanation on these lines may be made to account for certain of the problems still before us.

⤝⤜⤝

CHAPTER EIGHT

The Gargoyles of Notre Dame

⤝⤜⤝⤜⤝

I HAVE CHOSEN to take the year 1215 as a landmark, specially on account of its Lateran Council. This (the fourth) is important as the occasion when the Western Church produced its final answer on the subjects of dispute between itself and the Albigensians (the time being intermediate between the first and second Albigensian Crusade). It was the time when the movement away from "feudal" Christianity (described in appendix B) became official; and something was then done to clarify the Church's view of the devils. These, it was emphasized, were part of the same creation with man, and created good, falling from Heaven by their own sin.[1] But the Council also paid a great deal of attention to the state of the Church and clergy; the danger of heresy and new movements of piety both required a certain washing of dirty linen, and in any case there were certain standard complaints that crop up in council after council. Thus, in chapter 16, those clerks were condemned, as they had been before and would be again, who frequented taverns and practised secular trades, worst of all the trades of player, minstrel or clown.

This canon was a relatively early one on the subject, and others through the century grew fiercer and more specific. In fact, the tonsured clerk who, failing to find a benefice, took to the degrading life of a strolling player while still claiming his privilege of clergy was becoming a major social and disciplinary problem for the Church in this period. It was, essentially, a problem with which our own age is not unfamiliar: the problem of the unemployed, underemployed or unemployable "white-collar worker"; the intellectual, spoilt by education for manual labour, had become by too much and too cheap education a drug on the market. The wave of enthusiasm for learning,

[1]Acts, 2nd year (1216), cap. 1 (vol. XXII in Mansi).

which produced the first great universities in the twelfth century, brought it about by the beginning of the thirteenth that there were too many poor scholars chasing too few benefices, while the attraction of a degree and the brilliant career to which it might be the gateway was still enough to make small beneficed clerks restless. The poor and ambitious from all over northern Europe drifted to Paris to the Schools; starved there till they could no longer endure it; and drifted away again, mostly without their coveted degree but with a deep contempt for the rustic and unlettered, to find, almost certainly, that the stay-at-homes had slipped into preferment before them, and the rich, who could afford to read Law, stepped into better places over their heads. If they managed to reach home again, their chances of not slipping back into the peasant class from which most of them sprang were remote. Often they were ashamed to return, or had not the means. The scholar's profit for his trouble was education for its own sake; a certain verbal quickness of wit that the Schools fostered, a retentive memory, whatever of arguments or verses that memory had salvaged from the books he had left in pawn, and an intimate knowledge of the drinking songs of the Quartier Latin. Add to this the training in music and singing that was the basic professional asset of clerks in minor orders, which therefore he probably had from his school-days; and a certain traditional claim to charity, and the spoilt clerk's line of least resistance is charted. The claim to alms was a rapidly wasting asset as the social scandal grew, and Church councils were driven in despair to class the wanderers as work-shy degraders of their cloth. The clerk turned *jongleur* was an idler and a renegade to the comfortable, and if he demanded the hospitality owing to the genuine poor student he was a fraud; a state of mind, natural indeed, which did nothing to heal the vagrant's sense of grievance.

Miss Helen Waddell, in *The Wandering Scholars*, has given a sympathetic picture of their case. This fascinating work was, indeed, intended, as its title suggests, to be a history of the clerk-turned-minstrel, the "clericus vagus." The author in the event was beguiled by the early birdsong of mediaeval lyric into writing quite a different book; but the one chapter that remains to tell of the "Ordo Vagorum" still stands without a rival for the light it throws on this little-known but highly significant facet of the thirteenth-century social scene. The problem belongs to the thirteenth century, at least to this extent, that the twelfth created it, the fourteenth solved it, and it was the thirteenth that threw up its hands in helpless horror. It was created, as I have said, by the illusory attraction the universities, especially

Paris, held out to the starveling sub-deacon; it was solved, more or less automatically, by the Black Death and the growth of small, local universities in closer touch with the "placement field." This decentralization of course helped not only because it brought demand and supply into contact, but because it directly cut down the population of wandering scholars, scholars having now less far to wander. By the sixteenth century, Scots undergraduates around whom the tradition of the trudging poor student still hung were walking home on "Meal-Monday" to replenish the sack of oats for their porridge; frugal as they were, theirs was a very different kind of poverty from that of their forebears who had tramped over Europe, begging their bread on the way, to sit in the straw of the Paris lecture-rooms.

It was thus chiefly in the period that separates the crushing of the Albigensians and rise of the friars from the beginnings of the witch-terror that the Church turned the searing blast of its displeasure against this small fry. For the wandering scholars were rebels, in spite of themselves indeed, and indeed against ecclesiastical discipline rather than against Christianity, but none the less rebels, malignants who made the "haves" conscious of the "have-nots" if only as a nuisance. From the point of view of the hierarchy, the *vagi* who took to the low arts of the joculator were letting down their order, making themselves a scandal, flaunting their idleness and debauchery while boasting the protection of the tonsure. From the point of view of the *vagi*, the hierarchy were simoniacal deniers of Christ, Dives to their Lazarus. So the Church in its councils thundered, and the poor clerks glibly lampooned the thunders; they formed their own Order, in mockery of the regular clergy, had their own bishops and councils, their own rules and canons, their own Gospel and their own Creed. The Church begins to condemn, not vagabonds in general, not simply clerks turned "ribald" or "buffoon," but in a special and technical sense "Goliardi" and "Eberhardini," members of a suspect organization or organizations. The wandering scholars (*vagi scholares*) are condemned, at Salzburg in 1291, as a "sect";[2] the canon, after reciting the details of their scandalous lives, goes on to say, "inveterati sectam suam non deserunt"—words that would not come strangely in a pronouncement against positive heretics. The goliards, indeed, were not heretics; but they were, they had been for long, a "sect," or as they called themselves an "order," an organized group with at least what purported to be rules and observances and some who at least claimed to be officers and rulers among them. There may, indeed, have been

[2]Quoted Waddell, *Wandering Scholars*, appendix E, p. 267. Mansi, xxiv.

more than one of these burlesque *ecclesiolae*. Miss Waddell points to a reference to a "bishop of the Eberhardini," defined by context as an actor, in 1204; and prints a mock "indulgence," or release from the importunity of beggars, granted in 1209 by the "archprimate" of the *vagi scholares* of Austria.[3]

The language of this and other *jeux d'esprit* that Miss Waddell has examined shows pretty clearly that the organization of the goliards was a burlesque of the Church, and their pretended official acts (for the most part) merely satires against their enemies, the clerics in high office. Theirs was purely a protest of the "have-nots"; there was nothing anti-Christian or even heretical about it. It is true they made songs on the names of Roman goddesses, true that old-fashioned moralists were ready to call all such *literati* heathen; but this sort of thing has been a commonplace of literary history down to the day before yesterday. Circumstances made the goliard an outcast and something of a rascal; he resented these circumstances, but he did not rationalize his resentments against Fortune, against Bishops, against the way of the world, into any creed of a separate goliard god. At worst, he attacked the hierarchy, justly or unjustly, for the same kind of faults that the fourth Lateran Council itself had complained of; he did not seek to make Christ again a scapegoat for the sins of His Church.

This at least is what the goliard buffooneries seem to suggest.[4] It remains important, to our purpose, that we have here an example of that "parody of Catholicism" that the Anti-Sadducee School is inclined to see in witchcraft, and especially in the Black Mass. If we cannot relate it to witchcraft by any closer tie, then the theory of "Catholicism parodied," as an explanation for any element in the cult, will become slightly harder to maintain; for the theory will have to stand comparison with a known example in approximately the same region and age. Can we, in fact, construct any hypothetical link between them so as to seem reasonable; and will it help to explain anything if we do?

It must be admitted that very little can be positively stated about the *Ordo Vagorum* beyond the fact that it did, in some sense, exist. It was always a movement that Authority disapproved of, and therefore has this at least in common with the witch-cult, that its whole history was more or less secret and the only evidence to emerge about it did

---

[3]Account book of Bishop Wolfger of Passau, Easter 1204, Waddell, *Wandering Scholars*, appendix B, p. 238; text and translation of "indulgence," *ibid.*, appendix C, p. 239; and cf. appendix E, p. 263 (cap. 16 of Salzburg council of 1274) for the nature of the nuisance involved.

[4]Waddell, *Wandering Scholars*, cap. 8.

so accidentally and is not to be relied on as typical. We have to guess at both, and of course we can make our guesses point the same way; we cannot claim to prove anything by such means. Still, we have the time-context of the goliards, and we know a good deal about their educational and social background. This, I should say, entitles us to be fairly confident about certain aspects of their history. The positive evidence assembled by Miss Waddell does not very clearly point to a high degree of organization among these vagabonds; nor does it do more than hint at the nature of such organization as they may have had. We are forced back on *a priori* reasoning; but this, I think, can take us some way. We can, for example, assume that there was in fact an organization. The documents point to nothing much beyond a solemn farce, rules written in the spirit of mockery and titles and offices assumed for convivial occasions. One meets with this kind of thing today in undergraduate cliques, and it was commoner in our grandfathers' time; burlesque "orders" and "chapters" are likely to have been formed by the students anyway. Were the vagabond students an "order" in any more serious sense? There is little indeed to suggest as much, unless it be the "indulgence" of the "archprimate" already referred to. But on *a priori* grounds one would say that there *must* have been a brotherhood with fairly rigid obligations on its members, to combine for mutual aid and protection a class, such as the wandering scholars, who had no other protector. I suppose the line of argument on which I rely is tolerably familiar. The thirteenth century was everywhere an age of tightening bonds of class solidarity, the height of the age of guilds and sworn communes, the formative period of political organizations of "estates." But besides that it was an age when men needed protectors; merchants who ventured out of their home town, or clerks who went to study at a distance from their diocese, banded themselves together from sheer necessity, since they were deprived of their natural protector, lord or bishop. The goliard clerks were trebly so deprived, being distant from their homes, having abandoned their university (itself just such a mutual protection group in origin) and being frowned on by the Church, which would otherwise have been their natural resort. They were in extreme danger of losing all recognized place in society, of becoming, in mediaeval conditions, pariahs compared with whom the "stateless" of our day are privileged. Members of the Sacerdotium whom the Sacerdotium disowned, members of the Studium following an incompatible way of life, foreigners wherever they went, they had much more need than the

Freemasons for a secret organization committing its members to mutual succour and comfort.

Secrecy, indeed, was a necessary condition of their society, while to the Freemasons it was largely accidental. The masons, travelling from place to place where their skill was required, could not maintain the ordinary kind of exclusive town guild, but a guild of some kind they had to have. The society they formed was surrounded by a veil of secrecy only because it was necessary to be able to tell a brother of the order from a false claimant when the "lodge" at work on a particular site might be drawn from several countries and unknown to one another. This was also a consideration with the goliards, as they were also wayfarers; but in addition they were living under the ban of Church councils, and the clergy were forbidden to befriend them.

The *Ordo Vagorum,* and the Eberhardini if, as is rather improbable, they were not in fact the same, must have been quite serious secret societies, with passwords and so forth, whose members were pledged to stand by one another wherever they might wander, societies which, like the Masons, were adapted to organizing a local cell on the spur of the moment wherever a sufficient number of initiates happened to foregather, and which, besides this, had a permanent framework of communication and control which spread its net from some French headquarters over much of Western Europe. Given the circumstances of the outcast goliard clerks, this is what we should expect to find in that age. The positive indications, such as they are, do point to the existence of local officers, such as the "Archiprimas" Surian and the "Lord Bishop" who took alms of Wolfger of Passau. The language of all ostensible acts and formularies of the "Order" apes that of the Church, as was natural to the Church's impenitent prodigal sons. This language is certainly parody; but whether for parody or imitation, the Church was the goliards' undoubted model.

Given all this, and given that the order is first heard of at the beginning of the thirteenth century and cannot then have been old (for the universities themselves were young), precisely what part of the Church's organization did they follow? There is little reason to doubt that as the Order evolved from casual buffoonery to conspiracy, and as it spread beyond the immediate environs of Paris, it drew most heavily for suggestions upon the new rules of the friars. These were the popular and rising orders of the day, and were specially in evidence in the universities. Their rules were expressly designed for societies of wandering poor religious, for tonsured beggars; and they differed from existing orders in this and in their more effective central organization. The monk was a member of a settled community, the self-governing abbey; the abbey might owe obedience to a larger order or "family," but it was itself the society to which the monk's loyalty was owing. The friar, on the other hand, was first and foremost a member of his order, and of its local convent only incidentally. The order had a chain of command through its general and provincial chapters that practically did away with the convent's independence, making of it not a state in a federation, like a Cistercian house, but a unit in any army. I use the words "convent" and "house" advisedly, and they express a related dichotomy: whereas one might reasonably think of a monastic community as a *building*, as something fixed and local, the basic community of friars is the convent, the company of men whose essence is unchanged though it should move its quarters.

Since the first days of the friars, these two religions have strongly influenced one another, and the contrast nowadays is by no means so clear; but at this time the friars were still primarily wanderers, and indeed wandering scholars. It is of interest to note that when they began to settle down the word "convent," from meaning the community itself, came to mean the building it occupied; and this I suppose is what one generally means by it today. But the goliards were never faced with the temptation to become a claustral order; from necessity, they followed a life closely similar to that of the primitive Franciscans without the vocation, and it seems most probable that they based their rule on that very fashionable model. (Simply as an organization, the new kind of order developed by Francis and Dominic was a great advance on earlier efforts, and widely imitated, even by such as the Carmelites whose way of life was that of conventional monasticism; it may even have influenced secular governments to some extent.) The *Ordo Vagorum* is first heard of before the orders of friars came into existence, and therefore originally cannot have followed their customs; but the considerations that would urge their adoption are so strong that it must be reckoned more likely than not that the goliards adopted them. It is in any case reasonable to suppose that the Order was formed of local or peripatetic cells, that perhaps might be set up *ad hoc* on a convivial occasion, linked in provinces and subject to some kind of General Chapter. If the friars furnished the model, one would guess that the name for a cell was "conventus" and the qualifying number thirteen.

Thirteen—based, of course, on the number of the Apostles—was the ideal number of a community of friars; and in this the new orders were looking back to a very ancient tradition of the Church, according to which a religious body or congregation needed to be at least of this number in order to function as an independent entity and elect its own head. Thus, ideally, an Archbishop should have at least twelve suffragans, an abbot at least twelve monks under his rule. A particularly noted example of this feeling is provided by the first community set up by St. Benedict at Monte Cassino, which (we are told) contained thirteen small houses each of an abbot and twelve brethren, all under the superior government of the saint himself. The word "conventus," applicable to any community of regular religious though specially used of friaries, could also be used to express this qualifying minimum of thirteen members; and therefore would be specially natural when used of a body actually numbering thirteen.

If I am right in supposing that the goliards would naturally adopt the organization of the Franciscans and Dominicans, they adopted this detail. If I am exaggerating the influence these orders are likely to have had, this much is still probable, given that the *Ordo Vagorum* mimicked the *language* of the Church, was familiar with its internal discipline, and made a special point of claiming (ironically) to imitate the Apostles.[5] In that case, we have not only a society that mocks the Church and possesses the learning to parody it effectively, but an organization that ramifies through France and the neighbouring countries, based upon the coven of thirteen and even, probably, using the actual word "coven" (which is certainly derived from *conventus*).

It would be unwise to rest much on this point, for the word "coven" in a witch context makes a late appearance and is, to the best of my knowledge, confined to post-Reformation Scots evidence.[6] However, it can hardly then have been a new imported term, for there can be little doubt the word if not the thing was borrowed from Christian monasticism and therefore can hardly have been borrowed, in Scotland, later than the Reformation. As for the thing described by the word—a cell in a religious order or community, of thirteen members ideally—this need not have been monastic or even Christian in origin, since thirteen (a leader and twelve) is a rather popular number in the myths and cults of many religions besides the Christian. But it obviously could be borrowed from Christianity, and we do not know of any other religion from which it could have been borrowed in the

[5]*Carmina Burana*, 195, and Waddell, *Wandering Scholars*, pp. 186–8.

[6]Murray, *Divine King*, appendix 7, p. 253, alleges some earlier examples, but in these instances there is no connection with witchcraft; the word is simply used for "company" or "faction." As such it is philologically interesting, but irrelevant to the present discussion.

relevant time; so the economy of hypotheses requires us to accept this as the best available explanation.

A sacred thirteen is always a sacred twelve plus an even more sacred one; every sacred twelve is thus a thirteen in potentiality. Thirteen in itself has no great mystic significance for mankind at large; there are those who insist on looking back to a hypothetical race of ancients who counted the year as thirteen Customs of Women instead of the more usual twelve lunations, but this is an aberration of perverse ingenuity unbacked by concrete examples. Examples of sacred twelves are very numerous, and I should be perfectly ready to believe that thirteen was, on that account, a sacred number proper to a ritual college in any or all of the pre-Christian religions of Western Europe. But it is quite unnecessary to look so far back for an explanation, when the Christian significance of the number was so much more widely known than any detail of paganism can have been to Europe in the Middle Ages. It takes real determination to follow Miss Murray in reading a pagan interpretation into specifically Christian uses of this number; or to hold that, given it *has* a Christian significance, this cannot be the explanation of its popularity "with all classes" in the Middle Ages, whereas the number of the witch-coven, apparently, can.[7]

So far as the word "coven" indicates anything, then, it indicates Christian influence; adoption of the language of opponents (which does occur in the history of religions; the word "Christian" is an example), adoption of institutions complete with the name, or influence from renegade Christians. Of course, the last is the suggestion I should prefer to adopt for the purposes of the present chapter. I do not, however, want to read too much into the word "coven," both because of its late appearance and because it is not quite unknown in a sense approximate to "conspiracy," and we cannot exclude the possibility of pure coincidence although the arguments the other way seem much more forceful. In any case, a word is not much to hang a theory on, and the theory—that the goliard society was the parent of the witch-society—may not seem intrinsically probable.

Nevertheless, the goliards could supply several things which it concerns us to look for. Their society flourished in just the period when the Inquisition was growing up and before it began attacking witches; the period when the Cathari and Waldenses were being hunted and becoming convenient pegs on which to hang any kind of

[7]Murray, *loc. cit.*

superstitious calumny, when the old wives' tale of the Canon *Episcopi* was being transformed by the experts into terrifying truth. The society in all probability had an organization very similar to that which is reported of witches—of some witches—in the seventeenth century; an organization based presumably on that of the friars, modified by the necessity for secrecy. The goliards were opponents of the existing state of things in the Church, and of its leaders, without being moral reformers in the sense the Waldenses were, and they possessed a vastly more intimate knowledge of Christian doctrine and liturgy than the ordinary humble heretic. Many among them, though certainly not the majority, were probably actual priests; but the typical member of the society would be at least in minor orders, know Latin, and be familiar with a priest's duties. He had, it is safe to say, hoped to become a priest, though hardly for reasons we should regard as respectable; his ambitions would be fixed on some capitular office rather than on a parish, that is, if he stopped short of imagining himself as bishop, cardinal or pope. The majority of the Order, no doubt, wryly accepted a kind of vocation to unholy poverty, to clowning at markets, singing in taverns, and being grateful for a place in the straw not too far from the hearth. But in the nature of the case it must have thronged with much more savage rebels, men bitterly wounded in their ambitions, and spoilt priests jealously retentive of their clergy. If we are looking for celebrants of the Black Mass, we need look no further.[8]

While we are about it, we might as well note that most of these could and doubtless would have performed a Mass, Black or other, for a consideration; that is, they would know how to, though in most cases they would not possess the requisite priest's orders. It is hardly a point on which we ought to dwell, for it is not established that witchcraft and the Black Mass have any necessary connection; though I think it is clear that the Black Mass, meaning some ceremony based on the real Mass, could be and probably sometimes was grafted onto the Sabbat towards the end of the latter's evolution. A good indication of this, if it can be trusted, is the confession of Madeleine Demandouls of Aix, quoted by Miss Murray from a Jacobean propaganda pamphlet.[9] By this account, the local witch-master, Louis Gaufredy, "did first invent the saying of Masse at the Sabbaths, and did really

[8]I do not of course mean to imply that there were no other probable celebrants, nor that such a trade would ever attract more than a handful of the wandering scholars, but only that in their situation they were peculiarly prone to temptation.

[9]Murray, *Witch-Cult*, p. 149, note 2; quoting "Admirable Historie of the Possession and Conversion of a Penitent Woman," by Sebastian Michaelis, London, 1613.

consecrate and present the sacrifice to Lucifer"—and sprinkled those present with the consecrated wine—"at which time every one cryeth, *Sanguis eius super nos et filios nostros.*" (I suppose the word *filios* inspired Miss Murray's comment that "the use of this phrase suggests that the sprinkling was a fertility rite."[10]) This was said in 1610; in the knowledge of the deponent, the rite was an innovation in that coven, and a consciously anti-Christian one (which, of course, is the real significance of the Vulgate text), for which an educated witch-master was responsible; presumably he was a priest, if he "did really consecrate." Therefore (if we accept this piece of evidence; a translation in a propaganda pamphlet is not the most perfect authority), the Mass was not an essential part of the rites, but might be introduced by a learned leader as an improvement. At Aix, this seems to have occurred around 1600; in other places something of the same general kind may have occurred before.

It is not, however, only or even mainly as possible celebrants of Black Masses that I would regard the goliards as important to the history of the cult. After all, the instance just quoted indicates as much as anything the *absence* of the Black Mass from, so to speak, the Canon of the Sabbat. Neither do I wish to suggest that the order itself developed into the witch-cult, or that its members as a whole were absorbed into a witch-cult already existing. On the whole there was little that was actually nefarious about the goliards, except from the specialized point of view of Church disciplinarians; and probably nothing that was pagan in more than a literary sense. But it can hardly be doubted that individuals would be attracted to the *Ordo Vagorum* who would also be attracted to the role of witch-master; and such people would find in the order advantages not precisely those for which it had been designed.

There are two points here to be considered, of which I will take the second first as the shortest dealt with. The *Ordo Vagorum* was a secret society, and one that covered a fair amount of ground. The strolling way of life of its members, which imposed upon them an organization adapted to wide dispersal, also enabled them to preserve contacts over wide distances in a world without the swift communications on which we rely; there would always be somebody going in the right direction who could carry a message, and those summoned to a council in another country would have no elaborate preparations to make. But the society, which must in any case have had secret passwords and so forth, could only preserve itself if it was understood that

[10]Murray, *loc. cit*; cf. Matthew 27:25.

members should co-operate with men they did not know, who knew the passwords. Dispersal itself, even without the need to avoid the eye of Authority, would necessitate this much, as with the Masons' society. But such an organization, however innocent its original purpose, must run the risk of being exploited for sinister ends; and any secretive group, especially one that gives succour to the fugitive and social outcast, will naturally attract recruits of questionable moral standing. Again, the history of Freemasonry presents an instructive parallel. That order has now the reputation, on the continent, of nursing sedition and undermining Christianity; and while we need not believe the fantastic stories against it that are spread by French Catholic propagandists, there is substance in the basic accusation, if only because those who become Masons in France do so with the society's lurid reputation in mind. On account of their rather childish fondness for mystification and cryptic mummery, the Masons have also attracted many searchers after the occult, and have, I believe, even adopted at the instance of these eccentrics a certain amount of Rosicrucian parrot-language, so as to deceive many men whom one would have reckoned sane, notably Rudyard Kipling. It is dangerous for a friendly society to indulge in this kind of make-believe for grown-ups; when it gives itself airs as if it possessed the esoteric clue to the universe, it is likely to draw into its net some very odd fish, and when it behaves as if it existed for an undeclared dark purpose, it may get a very dark purpose thrust upon it. This seems to have been the fortune of the Ku Klux Klan; originally an elaborate joke, like any of these zoological Ancient Orders that put colour in the lives of business men, the sinister suggestions of its ritual were so interpreted by the first recruits that it came to be looked on, from within and without, as a sort of *Vehmgericht*; and as this took place in the Deep South in the period of "Reconstruction," when the Southern whites felt an urgent need, emotional as well as practical, for an engine of covert violence against their former slaves, the Klan developed as a proto-Fascist conspiracy.

This sort of thing can occur even to a quite public and overt organization, such as the American Legion, not to mention Communist-front cultural clubs and Catholic-Action-front Labour movements. But I think it need not be argued at length that only a secret society can be readily adapted to the needs of a magician; we only need to be clear that this kind of internal perversion of an organization from its true purpose, or use of it as a cover for nefarious activities, can and continually does occur.

This brings me to the other point I mentioned a moment ago: that the *Ordo Vagorum* would be likely to contain potential witch-masters. The members of the order were unsuccessful priests, men who had given much time and pains to acquiring the professional skills of the ecclesiastic, and who were now forced to regard that time and those pains as thrown away, unless they could find a new use for the skills they had no chance of legitimately practising. Of all who were unsuccessful in the scramble for preferment or long struggle for a degree, only those who were unable to slip back into a respectable lay trade became wanderers and joined the order (though the tonsured clerk who took to lay business without giving up his clergy was also condemned by Church councils).[11] They begged their bread, or sang for their supper, as minstrels, tumblers, and clowns; it would be only natural to expect that they supplemented their repertory of jigs and tales of bawdry with other resources, not unknown to the fairground, in which their claims to superior education could be an asset; if they became fortune-tellers, three-card men, quack doctors, and the then equivalents. One feels that some must have done so. The superstitious would naturally tend to regard any educated man, especially a tonsured clerk with Latin at command, as something of a magician, something of a doctor, something of a priest; and the goliard must often have found himself in need of supper and a bed in some village where these skills would command respect but almost everybody could sing and dance. A little conjuring on the side would be a natural addition to his repertory; and on occasion he may well have been presented with a ready-made opportunity to cash in on credulity. Consider, for example, that the only actually sacerdotal function of the clerk in minor orders was exorcism—casting out devils.[12] The Apostolic power to command the Devil was the inheritance of the sub-deacon equally with the pope; the "Eberhardine" was not even guilty of fraud if he claimed it, and how easy fraud must have been for him in other ways! It would be equally easy for us to imagine a dozen ways in which a goliard, without any fixed plan or ambition, may have found himself a sorcerer.

Time and again some unbeneficed wanderer, who had perhaps sat under Aquinas, would tune his rebeck on the green of a village whose priest had never been near the place; where the pluralist incumbent himself lacked ordination, and had perhaps put in a curate without

[11]Waddell, *Wandering Scholars*, appendix E, *passim*.
[12]That is, they bore the *name* "Exorcist." Their functions as such were in practice confined to the ceremonial carrying and sprinkling of holy water.

Latin enough for a choirboy, and perhaps forgotten to put in any curate at all. I do not wish to enter into the controversial question whether that kind of laxity was typical in this age, but certainly it could occur and was hardly rare.[13] Imagine the cruel irony of such a chance; imagine the clamorous need of the simple peasantry for the man who could pronounce the words of power; who knew the secret of the prayers for rain and harvest, who could drive out ghosts, bless the mysterious lucky water that kept the threshold safe, and curse the evil spirits that sent disease and death. There may well have been men who possessed themselves of neglected livings by the direct method; and they are hardly to be blamed. Perhaps at their first arrival they would find a soul in danger of dying unbaptized or unabsolved; and even the canon law would recognize their right and duty to step into the breach. It would be, quite probably, by an invisible gradation traceable only by the expert decretalist that orders assumed for an emergency would pass into orders assumed by flat imposture, and they in their turn into claims to magical power. The self-made priest I here postulate would probably make this last step, because he could not simply slip into the empty parsonage; whatever else of pastoral care an absentee might neglect, the tithes would still be collected, and the interloper would have to devise an alternative source of income. He might, for instance, charge for imaginary prayers of special power,[14] or manufacture Christ's body in the bread for use in talismans; Mass-production, as one might say.

Then of course, the day would come when ecclesiastical authority, archdeacon or outraged incumbent, would arrive to eject him, and make him, so to speak, an anti-Rector in flight, with a vendetta to pursue and the sympathies of the people; or without their sympathies, and with a strong need to recapture their respect. If he stayed in the same district, it would be as a magician; if he passed on to another, it would be with useful lessons learned.

Elsewhere, a goliard who had taken to charlatanry and fairground hocus-pocus as a more paying game than the jongleur's would have come into direct contact with his business colleagues, the village goëtes or hagwives, and would overawe them, instinctively, with a display of abstruse jargon; claiming, as a literate fraud naturally would claim,

---

[13]The question is, of course, controversial; a good deal of the controversy is conveniently thrashed out in the later volumes and appendices of Coulton, *Five Centuries of Religion*.

[14]In this connection it is worth noting that an unofficial formula of exorcism was included in the Benedictbuern MS *Carmina Burana*; Waddell, *Mediaeval Latin Lyrics*, p. 198, "Omne genus demoniorum...."

to have learned his art from Hecate or Hermes Trismegistus or some inconceivably ancient and remote authority, to have read lost books or travelled far in the mysterious East. Suppose that every now and then such impostors were taken at their own valuation, and accepted by a local group of *veneficae* as distinguished masters of the craft. Suppose it happened now and then; is this much unlikely?

Or imagine the wandering scholar whom a local churchman, obedient to canons and the anathemas of councils, refuses alms, and tries to hale to the official's prison to be forcibly shaved as a disgrace to his tonsure. Might he not claim acquaintance with the Devil, as a reason why none should dare to lay hands on him?

The thirteenth century opened with the Church's first military offensive against the Albigensians. As they were dualists, their fiercest opponents condemned them as devil-worshippers; and the Dominican Order, whose wits were first whetted on that heresy, came away from the crusade obsessed with the problem of Satan. The Dominicans became the most sought-after teachers in Paris (and, later, in all northern universities), as well as the most controversial. As the century wore on, the new recruits to the *Ordo Vagorum* must have been increasingly imbued with the new scholastic Anti-Sadducism; as theology dominated the Schools far beyond humane letters, the wandering scholars must have been ever less inclined to make their living out of lyric verse and more tempted by a diabolism in which the later generations must have come to believe. Thus, if here one and there another had become accustomed to make pretensions of supernatural learning, and live on those pretensions wherever possible, it is reasonable to believe that they would find themselves the objects, inside the Order, of increasing respect; they would not find it difficult to attract candidates for initiation into the craft of magic.

Even without this, the society was organized for surreptitious communication, and if two or three who in different ways had taken to charlatanry should meet at any time it would not be difficult for them to arrange future co-operation. If one, or two, had made contact with some existing group of witches, they could pass on what they had managed to learn of the practices of such people, and the way to go about gaining their confidence; others might trade for this information a useful conjuring trick or two. From such contacts, which the secretive sworn brotherhood of goliardism would make easy to preserve and renew, a college of witch-masters may well have grown. If it ever became formalized as an order within the Order, the existing organization would presumably be imitated *mutatis mutandis*, and perpetuated, as something private to the witch-society, after the supply of learned men to the profession of tramp had dwindled and the *Ordo Vagorum* thus decayed.

When this took place is again a matter for guesswork. Councils throughout the fourteenth century continue to condemn minstrel and vagabond clerks, *Eberhardini*; but the problem does not seem to have been crucial, and the language employed seems to be copied from earlier texts.[15] After the middle of the century it seems clear that Europe was complaining of a lack of educated men rather than an excess, and the dawn of realistic literature in Boccaccio and Chaucer leaves the goliard without a mention.[16] Even if the Order survived, I should guess the witch-masters were no longer using it; it would not have taken them long to set up their own organization and induct their own pupils, who perhaps would not always qualify as wandering scholars. The parent Order had existed in some form or another as early as the first years of the thirteenth century, and the offshoot would need little time to grow. It would have the advantage of all offshoots, of an organization and a like-minded pool of recruits ready made.

I suggest that, in some such manner as I have here sketched out, a group of goliards, spoilt clerks, who had turned to sorcery as a more appropriate outlet for their talents than minstrelsy, came into contact with surviving groups of witches in the course of their wanderings, fairly early in the thirteenth century, and were already in contact with one another through the existing brotherhood of goliards, an under-cover order framed, partly in mockery, on the model of the friars. I suggest they were able, by virtue of their superior education and of the knowledge they pooled with each other, to gain acceptance by witches as masters of the craft, in several places where the cult held out; and that they may have organized it and welded it into a ramifying international secret society more or less on the model of their own. From this time the regular coven with its regular meetings, its constituted officers, and its rigid discipline may have come into being; from this time thirteen is taken as the standard number in a cell. If any

[15]For instance it would be unwise to assume that because a Magdeburg council in 1370 spoke of wandering clerks "qui eberhardini dicuntur," this name, which had appeared in many previous councils, was still in actual use; it may have become merely a clerical technicality (Waddell, *Wandering Scholars*, appendix E, p. 270).

[16]At least in our sense. Chaucer's Miller is described as a "goliardeys" in a context which makes it clear that his indecent conversation, not his skill on the bagpipes, is referred to (*Canterbury Tales*, Prologue, 1. 560). "Goliard" however was not in the Middle Ages a technical term to the extent that it is in the language of Miss Waddell.

shadow of this organization existed before in one place or another (as it may have done), now it had a chance to become general; for now uniformity became possible, and now itinerant witch-masters carried out their visits of inspection in their allotted circuits and met together to consult on the affairs of the craft and exchange the fruits of their learning and experience. Any practice that had formerly been purely local might now become the custom of the society as a whole; there is a movement towards standardization, even perhaps towards an attempt at logical coherence. As the witch-masters of this generation would be learned men by the standards of the time, there was an opportunity not only for exchange of knowledge but for borrowings from outside; possibly borrowings from those heresies which the Inquisition were already prepared to confound, by way of diabolism, with sorcery. It is also likely that the new witch-masters would tend to emphasize and perhaps exaggerate the place of Satan in the cult; for it is certainly as Satan that they would regard him.

Indeed, it is by no means impossible that all memories of old horned gods had been lost by this time, and that the goliard quacks introduced the god, thinking of him as Satan even if they scrupled to name him openly. They would be inclined to regard Satan as a source of supernatural power, as the question was then one much argued in the Schools; and they may well have used impersonation of the Devil as a weapon when they wished to save their skins, wreak vengeance, or extort money from some hostile community. The familiar iconography of the Devil was by this time fully established; and the typical trades of the goliard included acting. (It is not even particularly unlikely that the Order, or individual members of it, may have possessed Devil's costumes for purely dramatic purposes; Satan was, after all, a popular character on the late mediaeval stage.)

The new witch-masters can hardly have been the originators of the Sabbat as a whole, or of the dances, nor the inventors of the ointments. I doubt if they were in a position actually to recruit circles of local witches, at least at first; and I am prepared to believe that the horned god already existed, and that most witchcraft techniques were much older. The actual practice of sorcery they would probably pick up from their followers in one place, even if they passed it on to other followers elsewhere. The great importance of the new development, as far as sorcery is concerned, would be in providing a medium whereby one witch-group could convey traditional knowledge to another. Even so, there are aspects of the cult, or beliefs about it, which if they correspond to reality are easiest explained as the innovations of educated initiates. The Black Mass, of course, is one, and the *osculum infame* another. The name "coven," if not the thing, can be quite definitely assigned an external origin; and the thing itself, in the rigidly organized form it seems to have had latterly, may well have been created by this process and, most probably, only became universal by its means. The *name* "Sabbat," though in this case not the thing described by it, is another instance.

Sabbat, we are told, may have many origins but is certainly not related to the Hebrew *Sabbath*. On this point there is an astonishing agreement between Miss Murray, the Rev. Montague Summers, and Mr. Pennethorne Hughes, as well as Michelet who seems to be ulti-mately responsible, and certain unnamed etymologists to whom vague reference is habitually made. Of course, they are mistaken; *Sabbat* conceivably does not derive from *Sabbath*, but the probability is they are both the same word, and certainly the contrary has not been proved. The distinction in spelling is a very recent development, not observed in the age of persecutions itself; the distinction of sound would not exist in French or seventeenth-century English; in mediaeval Latin the two words cannot be distinguished at all; and the distinction of meaning is a mere nuance. In these circumstances it is rash to urge that the arm of Coincidence is long, and *s'esbattre* or *Sabazia* intriguing possibilities. "O quanta, qualia, sunt illa sabbata," wrote Abelard in the twelfth century—using a form identical with that associated with witchcraft, certainly referring to the Jewish usage, and taking the word to mean, not only *Saturday* (the usual mediaeval sense of the word), but in general a day set apart, a holy day.[17] Clearly, the word can be applied to the major witch-festivals in this sense; it was probably applied to minor witch-festivals also, and the word *Esbat* no more than an unrecognized Basque morpheme, but of course it is as easy to suppose that *Esbat* is a crude back-slang coinage from *Sabbat*.[18]

It may perhaps be objected, why should these spoilt clerks import into the cult the modifications I have mentioned? If they had the chance to become witch-masters, and found it served their turn, doubtless they became witch-masters (and neither of these, I would maintain, is hard to believe); if they became witch-masters, doubtless it was convenient for them to tighten up discipline among their followers and to devise organs of mutual co-operation; but what need

---

[17]The classical Latin for this would be *feria*, but in the Middle Ages this, by the medium of subsidiary senses, had come to mean a week-day.

[18]In view of the distribution of the words, it is fantastic to suppose the contrary, that *Sabbat* was derived from *Esbat* (Murray, *Witch-Cult*, p. 97).

was there that they should bring about any *ritual* changes? The short answer is that they needed to back up their own position; to make themselves necessary to witchcraft, they had to persuade witches that the special knowledge they possessed was necessary to witchcraft; as masters, they had to have something to teach. Actually, I should imagine it was a complex psychological need of their own as well that the cult under their guidance should be a cult of just such a nature; but this is not a necessary hypothesis. The rites must employ a certain amount of dog-Latin, because they knew Latin and the village hag-wives did not, and because peasants were ready to regard Latin as a language of mysterious power. There had to be rites of sorcery that they were the first to tell the coven about, and therefore they drew on the scandals that circulated among the clerical public about the devil-worship of heretics. But also, they as more or less educated men, rationalizers, needed to believe that the cult was a cult of the Devil, because they could not believe in any other supernatural power to which the Church had not better access than they. This of course is to assume that these shamans were half charlatans and half true believers, partially their own dupes; but this, after all, is a very common mental condition. In any case, whether they took it seriously themselves or not, they would naturally still incline to the belief that their dupes were worshipping the Devil, as the only source of malign spiritual power, and therefore that a cult of the Devil was what they were required to concoct as the spiritual leaders of these *maleficae*.

Today, of course, the first essential of a convincing liturgy for diabolists would be an order of the Black Mass. But though such a rite might easily develop in the conditions I am presuming, given the time-context it would not be necessary, for the Black Mass might occur to any devil-worshipper independently if he started from a Christian background, but as a legend about devil-worshippers entertained by Christians it was only on the point of beginning to grow in the thirteenth century. On the other hand, such a liturgy would need to contain the *osculum infame* and something in the way of "nameless orgies," probably preceded by some kind of common meal; for these were already believed to be practices of diabolists at least by the middle of the century. They were first imputed, as I have said, to the Cathars and Waldenses, and these were in some sort also regarded as followers of Satan; they had since been attached to explicit devil-worship by an extraordinary chain of mental confusion for which the principal responsibility rests on the repulsive Conrad of Marburg.

Fortunately, Conrad's defects as a man and an Inquisitor are so manifest as to be common ground between Protestant and Catholic historians, and I need not go into his career at length. Suffice it to say that he was a violent fanatic, and (though a secular priest) was head of the new-formed Inquisition for Germany in 1231–3, at which time the Emperor Frederick II was showing zeal to stamp out heresy in his German lands, not so much because heresy was rampant there as because Frederick was in grave need, politically, of emphasizing his own orthodoxy. It was a task after Conrad's heart, but it must be admitted that his knowledge of heresy was slight and of judicial method much less. Probably there were in fact some few heretics in Germany even at this early date, more or less of the Waldensian persuasion; according to public repute there were at least two groups: the unimportant Steadingers, peasant rebels whose real objection was to paying tithe, who attempted to colonize the wilderness where feudalism had not penetrated and who were the occasion for a small crusade, and a group of petty burgher puritans in the city of Strasburg whose preacher was alleged to have entertained opinions we should call "universalist," holding not even Satan to be irreparably damned. This latter group were in mockery called "Luciferians" on this account (from the name of a very trivial fourth-century schism which in fact referred, not to Lucifer the fallen angel, but to a tiresome bishop of the same name).[19] The word "Luciferian" seems to have had a startling effect on Conrad's impressionable mind, inflamed as it evidently was by reading anti-Cathar propaganda; probably the "Contra Haereticos" of Alain de Lille, since he is not likely to have known of the more factual work of Pierre de Vaux de Cernay. From Alain or some similar author he learned how Cathars got their name from the obscene homage they paid their devil in the shape of a cat or of a goat, and how their assemblies were disfigured by sexual licence. What could be easier to believe of "Luciferians"?

Inspired with a proper zeal to rid Germany of these depravities, Conrad is said to have declared that it were better a hundred innocent persons should perish than one guilty escape. According to the protest addressed to the Pope by the German bishops when they came to realize the extent of the danger, Conrad was in the habit of offering

[19]Oddly enough, Bishop Lucifer differed from the Church of his day mainly in demanding greater severity on heretics (Arians), and would have had much in common with Conrad. For all this subject, see the article by E. Amann, on "Luciferiens" in *Dictionnaire de Théologie Catholique*.

all suspects the simple choice between confessing to the whole rig-marole of obscenities or of going straight to the stake as obdurate heretics. This struck them as the wrong way to go about it, because members of the nobility had been accused; before they intervened, the number of humble victims had probably run into four figures. In 1233 the hunt was called off and Conrad shortly afterwards murdered to the general relief.[20]

Whereas we are usually in some doubt how much credence can be given to the Confessions secured by the Inquisitorial process, it is evident that those collected by Conrad were of no value at all. But in the mind of that age, they shed a new light on devil-worship; these German heretics (real or supposed) supply a connecting link, on account of their name, between the Cathar bogey of the twelfth and thirteenth centuries and the witch bogey of the fourteenth and follow-ing, the common element being worship of the devil in one sense or another. It should now be clear that most of the stories that were told about the Sabbat belong to Satanism, and to witchcraft only if it was Satanism, and only if it took hints from a pre-existing popular idea of Satanism. These unedifying rites were not, in overwhelming prob-ability, ancient pagan practices, innocent of a Satanic intention, which were ignorantly transferred by sectarian propaganda *from* witches *to* heretics. On chronological grounds, it would seem that the transfer-ence, whether of real customs or of false accusations, must have been the other way.

There is, of course, an obvious objection at this point to my line of argument so far. If these accusations can be taken as absolutely groundless when they are applied to Luciferians, why am I prepared to accept them when they are applied to witches, and to erect a surely rather far-fetched speculative reconstruction of unwritten history in order to explain it? If the goliards had a hand in it, it can be shown that they might reasonably influence the cult in this way; but why need it be supposed that they or anyone had such a hand, when it is evident the Christian world was in any case capable of believing the things it believed about witches, with no necessity at all of their being true?

The reader may be ready to dismiss the whole body of later witch-confessions, even the most circumstantial, as nothing but the product of terrorist methods. I am prepared to discount about ninety per cent but not the whole; it is a matter on which I think we must ultimately

[20]Lea, *Inquisition*, cap. 6.

rely on taste or intuition, the *feel* of the language employed. It is hard to read King James I and believe there was nothing at all in it. It is almost impossible to believe witchcraft in the general sense was not practised; and though this hardly applies to the Sabbat, there are details connected with that which cannot be explained as scare-stories borrowed from anti-Cathar propaganda and misapplied. The propaganda has nothing to say about flying ointments, or round dances widdershins, or devil's marks, and would make out the heretics' assemblies to be indoor occasions of the greatest secrecy, as they presumably were. Nor is there any link between Cathars or Waldenses and the dates associated with major witch-ceremonies, April 30 and October 31. It really looks as if the witches did hold occasions of ceremony, and for what they did on those occasions we have only the indications of confessions—indications which point to the kind of ceremony we have been discussing. Of course, the same applies to Cathars and "Luciferians," and presumably their rites were actually less lurid; but we can presume this chiefly because they were Christian heretics who preached a rigid morality; there is nothing in the nature of witchcraft hostile to devil-worship, or to sexual licence upon an appropriate occasion.

As for the goliards, I do not rely upon them; I merely suggest them as the medium whereby certain details, that may easily be supposed to have been a part of the witch-cult, may most easily be supposed to have become such a part. Other media are conceivable, but I think none will work so well; certain influences might come from some hidden heretical group direct, if we are prepared to believe that the Inquisitors and pamphleteers were right about heretics; and something might have been contributed by the Freemasons, if there was any reason to suppose that their society was then already organized in the manner and degree of modern Masonry and was already prepared to play with occultism, which was almost certainly not the case.[21] As to the objection, which may and ought to be made, that the whole

[21]Although, of course, the secrecy of Masonry makes it difficult to be sure and impossible to quote adequate authorities, its history is not in fact so secret as its members would wish. It seems to be agreed, except by cranks, that the order as it now exists originated in Britain in the seventeenth century, spreading to France in the eighteenth, and though it may imitate, does not actually descend from any mediaeval society of working masons. Its mystical doctrines were adopted as an afterthought, and derive from Paracelsus via the Rosicrucians; that is, they are older than Masonry but not older than the sixteenth century. Masonry lacks a reputable historian; but the history of the *words* "Freemason" and "Franc-maçon" at least makes fairly clear the English, and relatively recent origin of the term in its modern sense.

hypothesis outlined in this chapter is a concoction *a priori*, I will admit it, but would maintain that any historical theory about the witch-cult has to be. Speculation, clearly stated to be such, is no crime.

Having got so far, I may as well run over some of the later developments as I see them. The "college" of witch-masters, drawn from the goliards' ranks, arose and reorganized the cult in the middle and late thirteenth century; the cult, as reorganized, stretched in a scattered way through France and Germany, probably extending into Scandinavia, Bohemia, and Hungary (though only just) but hardly penetrating into Italy nor yet to Britain. Outside the area covered, the more primitive traditions were still kept up, as also doubtless in pockets within the area, and witchcraft in these places continued to subsist without much in the way of organization or formal ceremonies; though of course it would exhibit certain parallels with the sect, as it had always done. Formal cult witchcraft only spread outside this area in a later age, where indeed it genuinely did so; Britain, including Scotland, had to wait till the sixteenth century for it, though when it came it was able, as at its first rise, to graft itself on to a local tradition.

The phase of fairly consistent central control, however, was only a phase. After the first generation the leadership was not able to preserve continuity of contact, and local branches of the sect again began to develop along independent lines. This was partly owing to the activity of the Inquisition, which almost immediately became aware of the new danger and began, around 1300, the witch-hunt that was not to end till it had outlasted the Age of Faith and the old Universal Church. It may also have been a factor undermining uniformity that the local witch-master, once the sect was fully organized, would naturally come to resent the control of a superior hierarchy as a limitation on his power; but only if he did not regard the remoter authorities as custodians of greater supernatural secrets than his own, and had been tempted (as for instance by resort to the Devil) to look elsewhere for the true source of power. But most important of all, the personal quality of the first leaders could not be kept up; there would be ever fewer learned recruits, and latterly each witch-master would know only what his own master had taught him. There was a dearth of rebel scholars, especially after the first great outbreaks of bubonic plague that left the Church with a clergy shortage; a shortage, as I have said, that was ultimately to be made good by the new local schools rather than by Paris, involving a certain loosening of the old international community of scholars. There was, on the whole, a lowering of intellectual standards at the end of the Middle Ages, not unconnected with these events; and the growing use of vernaculars in place of Latin would also have its part to play in destroying the "world-citizenship" of the clerk.

In places, perhaps, the witch-societies relapsed into their old informal state with nothing to show for what had passed but vague memories of foreign doctrines, and a few garbled spells borrowed from books or from long-distant, quite unrelated covens. Elsewhere the framework held; and, it would seem, most notably in the Alpine valleys, where a Church already reduced to a condition of extreme nervousness by the first great waves of popular heresy, continued down to the Reformation to cry out against the abominations of witches more constantly and more insistently than in any other province of Christendom.

I should like to say something about the numerous outbursts of popular fanaticism and religious eccentricity that marked the end of the Middle Ages and seem to have been an outlet for the psychological strain endured by a superstitious population in a time of recurrent and shattering epidemics. The fourteenth century was an age, certainly, when religious hysteria was in the air; this might make many become witches, and many others burn witches, and at any rate cannot have helped to preserve the remarkably sane and balanced mind the Church had hitherto shown. Apart from indicating the state of the public mind, however, they do not seem to offer any material useful for our purpose. An exception, perhaps, is the sect known as "The Brethren of the Free Spirit," of German origin, which seems to have migrated to Bohemia in the time of Huss and subsequently found its main centre in the Netherlands. Its beliefs were antinomian in tendency, and its principal claim to fame was the (alleged) Paradisal nudity practised at its secret meetings. Its interest for us is purely negative; in the fact that it was never confused with witchcraft. We know, as usual, nothing about it except what its enemies chose to say; what they say of its rites and tenets suggests that they could easily have represented its assemblies as Sabbats, but they do not do so. Given the precedent of the "Luciferians" and the fact that the conventional picture of the witch-Sabbat was now fully formed as it had not been in the thirteenth century, this is mildly surprising, and worth quoting as a very slight and indirect tribute to the objectivity of ecclesiastical judges in the later period, and thus a kind of corroboration of what they believed about witchcraft. At least they were not seeing a witch in every woodpile in the fifteenth century; after the Renaissance and Reformation, the same could hardly be said.[22]

I hope that in the course of the remaining chapters some remaining improbabilities in the line of development I have suggested for the cult may come to appear less improbable; may appear to be, not only within the bounds of possibility, but of the order of the things that happen in History. The most serious improbability for most people, I should imagine, is the concept of the self-appointed, educated witch-master, exercising a strong influence in and on the cult though coming to it from outside. All I can say in defence of such an idea is that, unless it could occur, the accounts we have of witch-beliefs and witch-practices make no sense at all. We have to try to explain a state of affairs in which syncretism could run wild; we are faced, in some of the most recent evidence, with more than spontaneous borrowings or unconscious imitation of other religions will account for. Wherever we find the Black Mass (and it would seem that at times we do find it) we may assume that a spoilt priest or at least an educated man has been absorbed into the cult; and there are other indications of education, or at least sciolism, of a quite unecclesiastical kind, in some recent and literary material which I am saving for the last, where it belongs in time.[23] Of course, the Murrayites would urge that witch-masters generally *were* educated; but they can hardly have got their literary training inside the coven. It seems to me most reasonable to suppose that on occasion a witch-group would accept as a leader, priest or shaman a man of like-minded pursuits who was as ignorant as we are of the real original nature of the cult but who had his own ideas of what a witch-cult *ought* to be. We should bear in mind the extreme difficulty that must have attended the preservation of an Apostolic Succession among witch-masters at a time—such as most times—when the educated in the main were either hostile or contemptuous. The witches, we may suppose, expected their priests to be more learned than themselves; even if we allow the cult from an early date to have included both sexes, it would be difficult for them to be self-supporting in the matter of candidates to the ministry. Consider also that the old rites would be kept up in most places by ignorant and gullible people, who firmly believed in their own incantations and were inclined to be superstitious generally. A quack could

[22]For a very highly coloured account of the Brethren of the Free Spirit, poorly documented (as is inevitable) but in its own way revealing, see Fränger, W., *Millennium of Hieronymus Bosch.*
[23]See cap. 10.

impose himself on such people with fair ease, and perhaps learn from them all he needed to impress the slightly more sophisticated witches he might find elsewhere with his credentials. Those who dabble in magic, at any level, are apt to deceive themselves, and commonly hanker after some higher authority, some deeper mystery than their own. They are not the best judges of a charlatan's claims, nor of Comparative Religion.

The witches, contrary to their own belief, were not exempt from any natural law, and their society was not exempt from the ordinary human expectation of development and change. An oral tradition is particularly subject to corruption and re-interpretation. Any hypothesis about the history of witchcraft which assumes the minimum of development from prehistoric to modern times is worthless. To be worthy of consideration at all, it must show certain developments to have been possible; to hold the field, it must show them to have been also probable. But here we must leave the present line of conjecture, for there yet remain views of our subject whose mere possibility has still to be examined.

CHAPTER NINE

The Powers of Darkness

FOR SOME CHAPTERS past we have concentrated wholly on an attempt to extract some sense from the historical and anthropological possibilities, on the assumption that these alone needed to be considered. But there remains the outright Anti-Sadducee view, the view that witches really adored a real Satan, and enjoyed, perhaps still enjoy, supernatural privileges as his devotees. There also, of course, remains the "Freudian" type of explanation, the view that the whole thing was a romp of degenerates. That the cult did itself degenerate, and into something of this kind, is I think tenable but not very likely; at least it involves, to my mind, a seriously misplaced emphasis. It seems clear that most of those who confessed to Inquisitors (except Gilles de Rais) could not be described as voluptuaries on the spree; they were either genuinely deluded or falsely accused, unless of course there was something in it, and they were genuinely persuaded of the truth. If they were, if the Devil really did give them his invaluable assistance in a career of wrong-doing, then of course their behaviour was very reprehensible but quite cold-bloodedly rational, and the Doctors of the Church can throw a more useful light on the Sabbat than the doctors of Vienna.

Most people today, of course, are not very ready to regard demonology as a science, or to consider as a serious question at all the abstract possibility of what the Anti-Sadducees assert. But there is a minority of the theologically convinced, and a majority, in our own as in most ages, avid for marvels. If all the argument on the point is left to the believers, and the sceptics' case allowed to go by default, we shall be doing less than our duty by an important part of the subject. Any man is free to pooh-pooh what he has never considered possible; but let him not call himself "scientific" when he does so. Bacon and

Newton turn in their graves when people say "science has disproved" miracle or magic.[1]

I am no theologian (come to that, I am no scientist), but I shall make what shift I can to examine this question from the point of view that alone can be called relevant. Assuming, as many people do, the truths of Christianity, could the Devil do what is reported of him in this matter of witchcraft, and if he could, would he?

I am not here concerned with the history of Christian thought, but with its cogency. For the authority of the Past, I must refer the reader to Authority.[2] For the Anti-Sadducee argument, I again refer him to the *Malleus Maleficarum* as the standard text on which such as Summers have drawn. As I understand it, the argument in its simplest form runs: if you believe that the Power of Good can perform miracles, why should you not believe the same of the Power of Evil? In a more sophisticated guise it would read: Lucifer, and the angels that fell with him, retained their angelic nature and therefore a degree of command over the temporal world proper to spiritual beings and supernatural from Man's point of view. Power, by the Divine Permission, was left to Lucifer to trouble fallen Man; God's providence in this is beyond our understanding but not unjust. The Devil, in fact, is the instrument of divine justice, whether he would or no; for God, so to speak, exploits his malice and his angelic power over nature, to test Man on earth, and after death to punish those who have forfeited God's grace. The Devil, therefore, has supernatural powers, under the Permission, and uses them most readily to bind men to his service; to which end he can and will bribe them with his thaumaturgies to sell him their souls; and all witches, warlocks, necromancers, and so forth, who can really perform what they claim, are bound to him by some such covenant. Conversely, those who have made that nefarious compact can perform what they claim; or rather, not they, but the Devil on their behalf.

A number of objections to this opinion have been aired in the past, some of which are considered in the *Malleus*; but I think few modern

[1]Science, being wholly concerned with what is by definition *not* supernatural, has nothing at all to say on the possibility of the supernatural.
   The point is forcefully argued in Lewis, *Miracles*, cap. 7; the reader will be aware that I differ considerably from several opinions of this author.

[2]The best recent Roman Catholic statements on the Devil are to be found in the volume of Carmelite studies called *Satan* (apparently no editor; 1951). I know of nothing comparable for other denominations, but in the context this is not necessary.
   The *Contra Haereticos* of Alain de Lille, already referred to, is largely concerned with this question and deserves a mention as having priority of time over most Catholic treatments of it (twelfth century).

Anti-Sadducees have been readier than those of the Bluff way of thinking to consider the question still open, wide enough for objections on the other side to be visible. It is therefore still appropriate to make some rather elementary points. I shall, however, make the most fundamental first.

There is a Kingdom of Heaven; there is, at most, a Republic of Hell. That is to say, the Christian system of belief, admitting the possibility of fallen angels, does not admit the possibility of a Power of Darkness who represents Evil as God represents Good, who rules in Hell by the same indisputable right that God rules in Heaven. Nor, of course, would any leader among fallen angels wield supernatural powers, or even exist, but by God's permission. Christianity rejects dualism. But actually (though this I think is as far as dogmatic formularies would go) we can go further. There is no room, in Christianity, for personified abstractions. The Christian faith is beyond all others in its emphasis on the concrete; its defenders would claim that it is higher than the "higher" religions, but certainly in a sense it is more pagan than the pagan. A God who is a fully human man, born at a definite place and time; a "dying god" who died, not annually in the form of corn, but literally, on a specific day of an approximately known year, in a specific place and for complex political reasons; who afterwards rose from the grave, not in any spiritual sense but bodily, and by so rising brought to mankind the hope of just such physical resurrection—such a God cannot stand opposed to, does not belong in the same order of ideas with, an allegorical figure out of a cartoon, a draped and man-shaped adjective. In the sense in which one would repeat the Nicene Creed, I Do Not Believe in the Devil. The Devil occurs in the Bible, in a very insignificant role, primarily as a figure of speech. Those to whom the Gospel was first preached, especially those Jews of the Diaspora with whom Paul was chiefly concerned, were familiar with the idea of a Spirit of Evil, ultimately from Persian sources; it was not really part of their own tradition (the Satan of the Old Testament is a very shadowy figure) but it was then fashionable as a philosophic concept. The early Church had a great deal of trouble to rid itself of the gnostic aberrations that took their rise in that fashion. Thereafter the exact character or status of the Devil was a vexed question for many centuries; but it was always a marginal one. It does not affect the essential beliefs of Christians whether there are any devils or not, just as it does not affect their essential beliefs whether the soul can survive without the body. Popular Christianity has become so infected with simplifications that many people imagine these questions are indeed crucial; but that is not our present concern.

The view that God created, besides Man, a higher order of rational beings to form, so to speak, the army of Heaven, and that some of these revolted and became "devils," has very slight and uncertain Biblical foundations but has gradually gained general recognition. It is, however, rather unlikely; for if other rational beings besides ourselves threw off their obedience to God, surely Christ would have died for them also, and God would not treat them as enemies, seeing by His Grace He is ready to pardon us? Still, let us allow this opinion. What reason, beyond very vague and metaphorical expressions of Scripture, have we to suppose that the rebels are an organized army with a leader? There is nothing in the nature of the case to demand it; and some speculators, wishing to show mercy to the fairies, have allowed that angels might have taken part in the mutiny who took no subsequent part in Infernal politics and occupy a neutral position, in secret, here on Earth. Most references in the Scriptures that are construed nowadays as referring to Satan have not always been so interpreted and probably ought not to be so (the serpent in the Garden of Eden, the beasts of Revelation, the tempter of Job, were probably not princes of Hell in the minds of those who wrote of them). The belief in an arch-fiend is really very thinly grounded.[3]

There are other difficulties about Hell and Devils generally, before we come on to Black Masses and Covenants and so forth. There is, primarily, the whole question of Evil, and Sin as the extreme evil. The Devil tempts Man to sin; who then tempts the Devil? If he fell without any external prompting, could not we have done so? The Devil, so far as I can see, serves no useful function; even as a hypothesis, he is glib and incomplete. And I entirely fail to see how God can be fancied as employing His worst rebel as a gaoler. The Devil punishes Man for his sins; who punishes the Devil? If he punishes himself, in wilful isolation from Grace and self-consuming pride, is not every sinner thus his own tormentor? In any case, if God is just, Hell is not a place of punishment; for punishment of souls for sin must be just also, and imposed by the just, not by the unjust; the devils must needs be untrustworthy ministers of a good purpose. If

[3]Bamberger, B. J., *Fallen Angels*, traces the rise of the idea of a Prince of Evil in Jewish tradition and exhibits some errors of interpretation on which it was based. Note, however, that he is mainly concerned, not with the existence of Satan but with the myth of his expulsion from Heaven.

without their will they are constrained to torment those among men
with whom they have most sympathy, and it must indeed be galling
for them, then I suppose that punishes them; but in that case the
devils are not the real executioners; there are taskmasters above them
whom they dare not disobey. But then, what becomes of their
rebellion? And could not these gaoler-angels just as well force lost
souls to take turns stoking the fire? I see no need for devils in a place
of punishment, except as prisoners. But is there, can there be a place
of eternal torment in God's scheme? Surely not; for finite sin cannot
entail infinite torment by any decree of a just god; and original sin,
which is infinite, is sin only in potentiality, not incurring actual pains
but simply standing between Man and the Beatific Vision. This much
is agreed by the theologians, who no longer think credible an eternity
of fire and brimstone for the merely unbaptized. In any case, to call the
justice of God "inscrutable" is not to say that it may, perhaps, be
unjust while remaining just; Hell, as a place of punishment, is merely
nonsense.

Hell may exist, in the sense "absolute exile from Heaven," but such
exile can surely not also involve some measured pain externally
imposed. Purgatory may exist; souls, ultimately saved, may require
purgation, in a sense punishment for sin, but punishment with an
end to it. In justice, all punishment must have a term and a purpose;
and in Christian ethics the punishment of souls must end in the bliss
of Heaven, for if the end were only the cessation of pain, that pain can
have had no purpose but to satisfy God's revenge, and we believe that
He does not revenge Himself. (And otherwise, the death of His son
would be not satisfaction but a new offence.) I am sorry to have to
allow Purgatory, for in common with most of my church I am on the
whole a Protestant and for the rest would rather side with the Greeks
than with the Latins; but I see no help for it. Hell, I suppose, is the
refuge of those not able to face the sight of God and the pains of
purgation; it must be, precisely, a place of no punishment, nor much
of anything else except bad company.

I see no reason, then, why God should be supposed to have given
some spokesman of the fallen angels some kind of warrant to trouble
Man, or left him any shreds of miraculous power. Strict miracle,
indeed, he cannot be supposed to perform, unless he has some divine
purpose to fulfil; there seems no such purpose that he would be fitted
for, and are devils in any case fit to be trusted to carry out any kind of
policy? The will of God is inscrutable; but the thousand wills of the
devils are merely incoherent. Good is consistent within itself; no abso-

lute good is incompatible with another absolute good. Conflict only
arises between relative goods, that is, precisely where there is also an
admixture of evil. Evil, on the other hand, is never at unity in itself;
one evil always fights another, as how should it not, for is not dis-
unity itself an evil?

Indeed, for this reason, there can be no absolute evil at all; or
certainly no consistent will to absolute evil. Evil, simply as such,
cannot be pursued as an end; if Satan wishes to encourage some particular sin, he will have to make a truce with some particular virtue.
Satan himself cannot be absolutely evil, and remain effective. To
suppose him formidable is to suppose him strong, intelligent, determined; and that is better than to be weak, foolish, and inconstant.
What is better is relatively good; without the assistance of relative
good, Satan would be powerless. Indeed, he could not exist, since all
things that exist are God's creation and created good, and mere existence, since it proceeds from God's will, is better than non-existence.

That which is good in itself does not cease to be good in itself
because it is used for evil purposes; beauty is still beauty, though a
snare; skill remains skill though the handmaid of crime; knowledge
is still knowledge though twisted to support a lie, and they remain,
in themselves, better than ugliness, ineptitude or ignorance. Even
moral goodness so perverted remains intrinsically good. Courage is
still admirable though a burglar needs to possess it, and the patience
required to pick a lock is a virtue though in the man who so misuses
it it is found in conjunction with avarice, which is a sin. The commendable qualities of Satan, if any, are to be commended; and if
he has none, he is not to be feared.

A quite random study of the imaginative literature on moral
themes will make this clear. It is a familiar problem that the bad
characters in books are more convincing than the good, but it is a
much worse problem to draw the portrait of a convincing and really
horrible devil. In fact, it cannot be done. Consider how Milton was
thwarted in *Paradise Lost*; to make Satan a possible character on the
epic scale, he had to make him heroic; show him wholly evil, and he
would be merely laughable, a squalor self-fettered in slime, and there
would be no Adversary and no plot. Critics have been known to assert,
on this ground, that Milton really sympathized with his Satan. But
how otherwise could he possibly have been represented, in a work of
serious moral purpose? The Middle Ages, by and large, had preferred
to let their Devil exemplify a wide range of vices, and in consequence
he became for them a mere grotesque. A sickly misshapen goblin out

of Hieronymus Bosch, vicious but impotent, or a grand operatic Prometheus; these are, more or less, the alternatives.

Every real person combines virtues and vices; thus far, we are all more devil than angel. Therefore villains are commonly made complex and interesting, like real people. Perfect characters are not interesting, because there is no conflict in them; we know what they will do, and what will happen to them. That is what Fiction means. But outside fiction the best people we meet—not necessarily the church-going, but the generous, the courageous, the determinedly honest—make more impact than the ruck of *hommes moyen sensuels*, the moral plebs to which most of us belong. Villains, in real life, hardly matter; they are, by and large, people about as morally slack as ourselves in different circumstances.

If we can once get beyond the Sunday-newspaper idea of Sin and consider the subject as a whole, recognizing that one sin, Sloth, is a condition of most other sin, and one virtue, Fortitude, a condition of most other virtue, we can accept virtue as strength and vice as weakness; which is what the words mean. Good is positive; evil is a declension from good, not something added to what was originally neutral. Evil is the absence or deprivation of Good, and as real as any other absence; as real and as unpleasant as a hollow tooth or a hungry belly. But it has no force of its own; it is a category set up at the Creation, of non-entity in opposition to created nature, which last as God's handiwork and as possessing real existence is good, and to which evil—always relative evil—occurs as decay and is experienced as disharmony.

Well, but even so, could not a fallen angel, a specially powerful and sinful though, perhaps, not universally depraved Spiritual Wicked-ness in High Places, be so ambitious to be a god that he would inter-vene in Man's affairs malignly and sell favours to the unjust? He might; but how should he come by favours to bestow? Angels do not work miracles, unless as the agents of God; Satan can work no miracle. It is a respectable opinion among the pious that, nevertheless, angels by their own nature have powers we do not enjoy, and these the devils retain. Another, less popular opinion that has also been held is that the devils, at least, learnt as angels and still remember facts as yet unknown to Science though within its sphere; their larger understanding, for example, enables them to predict the future, but rationally, not supernaturally. These suggestions, however, are very little help to the Anti-Sadducee; for what is not miraculous cannot run counter to a rule of nature, and one such rule is not hostile to another.

The Devil can in no circumstances manipulate the matter of our space-time continuum except as the properties of bodies in our space-time continuum permit, whatever his own nature originally was or however much he may know. If he takes physical shape on our planet, he is himself fully bound by all the consequences of a material frame as we ourselves suffer them; and without some physical vehicle for his will he can work no physical act, can impart no locomotion to rain-cloud or broomstick or bacteria. Indeed, without either godhead or organs of sense, presumably he would lack mere cognition. I do not say he has to occupy a human body, but he has to have a body, and be subject to natural laws. Of course, Heaven and Hell may have natural laws quite unlike our own; but if he trespasses into our world of nature, the laws we know will apply also to him.

Perhaps that is why he seeks to ally himself with witches; perhaps he uses them as media, and can only work evil through their agency. Perhaps; but it does not seem very likely. It does not appear that Satan ever, in fact, achieved anything by his association with witches that he could not have secured by merely tempting them in the ordinary way. It would be reasonable enough to suppose that he and they are less powerful for evil separately than they are together; witches, being human, can perform acts he cannot, but he possesses the knowledge that will make their malignancy really effective. But History hardly allows us to believe that a fiend of superhuman subtlety and virtually unlimited knowledge and insight has ever actually been in control of even one malignant; had he been so, surely nothing but miracle could have prevented him from conquering the Earth and establishing diabolism as a state religion. Can we seriously attempt to see any historical events in this light? The harm done by witches has not been shown to be of such a kind or extent as to make it easy to believe that they had the benefit of superhumanly good advice; and as to other men's crimes, we dare not flatter ourselves they have ever been more than fallen Man by himself is capable of.

But Lucifer entices witches with offers of thaumaturgic power to tempt them to their moral ruin; he buys their souls, and this, not the harm they may do, is his primary motive. How does he buy souls? What man can sell his soul, which belongs only to God by its creation as well as by Christ's redemption? And is the serpent so simple that he pays in good coin when he must know the bargain is void? The man who desires to sell his soul has renounced Christ and put himself in Satan's toils before the sale is ever transacted; and afterwards, as he has not the disposing of his own soul, it is still in God's Mercy as

it ever was, and if he repents he may be forgiven. That is still in
God's power to grant and nobody else's. So Satan allows himself to be
cheated; and we are asked to believe that he is more cunning than
ourselves! If he had any subtlety, he would make large promises,
exact a price, and refuse to deliver the goods; then the victim would
certainly repent, but his repentance would be of no moral value.
To give Faust what he asks for is to run the risk that Faust may
repent indeed, and become a saint. It is always dangerous for the
Devil to convince anyone that he thoroughly deserves damnation; his
best policy is to persuade him the other way.

Actually, it would seem that the whole idea of the covenant with
the Devil originated outside witchcraft, in *magia* or pseudo-philosophic
occultism of the study and library. It seems to be a perversion of the
old idea of *coercing* the gods, which is a natural hope for magicians
to delude themselves with in times when reverence is on the decrease.
In Christian times, of course, it is the Devil that one seeks to bind to
one's service by ceremonies and words of power; for to coerce Christ
would hardly seem respectable to a magician who liked to think of
himself as "white." How "white" this dream was, morally, and the
means whereby it developed into the idea of a bargain, have been well
traced by Dr. E. M. Butler in her *Ritual Magic* and *The Myth of the
Magus*, and both because these books exist and because it is not
directly germane to my subject, I shall follow that topic no further.

A closely parallel phenomenon to the Faustian compact is the Black
Mass, again a preserve of the armchair kabbalist rather than of the
witch; and as such it has lasted down to recent times, if not indeed
to the present. The Black Mass does seem to have played a part in
witchcraft, at least latterly; come to that, so does the compact,[4] but in
all probability both were innovations by educated witch-masters in the
Renaissance period, when the Faust legend arose and became
extremely popular. I have already indicated some of the problems
that beset any study of the Black Mass on account of the vagueness
of the term; it has a history of its own, which is the history of a legend
rather than of a rite, but I doubt whether it will ever be, ever can
be, properly written. Mr. H. T. F. Rhodes has attempted it,[5] and his
account can be relied on for that latter part (from the late seventeenth
century) which derives mainly from police records or recent biographi-
cal material. For the much more interesting period in which the idea
grew up, Mr. Rhodes relied unduly on the picturesque imagination
of Jules Michelet, that well-known prose stylist of the Romantic

[4]*Witch-Cult*, p. 79 ff.   [5]*The Satanic Mass*, see Bibliography.

period, who intermittently held academic appointments under Liberal governments but whose contributions to our subject must be reckoned the work of an anti-clerical rhetorician rather than of a historian. Mr. Rhodes himself is a criminologist, and can throw useful light on pseudo-occultism considered as crime; but he does not dispose of the question which alone concerns us, whether in fact there is any other light in which to consider it.

An affirmative answer to this question has been too often assumed, by such as Peladan, Huysmans, and Waite in the nineteenth century and Crowley in our own times; they take it for granted that there is a true tradition of the Black Mass somewhere to be found, and all that is needed is to find it. But it is quite possible that this has been in the minds of *all* the mystagogues, *all* the framers of diabolic liturgies, *all* the self-taught magi. Hearing of the Black Mass through the invectives of Inquisitors, they fell a prey to the inherent confusions of the idea. Believing it to be a rite of deep satanic significance, and believing it to be an invocation of the Power of Evil, they set themselves to work out what it *must* be like, to reconstruct what they could not discover and professionally desired to know. It is most unlikely that there has ever been one tradition, one canon of the Black Mass; rather, a number of charlatans groping completely in the dark have ventured to celebrate a version that seemed to them to have the authentic ring. Very few have been found to assert positively what it was all about, what exactly it was thought to be for; I have tried to indicate that there is no easy or obvious answer to that question. Yet the idea, however ill-understood, has long exercised a strong fascination; it carries with it an aura of recherché vice to people who have no formed picture at all of the meaning of this hypothetical ceremony. (This is an assertion that the reader might care to try out on his acquaintances.) If the layman and the scoffer are intrigued, how desperately the would-be magician must long to learn more! There seems little doubt that in modern times some have attempted to fabricate a canon synthetically; a good deal of one, if my memory serves me, is quoted by Michael Burt,[6] the quotation being probably from Aleister Crowley, who based his reconstruction on the assumption that the original Black Mass was essentially an act of conscious worship of the Evil Principle and gnostic in inspiration. There seems no reason to suppose that there ever was any genuine original to imitate; no reason to doubt that the Black Mass, originally, was no

[6] *The Case of the Angels' Trumpets.* The works of Crowley are (justifiably) not easy to consult, and I cannot swear to this.

more than one of the jostling metaphysical misconceptions in the less balanced of literate minds, and if it has acquired a sort of reality in addition, this it remains. Probably it *has* acquired a sort of reality; that is to say, if there is no genuine model to imitate, a rite of Crowley's devising is as genuine as any, not to count the special case of the Black Mass developed by mere mountebanks to impress their customers, and framed solely on the lines of what the customer was believed to expect. The busy trade in deliberately horrific mumbo-jumbo in the Paris underworld of the age of Louis XIV is a case in point, and one where we cannot doubt the truth of the occurrence in view of the police investigations that proved so embarrassing to everybody when Mme de Montespan was found to be implicated. From their different points of view both Mr. Rhodes and Mr. Charles Williams[7] have dealt faithfully with this scandal, which is nearly unique as a *cause célèbre*. I cannot think that this whole question is of more than marginal interest to the problem of witchcraft, unless you classify all charlatanry as such; and it is still less relevant to the reality or otherwise of the things witches believed in.

There is very little doubt that some have tried to enlist the Devil's aid in their affairs, and have been prepared to pay the price traditionally exacted. I must say I fail to see how anyone could think it credible that Satan, though possessed of almost unlimited powers and only for that cause a desirable ally, and though presumed anxious to strike such bargains, should require to be summoned by an elaborate ceremonial known only to the few; which is a prominent feature of the popular tradition. Surely one should only have to state such a desire to bring Mephistopheles on the scene at a run, blank contract-form in hand? But Faust still draws his circles and burns his candles, because the whole original point of the legend was the fatal conjuration of the Devil by a proud philosopher who dreamed of making a servant of him. Compact, by which the Devil earns a *quid pro quo*, is a development upon this idea, and the two themes shade into one another.[8] So the apparatus of laboratory hell-raising, the pentacles and assafoetida and Holy Water and what not, remain in the backs of the minds of the literate public, to make periodical emergences in novels or on the stage, although there is never any clear reason given what they are supposed to be for. The man who wants to dabble in necromancy will no more question the necessity for the jumble of accretions

---

[7]Whose treatment of the Black Mass, in his *Witchcraft*, is to be commended as a balanced statement of a specifically Christian point of view and not unduly credulous.
[8]Butler, *The Myth of the Magus*.

in which the word "magic" is entangled than an unmechanical driver will criticize the inwards of a car. For magical purposes, you draw pentacles on the floor. It is well known.

Now, it is most likely that no genuine learned tradition of *magia* exists, because it is most likely that *magia* is nonsense. Therefore, everybody is really in the dark about it, everybody is outside; but there are those who believe there is an inside, and are anxious to get there. So, hopefully, they mix together anything they can find that carries magical associations and make what sense of it they can; they draw pentacles on the floor, they light candles and hope it will not matter that they were not moulded from the fat of unborn babies, they choose a Friday or a night of New Moon or some other occasion to which a superstition of some kind—any kind—attaches, they sacrifice black cocks and white hens, they burn assafoetida, they invoke the obscurest gods they can think of and draw the signs of the zodiac wherever it occurs to them to draw them. The ritual evolved in the private mind of the aspiring magus will be, in essence, not a scholarly attempt to come at the real point of "magic," disencumbering it of mental associations, but the precise opposite: it will be the cluster of associations itself, delicately lifted into the half-light with all its cobwebs still on it, in which, perhaps, the true original heart of magic lies concealed. In case there should, in fact, be nothing there, the sorcerer will never dare prod and examine the dusty conglomeration; rather he will go out to search for new shreds of anthropological bafflement to wrap his treasure more securely against the light of day. His instinct will be to cling to any and every superstition in case there might be some great potency in this one or that, or at least in the other. Because he does not, really, know what he is about, he will not run the risk of omitting what *might* be an important element. This is the impression given by the surprisingly large number of books that have been produced, that claim to give the low-down on ceremonial magic; all, of course, invite the same kind of objection as the books that instruct one how to make a million dollars.[9]

In the century or so that preceded the rise of experimental science, that is, in a period just about contemporaneous with the fiercest witch-hunts, there was a great interest in the pseudo-philosophical short cuts to universal understanding, in all those learned pursuits that explored the boundary of the physical and the metaphysical—in astrology,

[9]See Bibliography, s.v. Barrat, Levi, Ahmed. A useful parallel is supplied by the enormous wealth of alchemical texts dating from this period; on which see (*cum grano salis*) C. G. Jung, *Psychology and Alchemy.*

alchemy, kabbalism, and every kind of "-mancy." We should not laugh at these vain enquirers, whose curiosity was a manifestation of the same temper in the times that was to make laboratory experiments a usual hobby for gentlemen a little later; the alchemists were paving the way for the first inductive scientists and were often the same people. But there was a lot of hocus-pocus attempted as well, and the spirit of universal curiosity made many mountebanks, and some rich mountebanks. The magic that had some pretensions to be scholarly, philosophic, "white," was very popular at that time, perhaps especially in the Protestant world that was not committed by the authority of the Church to supposing all magic necessarily diabolical. Faust's university was also Luther's. Side by side with propaganda against witches, the age was prolific of rumours, by no means always hostile, of wizards; Paracelsus was chemist, alchemist, theologian, and Platonic mystic, and Bacon was a near-contemporary of Dr. Dee.

Now, the people who would naturally take the keenest interest in reports of great success by any necromancer or astrologer would be the witch-masters. Witches themselves, one imagines, are generally conservative; but no institution has the power to survive unless it can contain both a conservative element and an inlet for change and adaptation. I have already suggested that it was part of the witch-master's function to make suitable innovations as they might be required; his historical function, that is to say, for it is not likely it was ever consciously regarded as a duty of his office. It is highly likely, therefore, that in the Renaissance period the older magics were infected with new doctrines conceived in the astrologer's study. It would be reasonable to suppose that this was so especially in Britain, for the sixteenth century is the first to produce any clear indication that the organized Dianus-cult had reached these islands. It seems the easiest explanation that the organization was introduced from the continent at this late stage, to impose itself, as I suggest it did across the channel in the thirteenth century, on a number of local and family groups of quite unorganized and not particularly pagan rural wise-women. If Esbatarianism, so to call it, was new in the reign of the first Elizabeth —and any other supposition would be very hard to square with the evidence, negative as it admittedly is—then we should expect to find it much more influenced by quasi-scholarly ideas of satanism than elsewhere. We should expect to find the compact and the Black Mass more prominent than on the continent.

What we do, in fact, find, in England at least, is more emphasis than elsewhere on witch-mark and familiar. I imagine this is chiefly due to the difference in judicial procedure, which necessitated proofs secured without the use of rack and strappado. In Scotland, where these devices were available, the seventeenth century was to produce perhaps the most classically complete body of witch-confessions in Europe; the organization by covens of thirteen, the renunciation of baptism, the internal structure and discipline of the coven, the homage paid to the "god" and the general course of the Sabbat emerge more prominently and more uniformly in the Scots accounts than for any other whole national territory, although most of the details had previously been reported on French soil.

This, of course, suggests two possible explanations: that either Scots witch-masters, or Scots judges, were drawing their inspiration from France. Since France at this date was the ordinary source of Scots fashions one can say this quite confidently of the judges, and it is probable of the witch-masters also if they were at all commonly educated men. Since the first Scots *cause célèbre*, the North Berwick case of 1590, yielded strong indications of complicity by the Earl of Bothwell, it is reasonable to suppose that the ultimate leadership of the cult in Scotland in the immediately post-Reformation period was aristocratic and well-informed, and indeed largely political in purpose; quite capable, then, of being influenced by French ideas and even of reading the whole thing in a book.

Persecution of witches, in both Scotland and England, was a new movement in this age, and the panic seems to have been worked up by Puritans in close contact with continental ideas, especially Swiss, as a result of their exile in the last days of Catholicism. So close is the connection between witch-hunting and Reformation in the British Isles that it comes as something of a shock to read, in Scots dittays of the Civil War period, that witches were charged by virtue of the act of "our late dread lady, Queen Mary." (It also has an odd sound to find witchcraft described as "abominable superstition" in these same documents.[10]) Both Elizabeth and Mary, Queen of Scots were forced into legislation by Protestant Parliaments; neither act produced any clear evidence of the kind of thing the reformers were looking for during their reigns. Prosecutions for ordinary village sorcery touched a new high, but the organized devil-cult was not heard of till the North Berwick case under James VI, and in England the first scandal capable of catching the popular imagination was that of the Lancashire witches in 1613. In fact, the discovery of any evidence of this depravity was preceded, in both countries, by a long period of Puritan agitation

[10]Ewen, *Witch Hunting and Witch Trials*, appendix 5.

against it. This of course casts a good deal of doubt on the later cases; judges and kirk sessions found what they expected to find, and by the time they found it witnesses had had time to learn what was expected of them. There can be no doubt whatever that a large quantity of the evidence was false, the fabrication either of personal spite or of the cupidity of witch-finders, who at the height of the panic (in the 1640's) depended on the trials for a livelihood, like professional ex-communists in America.

Indeed, the McCarthy panic in that country makes the whole period somewhat easier to understand. We have seen how, given a wide-spread fear of a necessarily secretive crime, self-appointed investigators quite incapable of proving an accusation by the ordinary forms of law can gain acceptance as saviours of their country; how the testimony of the confessedly culpable is preferred to that of men of repute provided it points to guilt; how presumption of innocence can be thrown over-board, and a man tainted in perpetuity by the fact of having been accused; how legal safeguards designed to make justice accurate can be openly condemned as a fetter to prosecutions; all this, not in the most backward but in one of the most civilized states of the day, not in the newest and most unsure democracy but in one of the oldest, and in a country specially noted for its traditional and stubborn devo-tion to the forms of law. When journalists describe this kind of thing as a "witch-hunt," they are for once not using wild or emotional language; the analogy holds very closely. We can, however, claim for the English of that day, as we cannot for the Americans of this, that the panic hit them with less force than their neighbours. There hardly was a time when those in authority did not attempt to exercise some check on the hysteria, nor any time at all when the English witch could be as easily brought to execution as she would have been in Germany, France or Scotland.

One should perhaps modify that statement to admit that King James I was actively concerned to put witchcraft down; and the years just after the personal union saw the high-water mark of official and academic Anti-Sadducism in the Southern kingdom. It was unfortu-nate, though not quite accidental, that the same period saw the pre-paration of the Authorized Version; a fact which has committed English-speaking Protestants to a larger measure of belief in witchcraft and in the Devil than was strictly necessary. Even James, however, propagandist as he was, began as a sceptic and ended as at least a moderate. The North Berwick case, which had been a quite serious attempt on his life in Bothwell's interest, convinced him that the menace was genuine and grave; as a good Calvinist, he was more or less bound to admit the theoretical possibility. The publication of the *Discoverie of Witchcraft* of the English sceptic Reginald Scot stung his inveterately controversial spirit to a reply;[11] and when he reached the English throne, about the only way he was ready to gratify his Puritan subjects was to permit the passage of the act of 1604, that for the first time in England made the fact of being a witch a capital offence.[12] Witches could now be hanged (not, of course, burnt) on proof of sorcery, still by ordinary jury trial; it is remarkable to note that even then witches were menaced with less savagery than Henry VIII had shown to poisoners or ordinary religious dissidents,[13] and with a less unequal trial than those accused under modern Criminal Law Amendment Acts. It is perhaps even more remarkable that the first result of the new severity seems to have been a reduction in the number of indictments.[14]

Even so, James and his advisers came to fear that the danger of false accusations under the act was nearly as great as the danger of witch-craft itself. It speaks volumes for having intellectuals in authority that James preserved as balanced a mind as he did in the face of fears so universal and so natural to one of his timorous disposition. In his later years he was active in reviewing the evidence that had gained convictions, and on occasion was successful in destroying it;[15] such re-examination became royal policy, and was continued under Charles. It came to an end with the Civil War, when the Puritan party in both kingdoms got control of a government, and this period marks the peak of capital indictments. Surprisingly enough, however, the rule of the New Model Army brought in at least a partial return to the old official scepticism.

This was by no means admitted by Mr. R. Trevor Davies in his study of the relation between witch-hysteria and Puritanism.[16] According to his theory, there was an exact correlation between Roundheads and witch-hunters, Cavaliers and sceptics; this can even be regarded as the main distinguishing feature of the two parties, and the imputa-

---

[11]James VI, *Daemonologie*, first ed., Edinburgh 1597.
[12]1 James I, cap. 12.
[13]Protestants were burned under Henry and poisoners boiled.
[14]Ewen, *Witch Hunting and Witch Trials*, p. 101.
[15]Trevor Davies, *Four Centuries*, cap. 4, *passim*, relying mainly on Fuller's *Church History of Britain*.
[16]*Ibid.*, cc. 7–9.

tion of favouring witches, "suffering a witch to live," commonly laid on those who denied the existence of sorcery, can be seen as a possible contributory cause of the war if not actually the main cause.

As a study of the growth of the hysteria in its early stages, and its relation to other religious currents of the day, Mr. Davies' work deserves commendation. On the political issue, the theory would seem more attractive if the author had not attempted to prove it; for the proof is as pretty a tissue of anachronistic misconceptions and schizophrenic special pleading as it has ever been my pleasure to read.[17] Whatever the views of the Parliamentary Puritans, however, there is no doubt that Cromwell's army when it displaced them looked with a more hostile eye on the witch-hunter. It matters comparatively little that Cromwell intervened to save one suspect, or that another was released when one of his colonels detected the trickery of a witch-finder.[18] But besides these isolated cases, it is clear that the military authorities imposed a régime, throughout the island, in which the game of witch-finding was not worth the candle. The witch-finder just mentioned was hanged on his confession to twenty false accusations at £1 a time. Cromwell's rule is an interruption in the series of Scots causes célèbres. The English authorities, on their arrival in Edinburgh in 1652 as conquerors, found several culprits awaiting execution; so little respect had they for Scots legal traditions that instead of continuing the vigorous investigations of the former government they investigated the investigators, learning with horror, in their Sassenach ignorance, how the culprits had been induced to testify, and quashing the previous proceedings.[19] The Protectorate period almost brought a stop to the panic; in Scotland, however, there was a last outbreak after Cromwell's death, when the kingdom recovered its separate legal system. It is, indeed, to this last recrudescence that we owe the magnificently detailed confession of Isobel Gowdie of Auldearne; and, much as one would regret casting any doubt on the authenticity of anything so useful, it must be borne in mind that its usefulness to Anti-Saddu-

[17]More than one judge who opposed the Crown on behalf of the Common Law is classed as a witch-hunter on the grounds that he passed the statutory sentence on a prisoner convicted before a jury, which he had no option but to do. Pym is a witch-hunter because he made a rhetorical reference to "witchcraft" in a speech and because he probably took an interest in a case that occurred not very far from his native town. The Parliamentary troops are variously described as fanatically insistent on the truth of witchcraft and shamefaced about openly admitting their belief in it. Any known Royalist who was also a known believer was secretly not a Royalist; and so on.

[18]Cf. p. 43, note 6.

[19]Spottiswoode Miscellany, II, p. 91; quoted in Lea, Materials, p. 1338.

cees in an age of increasing doubt may not have been pure coincidence.[20]

In general, the suspicion that the details of a confession were suggested to a victim by a zealous examiner is never to be excluded; and the value of the evidence that emerges can only be gauged by a sixth sense in the reader, if he claims to possess one. Even in the seventeenth century critics were to be found who spoke of suspects protesting themselves ready to confess whatever their tormentors required, but ignorant what this might be; and of suspects who preferred a quick execution to the consequences of living under suspicion.[21] There must also, in a society obsessed by such a fear, be many people of unbalanced mind capable of convincing themselves in all honesty that they had committed the most lurid crimes; like the witch in Weirss-Jensen's well-known play (which was based on an actual case in Bergen),[22] or like Major Weir of Edinburgh, who accused himself, quite without prompting, of incest with his sister as well as Satanism.[23] There is no reason to doubt that many innocent persons were convicted, some on their own free confession; where evidence was found for a coven, this was on occasion, beyond a doubt, "guilt by association." In the notorious scare at Salem, Massachusetts, in 1692, a whole coven was revealed, with a fair quantity of detail about its observances, parody of the sacraments (in this case a parody of Calvinism), and so forth; but none the less for that, the panic was recognized as groundless when it was too late to save the victims; the evidence was, at bottom, the invention of neurotic children, and the magistrates publicly confessed themselves to have been in error. Even after the retraction by judges and witnesses, the incorrigible Cotton Mather remained convinced that the evidence was true.[24] A similar degree of obduracy had been shown by the judges themselves in the great Swedish scare of the "Blokula," in many ways a closely comparable case; indeed, the two may be directly related, and the little New Englanders have fed their imagination on the alleged experiences of the little Swedes.[25] We have to remember that pamphlet accounts of horrors circulated widely, and were regarded as edifying in devil-conscious Puritan circles.

[20]Her confession was printed in Pitcairn, *Criminal Trials*, Edinburgh, 1833.

[21]As in the case referred to on p. 194, note 19.

[22]Best known to the English-speaking public through the terrifying Danish film version, *Vredens Dag (Day of Wrath)*.

[23]Scott, *Letters on Demonology and Witchcraft*, pp. 319–22.

[24]Mather's pamphlet was reprinted as *Wonders of the Invisible World*, London, 1862. See also Burr, *Narratives of Witchcraft Cases*; Kittredge, *Witchcraft in Old and New England* is the most authoritative modern account.

[25]See appendix A.

It is also worth remembering that these same pamphlets have been the principal reliance, for want of a better, of modern investigators. They supply nearly all the information that Miss Murray so diligently collected, except for the official records available for Scotland. These, moreover, consist largely not of depositions but of dittays to the panel; that is to say, the evidence as the procurator hopes to make it appear. Here there is no question but that the form of confession expected is being placed before the panel in express words, though of course it would be based upon the results of a previous examination.

I suppose there is no need to go into the techniques of manhandling by self-appointed detectives which could to some extent take the place, in England, of judicial torture. The English evidence for Dianic rituals (as distinct from ill-wishing and so forth) would be so worthless by itself, and is so worthless as evidence for coven and Sabbat in England, that the means whereby it was extorted is of no immediate importance. It only needs to be mentioned as a corrective to possible patriotic smugness. If the English system excluded official torture, that is to say that it offered temptation to unofficial torturers, and that the fate of the victim depended on the bias of the jury. But as a confession was procedurally valueless, and guilt had to be established by third parties, evidence of cult-practices was naturally not forthcoming and we must do without it.

There is still another way whereby the spread of persecution may have itself created the evidence it sought. After the invention of the printing press, and especially after the Reformation had given it the function of recruiting the world at large into theological controversy, it was possible for any who could read to learn, fairly easily, what witches were supposed to do. Especially after Puritan preachers had assumed the mission of persuading the general public how just, how necessary, and how Puritan it was to hunt witches, few who took an intelligent interest in the subject can have failed to learn that witches in this place or that worshipped the Devil in the form of a goat and were subject to his commands; that they were summoned by him or his representatives to regular secret meetings at which particular blasphemies were regularly performed. On certain nights of the year great companies flocked to do him honour; they danced naked about him after they had kissed his buttocks in token of their abject servitude; they were examined by him what evil they had done, and were beaten if they had not done enough; they were instructed what evil they should next do; they feasted, and had carnal intercourse, either indiscriminately with one another or the women with the presiding genius and the men with *succubi* (or perhaps with any woman with whom the president was not occupied). All this, and much more equally interesting, came to the earnest enquirer with the full authority of Reformation behind it, while those who were prepared to give credit to the words of a known sceptic might learn from Wier or Reginald Scot the names of devils and the formulae of flying ointments. Is it not conceivable that sometimes witches and warlocks who had never previously known of all this elaboration may have been quick to take the hint?

In no country is there any evidence seriously worth considering of Sabbats and Esbats and the like until they begin to attract the attention of the spiritual police. In Britain the cult seems to have been a recent arrival, so recent that clear indications of it were not forthcoming until the hunt had been on foot for several years, and the hunt itself was a new importation from Geneva. In Scotland, where it seems to have been unusually highly developed and coherent as soon as it came to be heard of, it seems likely that the ritual society only came into being under the influence of its persecutors. It seems clear that Bothwell *was* in control of a large and powerful organization of covens; it is at least an intriguing possibility that his organization came into being actually as a response to the persecution—that learned diabolists and their politician employers reformed the cult to strengthen it in a time of emergency, and perhaps even picked up a hint or two about internal discipline in a politico-religious society from Genevan sources. (The "Devil"'s control of his followers seems to have been more autocratic than anything contemplated in Calvin's *Institutio*, but must, for example, have relied on an internal system of mutual espionage and "brain-washing" not at all untypical of the presbyteries of that time.)

I imagine the ordinary village witch up to that time had been in some sort of contact, more or less informal, with others of her kind; and that they had been accustomed, on occasion, to gabble half-understood invocations to forgotten gods, impartially with scraps of forbidden Mass-responses and the like, as part of a spell. They probably had, as was only prudent, initiation rules and recognition signals; and in places perhaps a group with common ceremonies and an acknowledged leader might be found. In this case such a leader would probably be a woman, which would make for some confusion if and when a system of male leadership was superimposed. The male leadership, the would-be local or national Grand Covens, would I fancy succeed in winning over and organizing the wise-women because, as usual, these latter

were leaderless and on the look-out for stronger shamans; because in
the conditions of the Reformation they had urgent need of a society
to organize resistance to the threatened suppression (as the goliards in
their time had had); and because those who now claimed to instruct
them could claim also very distinguished support—by the Earl of
Bothwell, who might soon occupy the throne of Scotland itself, and
even by the Devil.

There is no reason to doubt that these latest witches regarded their
god as the Devil, *gaffe* though it may have been to name him by that
name. Who else did they suppose he was? They were sorcerers, worshippers only on the side, and all gods must have been pretty much
alike to them. Naturally, they would be ready to ally themselves with
a god perhaps not altogether unlike one that their dimmest traditions
had spoken of; but they would have had little option, for they can
only have known of the Christian god and the Christian adversary.
When the servants of the former were threatening them with fire
above the earth and fire under the earth, of course they would seek
to ally with the latter, calling him by whatever name seemed diplomatic but not questioning his real identity. There was for these hag-
wives no *chichi* titillation in conscious blasphemy; worship, and
equally blasphemy, were means to an end. Their primary end was
survival; after that, power—the power to terrify the neighbours which
is, I suppose, the livelihood and emotional mainstay of most witches,
or, for a few, power, the sweeter for being wholly secret, in the
kingdom's affairs.

In the state of religious upheaval and resentment that the Reformation brought in its train, especially in the state of *canalized* emotional
ferment on which the extremer Puritans rely, the leaders of the cult
may well have seen a splendid opportunity for enlisting hitherto
undreamt-of numbers of dissidents into their hidden fold. The older
sorceresses, who cannot altogether have welcomed this, had accepted
the discipline of a highly dangerous secret society and must accept
its implications; in any case, they could bask in the glory of a new
status, as elders of the coven. This would secure the first object of all
goetia, in giving a sense of personal importance to the unloved carline
past her prime.

The new twist, however, could only preserve its essential form and
purpose as long as the central body could exercise its control; and I
suggest that this soon ceased to be the case. I suggest that, once again,
this time because of the strength of the persecution, the Grand Coven
was broken—I should judge this occurred after the scandal of 1590

when Bothwell's plots to murder James were revealed—and the cult, having been transformed in one generation by the activities of a ring of shrewd and educated warlocks who managed to seize control in special circumstances, in the next generation was deprived of their guidance while remaining the thing they had made of it. All this, if it happened so, must have been largely incomprehensible to the ordinary witch; expansion and reorganization, collapse in the centre, purges by external authority around the periphery, would be too much for the tradition to survive. For a time, till Law and Kirk managed to crush it between their millstones, the organization itself, or fragments of it, would last on to be a scandal to the last generation of Covenanters and a laughing-stock to the first generation of Deists. The magical tradition, half-remembered, half-guessed at, would still be handed down from mother to daughter in a secrecy even the coven knew nothing of. Perhaps here and there, when the terror had died down, the last to remember the cult—those, that is, to whom it had seemed in their own youth a revelation of incredibly ancient wisdom, too young as they had been to remember its beginnings—might meet and try to recreate the mystery from memory. Perhaps their daughters and a few they were sure of were still inducted through the rational eighteenth century, through the progressive nineteenth; perhaps they still are today. Perhaps, once again, some chance quack or amateur anthropologist has happened on the circle, and mounted the witch-master's empty chair, so that the cult in one place or another has taken the stamp of his mind, becoming in all but its indestructible essence edited to fit the quirks of a modern eccentric. I have suggested that this has occurred at intervals in the past; I see no reason to suppose that it will not occur at intervals in the future. The witch-cult may even be wholly a phenomenon of the future, though I do not think so; as long as witch-minded people exist, the cult does not need actual continuity, but only a claim to continuity such as they are predisposed to believe.

CHAPTER TEN

A Tell-tale in Their Company

I HAD ALREADY come to the conclusions set out in these last few chapters and was proposing to myself to round off with some judicious remarks on mass psychology and a telling appendix or two, when it occurred to me to wonder: is it not very remarkable that no effort has been made in our day to re-create the "Dianic cult"? Miss Murray's theory that witchcraft is entitled to serious consideration as a religion, and had in fact been the real religion of Britain till very recently, was put before the world in 1921. At that time the view was already popular that it did not in the least matter whether a religious creed was true provided it was truly *national*, rooted in the soil of the fatherland; and that, if it was not so rooted—if it was a foreign importation— mere truth was of no avail. Once depart from the traditional cult of the national gods, and a healthy national life was impossible; the "nation" being of course conceived as an immortal thing that History happens to, not the ever-changing product of a continuous historical process. This attitude would doubtless strike us today as "Nazi," but in the early part of the century it carried no such baneful associations. It was quite explicitly the theme of D. H. Lawrence's *Plumed Serpent*, and this is highly significant in view of Lawrence's influence over his age and also because it is an extreme case: the gods of his revived idolatry had nothing in common with the old Aztec gods except their names, and their worship was essentially a vehicle for Lawrence's private opinions on the psychology of sex. The view was gaining ground in the period between the World Wars that religion is, precisely, a sub-department of the psychology of sex. (So, indeed, in the opinion of the best minds in that remote epoch, was everything else; but religion especially.) More recently, Mr. Robert Graves has arrived on the scene, who openly desiderates a return to the old idolatry as he conceives it to have been. I cannot confidently say whether Mr. Graves actually believes that his White Goddess, in the plain and literal sense, exists. But he unambiguously affirms that we ought to worship her, and on much the same grounds as Lawrence; because it is of the genius of our culture to do so, because it is of the genius of every culture to worship the first gods it made, and she is ours.

Our age has seen very large claims made for the inner spiritual know-how of the unbeliever. One gets the impression that it is rather bad form to expect the pagan philosopher or poet to be as explicit as he is pontifical. The accusation of failing in this respect, however inappropriately, is still a good stick to beat Established Churches with, because it is well known that any and every stick may be used for this purpose. How sorry we should be for Quetzalcoatl or the White Goddess, if by any chance they should ever become Established!

But this is beside the point; my point at the moment being that it would be reasonable to expect high-minded people, in the 1920's, who were sorry to see England going to the dogs for want of a god she could believe in but were driven by the whole trend of their reading to suppose that this must be the case, to set out to supply that need according to the best anthropological principles. And as high-minded people in all ages have a bland and total disregard for the real character and content of the religions in which they choose to interest them-selves, we should expect further to find that the witch-cult as they would reconstruct it would be scarcely recognizable as a witch-cult. It would happily combine the more aesthetically tolerable *motifs* of several former creeds and the least controversial ethical statements of all ages. Gods with Persian names and Greek bodies would prove, on examination, to have thoroughly Bloomsbury minds; when England had been converted, there would be vegetarian Sabbats in Russell Square and nudist processional dances between the Museum and the occult bookshops; something of that kind. There would be a canon of the Scriptures including all the novels of Joan Grant, and good Dianists after all their incarnations would colonize new-risen Atlantis.

I say all this seemed *a priori* likely, and I was mildly surprised that it had not occurred. The acute reader will have noticed that my surprise proceeded from a false, or at least a questionable, premise. How was I to know that it had *not* occurred?

A revived cult such as I visualize would have no particular need to be clandestine; but it might well preserve a measure of secrecy as a matter of tradition, seeing it would be dangerously short of traditions otherwise. I confess I did not perceive the cogency of this until the proof was in my hands, in the form of *Witchcraft Today*, by Mr. Gerald Gardner. My own opinions were formed, up to the point we have reached, before I was aware of more than Mr. Gardner's bare existence, and I will confess that on first sight of his work I was led to class him as a normal Murrayite by the circumstance that Miss Murray had supplied him with an introduction. I now realize that this was hasty; beyond accepting each other on their own valuation as anthropologists in the same field, they disagree almost totally, though with true chivalry they affect not to notice this and hail one another as authorities—an unusual and edifying spectacle. The witch-cult described by Mr. Gardner as still existing is not that imagined by Miss Murray. I would not myself see this as necessitating that one of them should be wrong, for they deal with different periods and it is my whole point that the cult, being rudderless and incoherent at all but the subconscious level, is perfectly capable of having changed its form and its theories, rapidly and completely, an indefinite number of times. This, however, would certainly not be accepted by either of the authors I have named; both are convinced of the coherence of "Dianism" and would ascribe to it myths and rituals of immense antiquity. Both also relate it to a new reading of general history with the most categorical firmness; and Mr. Gardner is always saying, "witches did . . .," "witches did not . . .," "witches were people of such-and-such a kind . . .," though how he comes by this certainty he gives us no means to guess.

He has the peculiar merit, however, of speaking of the subject from inside experience. He claims to have been initiated into a coven, and, rather surprisingly, he is prepared to talk about it. I hasten to say that beneath a superficial appearance of extreme naïveté which in fact is merely stylistic, Mr. Gardner does not lack shrewdness nor put blind faith in what other witches have told him. He claims that vows of secrecy prevent him from revealing the evidence that would really silence objections; but he goes to the trouble of considering a number of objections, apparently his own, and does not seem to regard the arguments as closed. I get the impression of a man ambitious to believe more than his mind will let him; which, whatever the religion involved, tends to make one tortuous in the smaller arguments and sometimes strangely blind to the more elementary.

But whatever the state of our author's mind, I have reason to be grateful to it for the light his arguments incidentally shed. In particular, I was glad to read "the full text of the Myth of the Goddess" (for his coven is modern enough to have a female deity and, apparently, liberal enough to let him quote part of the secret liturgy). Mr.

Gardner thinks it is probably Celtic, though influenced perhaps by myths of Istar and Siva. It runs, in its entirety, thus:

Now, G. [Mr. Gardner is not allowed to reveal the actual name] had never loved, but she would solve all mysteries, even the mystery of Death, and so she journeyed to the nether lands. The guardians of the portals challenged her. "Strip off thy garments, lay aside thy jewels, for nought may ye bring with you into this our land." So she laid down her garments and her jewels and was bound as are all who enter the realms of Death, the mighty one.

Such was her beauty that Death himself knelt and kissed her feet, saying: "Blessed be the feet that have brought thee in these ways. Abide with me, but let me place my cold hand on thy heart." And she replied: "I love thee not. Why doest thou cause all things that I love and take delight in to fade and die?" "Lady," replied Death, "'tis age and fate, against which I am helpless. Age causes all things to wither; but when men die at the end of time, I give them rest and peace and strength so that they may return. But you, you are lovely. Return not; abide with me." But she answered, " I love thee not." Then said Death: "As you receive not my hand on your heart, you must receive Death's scourge." "It is fate, better so," she said, and she knelt. Death scourged her, and she cried: "I know the pangs of love." and Death said: "Blessed be," and gave her the fivefold kiss, saying: "Thus only may you attain to joy and knowledge."

And he taught her all the mysteries, and they loved and were one; and he taught her all the magics. For there are three great events in the life of man—love, death, and resurrection in the new body—and magic controls them all. To fulfil love you must return again at the same time and place as the loved ones, and you must remember and love her or him again. But to be reborn you must die and be ready for a new body; to die you must be born; without love you may not be born, and this is all the magic.[1]

The last statement would seem to have gone some way to purging the word "magic" of all but its most poetic meaning, which is I am sure very moral. The passage might, of course, be exceedingly ancient; and the present writer might be the Queen of Sheba, but he is not. I do not rely on the mere bogusness of language, which might be the result of translation; though it is noteworthy that this Authorized Version was, obviously, produced by someone with literary ambitions. I rely on the thoroughly unmythlike character of this myth, and on the content itself. Note that the narrative is exceedingly slight; almost the whole passage is taken up with the moral of it all, which in real myths (including those in the Bible) is precisely what lies behind and must not be confused with the actual story. Note how the personifica-

[1]Gardner, *Witchcraft Today*, p. 41.

tion of Death is both explicit and essential to what there is of a story; this is a mark of sophistication, but it cannot be an accretion with the ages.

But much more important than this, the whole set of ideas reeks of twentieth-century literary fashion. What the "myth" boils down to, what the main characters are supposed to have *done*, is in a line of descent from D. H. Lawrence: the heroine achieves some thoroughly vague kind of spiritual insight, she Understands, as a result of sexual intercourse. The preliminary flagellation is inseparably linked with this process, though it is not clear how or why; and this, I will grant, is strongly reminiscent of Rémy de Gourmont's *Phantome-Duplicité*,[2] a product of the late nineteenth century. I would not like to exclude the possibility that the myth was originally composed by a French *décadent* about the eighties; it has something of the right flavour, and literary forgery was then all the rage.[3] And it would be just possible at that time for such a person to know of the Babylonian legend of the descent of Ishtar to Hades; for of course Mr. Gardner is right about Ishtar, and the resemblance between the two episodes is too close to be accidental.[4] The Germans had then recently cracked the problem of cuneiform; but the results attracted no attention among English non-specialists until the twenties, and the whole feel of the passage would place it then rather than earlier, all else being equal. Modern archaeology has one other gleam of light to throw: the Villa of the Mysteries at Pompeii, one of the most recent important finds on the site, contains in the celebrated murals what could be an illustration to the second paragraph. This was recognized by Gardner, who claims that the worship portrayed in these murals was closely related to his own; and if there was any reason to suppose that the initiates of Boscoreale worshipped Tammuz, the other half of our "myth" might be known to them. Therefore, if we are prepared to accept our local witch-cult as Levantine in origin, the thing looks like hanging together. But is it conceivable that a story so unintelligible to most ages, and as a story so slight, could have been preserved through two millennia at the least of (presumably) oral transmission, and remain recognizably faithful to its original?

I find it hard to accept this myth as very ancient or in the least Celtic, or as a myth; but I am inclined to agree with Mr. Gardner's

[2]In his collection, *Le Pèlerin du Silence*.

[3]Consider, for example, Pierre Louÿs's *Chansons de Bilitis*, or the pseudo-Gospel of the childhood of Jesus "discovered" by Catulle Mendes. Colette, in *Mes Apprentissages*, has a good deal to say on the subject.

[4]On Ishtar, see any encyclopaedia, or Budge, *Babylonian Life and History*, p. 138.

suggestion as to its origin. "Perhaps it was coined to explain ideas and rituals already conceived, and to explain why the wiser, older and more powerful god should give his power over magic to the goddess." Perhaps it was. When? Not in ancient Babylon; the wiser, older, and more powerful god who gave powers to Ishtar was her father, Anu, and Alat, whom she visited in the underworld, was another goddess. It is germane to remember who the "old god" was in the mind of the author of this text, namely Death; and who had formerly been regarded as the god of the witches, namely the Devil. There can be little doubt that organized witches in the seventeenth century worshipped a male deity if they worshipped any, and this god was identified by most people (and in my opinion also by themselves) as the Church's Satan, who was also conceived as the Lord of the Underworld. So it seems likely that the end of active persecution supplies a *terminus a quo* for the change to a female deity. A *terminus a quo* for the text quoted would be supplied by the first translation of the appropriate cuneiform tablets; but since this need not have been a published translation, and since the interpretation of these documents was a process and not an event to which a single date could be assigned, the nearest one could say is "about 1880." This is to put it at the earliest, and a probable date would be much more modern (in both instances). The theoretical *terminus ad quem* for both is, of course, the date, unknown to the public, of Mr. Gardner's initiation; probably in the late thirties or early forties.

Though Mr. Gardner claims to be satisfied of the great age of the rituals he knows, it did occur to him that they might be modern concoctions. Apparently he asked the late Aleister Crowley point-blank whether he was the inventor of this, as of so much ancient tradition. He was persuaded, I think rightly, that it was not Crowley's line of country; and disposed, on stylistic grounds, of others about whom he seems to have had doubts.[5] He does not, however, consider the possibility that the inventor could be someone he had never heard of. He claims also to know from oral tradition that this particular cult existed in some form at the time of Waterloo. This, of course, would not conflict with my own view, unless the text quoted was equally old; but tradition seems to be exceedingly vague in this instance, detailed as it is in other respects.

Now, what sort of influence did the cult undergo to bring about this new change? And when is it intrinsically likely to have taken place? Answering the second question first as my custom is, I would

[5]Gardner, *Witchcraft Today*, cap. 4, pp. 47-8.

say that the goddess is likely to have taken over very recently, and to have been brought in by a new kind of educated recruit, the would-be mystic of the present century, products of popular occultism, anthropological novels (such as *Winged Pharoah* or *The Corn King and the Spring Queen*), and psychoanalysis. I doubt if at any date much before 1930 enough of the appropriate literature yet existed for many people to feel that to be truly pagan one must be "matristic." If these were the circumstances, then probably the myth was produced immediately the goddess was accepted as chief deity of the cult.

Fortunately, though we do not know her name, we do know who she is; for Mr. Gardner has let out another hint (the charge before initiation):

Listen to the words of the Great Mother, who of old was also called among men Artemis, Astarte, Dione, Melusine, Aphrodite and many other names. At mine altars the youth of Lacedaemon made due sacrifice. Once in a month, and better it be when the moon is full, meet in some secret place and adore me, who am queen of all the magics. . . .

For I am a gracious goddess, I give joy on earth, certainty, not faith, while in life; and upon death, peace unutterable, rest and the ecstasy of the goddess. Nor do I demand aught in sacrifice. . . .[6]

The style is much the same, though perhaps here it is a little more skilful. There are several points worth noting. First, that string of names. Those ladies, or rather four of them (Dione is a name of Aphrodite) were worshipped, when they were worshipped seriously, as different people. At the utmost, I will allow that identification between Astarte and Aphrodite occurred in a syncretic age; it was not original, and Artemis and the syren Melusine cannot be dragged into it. Lumping them together and calling them the Great Mother is not possible in religion, but only in Comparative Religion. If you believe seriously in Aphrodite you do not believe she is really Artemis; they may once in fact have been the same person in two aspects, but the worshipper who knows and accepts their separate legends will not believe it. (Myself, I doubt if they ever were the same; but I should be in a minority there today.) And did Isobel Gowdie of Auldearne know all this Classical Dictionary stuff? Would she have thought it important? Is it not plainly the product of an anthropologically minded age?

Then, those youths. Apart from the affectation of "Lacedaemon" (for Sparta; sciolism, too, in the context), why specially drag them in? Artemis has already been listed. The point *must* be the "due sacrifice."

[6]*Ibid.*, p. 42.

The reference, of course, is to ritual flagellation at the altar of Artemis Orthia; making two references to flagellation so far. There are, in fact, two others in Mr. Gardner's book, and some vague talk about "ordeals" and "frightening"; the context in every case is initiation. All this is at least mildly interesting, because there is no hint of it in any earlier account of initiation ceremonies. There is a good deal, in the accounts collected by Miss Murray, about the "Devil" beating his disciples,[7] but the context is always straightforward maintenance of discipline; as such, of course, it has no special interest because it was, anyway, the standard minor punishment most often employed in the countries and periods involved. It is really insignificant, but it might not seem so to a modern reader, to someone who was trying, from outside, to build up a picture of what a traditional coven was like and what it did.

There are, however, relatively few people who would seize on this element and expand it, making *ritual* flagellation a crux of the initiation ceremony (as we may reasonably guess it to be), inserting a reference in the solemn moment of the liturgy, that at which the goddess's names are recited, and justifying it by a legend, the very same legend that professes to explain the theogony of the goddess. The moving spirit behind the change would therefore seem to have been a person of that particular kind of specialized sensibility; it might, for example, have been Swinburne, and though I do not think it was (for there would surely in that case be also hymns and so forth, that Mr. Gardner could not mistake for anyone else's), it is not improbable that the actual author was under his influence. This, of course, puts a new complexion upon the change of sex, and casts some doubt on what I have said about the movement of fashion. For a masochist author, if male, is likely to be readier to worship a goddess than a god, and the more so the more the aberration is sublimated; the goddess would be, in fact, the sublimation. I am not altogether sure that there is any inevitable correlation between sexual delight in pain and glorification of the dominant woman; but one can see that a connection is reasonable, and certainly Swinburne exhibits both; in his work, moreover, his fantasy is represented, typically, by queens, goddesses, and allegorical figures who demand utter obedience or describe themselves in glowing terms, rather than by the more directly "Gruesome Ladies" of Leopold von Sacher-Masoch.

If so profound a change in the direction of the cult could be ascribed wholly to such a personal kink, there would be no need to look for any particular age in which it might occur, and in that case I should

[7]Murray, *Witch-Cult*, pp. 197–203.

ascribe the texts quoted, merely on literary flavour, to about the nineties; or perhaps to some late survivor of the "aesthetic" period. (Oddly enough, one could confidently so describe Montague Summers from the point of view of style.) I think we have to imagine some queer fish bred up on the last and most pagan Romantics as the most recent Magus, not necessarily of the whole of British witchcraft, but of that part of it with which Mr. Gardner has come into contact. (He allows that the covens he knows of know very little about other covens.) Magic, quite possibly, has become sectarian.

I imagine that the witch-master, typically, if he is to innovate, is trained in one group and afterwards either leaves it to return, or forms a new coven, or imposes himself on some other; for a prophet is not without honour, save in his own country. It is necessary that he should be accepted as more learned than his followers. The nature of the learning involved would, of course, make him an autocrat; where the leader is distinguished by greater supernatural knowledge and power, there is no room for democracy or doubt, and the sage must inevitably choose his own successor, because he will have to train him. Only a claim to still greater, still more esoteric science can upset the process, or a failure of the Apostolic Succession. Now, there is a point to be noted here, of some importance. If the group is united in the pursuit of hidden doctrines, and if moreover the knowledge thus sought is highly dangerous, then no initiate will expect to be admitted to the whole knowledge at once; it would even disappoint him. However long he studies he will assume the existence of a yet more esoteric level beyond; he will expect his teacher only gradually to reveal to him these deeper secrets. He will even be ready to discard, as meant only to satisfy beginners, what he was previously led to believe. This of course will not apply in genuine traditional witchcraft; I am supposing a tradition already undermined, and a candidate for magus status in a cult that may also contain humbler sorcerers. These, he will feel, are good enough to enact rituals (and rituals cannot easily be interfered with), but it is the adepts beyond them who understand partly why, and it is only the adepts beyond the adepts who possess the final secret that overrides all secrets, the last unquestionable real McCoy.

Now, if this is so, then clearly it is a simple matter for an innovator to go on making innovations throughout his whole career and never admit that he has done so; each time, he is merely stripping another veil off the unchanging ultimate secret. An established pundit of a sect of witches could be in charge for many years, and make many small additions and emendations in sacred texts, and then (perhaps when he had inducted a sufficient number of recruits of his own choosing) he might produce out of his conjurer's hat a new creed and a ready-made myth to go with it; a myth (who knows?) that would not suffer by its remarkable parallels in the most recent archaeological discoveries.

There are other possible answers to the question how and why the change took place. For example, I have been assuming the witch-master was a man, but much in Mr. Gardner's work suggests that the sect may have been reformed by a woman; a learned woman, after all, is nowadays a possibility. And it would be possible for the whole explanation to be contained in his suggestion that the "myth" was "coined to explain ideas and rituals already conceived"; to explain, specifically, a discrepancy between the actual practice of a coven and the literary idea of the cult, precisely in that the leadership was female and not male. The practice would be the natural outcome of persecution, throwing local groups of sorceresses back on their own resources; and perhaps was not felt as a problem till literate men began again to be recruited under the distant influence of Romanticism, when one of them supplied an explanation that seemed to fit. It will be seen that this hypothesis fits the basic facts well but leaves the details uncovered.

Then there is the influence of the mysteries of the ancient world, through the medium of such people as say "Lacedaemon" for "Sparta" and "Artemis" for "Diana." This is almost certainly a factor; the author or authors concerned are clearly Classical Romantics, so to speak, but their parade of classicism (brought out equally well by other fragmentary quotations of Mr. Gardner's, less germane to our purpose[8]) need not imply any actual knowledge of Greek or even Latin, and it is my guess their actual learning was thin. Unless they were very erudite, they would probably draw their ideas about the mysteries exclusively from the *Golden Ass* of Lucius Apuleius, and this would still be the natural main source if they were very erudite. In the tale of Eros and Psyche we might find a faint suggestion of that myth; and the deity of the *Golden Ass* is a Mother Goddess—one of the Mother Goddesses, for the author's contempt for the Syrian claimant should be a warning against all glib identifications—but still quite the closest foreshadowing of Robert Graves in ancient literature (so far as I am aware; and so far as any ordinary educated person is aware, which is here the point). It is noteworthy that the witch-

[8]E.g., Gardner, *Witchcraft Today*, pp. 25, 143.

goddess, in the charge I am still discussing, is not claimed as Isis, and as Ishtar only in her most Hellenized form; there was a limit to this man's syncretism, and it did not take in even the Northern Mothers, even Brigid or Freya. Lucius Apuleius may have suggested rites, and would encourage the tendency to doctrines of metempsychosis observable in Gardner. At any rate, the bent of the anonymous author's mind is not difficult to perceive; and its paganism is of a very literary kind.

One or two other points attract me in the "charge." I will pause, however, only to say that it is remarkable, and sorts ill with what we know of magic practices all over the world, that the goddess does not demand "aught in sacrifice"; but that it is thoroughly consonant with my own opinions and with what we know, for example, of Voodoo, that she gives "joy on earth, certainty, not faith, while in life." In other words, the immediate rapture or transport, however induced (it seems to be very tame in Mr. Gardner's lot), is its own end and justification; providing this, the goddess does not need to represent any particular spiritual or moral standpoint, to satisfy a questioning mind or to promise any more strictly mystical reward.

It would not be fair to Mr. Gardner not to refer to one other archive that he quotes: a warning, setting forth the precautions to be observed by witches to avoid detection and, if detected, to avoid incriminating others.[9] He recognizes that this cannot have genuinely referred to English conditions at any time; and I am bound to recognize that its English is less ambitious than that of the two examples quoted, and that it does indeed refer to the innocuous goddess-cult he describes. His view is that it is an uneducated translation from a continental source in the times of fierce persecution; and this is *prima facie* reasonable. However, he points out (and the text itself emphasizes) that witches do not keep old documents, but as a matter of policy copy what they require for their own use and destroy all dispensable relics. Thus, if he is right, we have to expect an extreme degree of textual corruption; he does not claim to have seen manuscripts of any age, and for example "goddess" may easily have been substituted for "god," leaving no traces. But I doubt if the text is genuine at all. It enjoins the frequent destruction of books, yet has itself survived after the tortures it speaks of have ceased to be feared, and in a country where they were never employed. Though the style differs somewhat from the texts already quoted, it still contains fancy archaisms that would presumably drop out if it had

9*Ibid.*, pp. 51–2.

in fact been constantly recopied from memory: "ye" and "aught" and "'tis" and so forth. It makes much the same feeble attempt at seventeenth-century grammar as the "myth"; and it seems to disprove the accusations made against witches with a suspicious neatness. It seems designed to create an impression of injured innocence, and I suspect that someone has been supplying the cult in its modern form with retrospective historical evidence.[10]

Certainly, there is nothing very terrible about the cult Mr. Gardner describes, nor anything very impressive either; but then, he is so vague. He emphasizes the nakedness of the worshippers, and the necessity (or at least desirability) of a coven of thirteen; he emphasizes the absence of obscene or horrific rites; but he tells us, in the end, very little. It is interesting to note that the ceremonies now apparently involve pentacles and candles and other indoor paraphernalia; the Esbat seems to have replaced the Sabbat completely. Mr. Gardner owns that he knows little or nothing about ointments. It all looks, nowadays, like a cosy and rather eccentric parlour-game for Yoga enthusiasts.

Of course, there may be other covens that have fallen out of contact with those known to Mr. Gardner, and they may have been more conservative. There may, also, be witches who have reverted to a pre-coven age, who are distinguished by no particular religious views but who preserve within a small trusty circle the old techniques of sorcery. It is possible that in some places the repertoire of traditional spells has incorporated features derived from the "Dianism" of the age of neurosis, but not from this newer "Dianism."

Nowadays, the really ancient folklore of Britain can seldom be studied in Britain itself so well as in the isolated pockets of primitive British stock in the North American continent. The "hill-billies" have preserved many folk-songs, for example, that English specialists in that field have been glad to record; and though the advance of technology, that has till now so strangely passed these backwaters by, is likely to swamp them in the course of the present generation, they still remained the most stubbornly conservative of English- (or Gaelic-) speaking communities late enough to attract the attention of the modern folklore student. If, therefore, any such student should wish to meet a witch, about his best chance is to go to Dogpatch and call

---

[10]Still, the text may well be corrupt to the extent of containing the exculpatory suggestions as an interpolation; the original form may have been more cogent than one that describes cannibalism and human sacrifice as "impossibilities" (together with flight through the air).

on Ma Yokum. This has, in fact, been done. In his *Ozark Super-stitions*, Mr. Vance Randolph describes his position in the local community in a manner startlingly reminiscent of a professional anthropologist describing his South Sea island. The Ozark mountain country of northern Arkansas is about the westernmost and most recent of these odd peasant enclaves in an air-conditioned world. It was settled about the first quarter of the nineteenth century, I should imagine from the eastern states rather than from Britain, but from just such regions of the Atlantic seaboard, regions of pure English or Scotch-Irish stock. The point is immaterial, for once such a community was established it attracted to it only such newer immigrants as were culturally akin to its founders.[11]

It is clear from Mr. Vance Randolph's account[12] that a witch-society exists in the Ozark country, along with Holy Rollers and other examples of religious eccentricity. He was not, of course, able to learn much about it, but interesting points emerge. The witch, typically female, instructs her own daughter in the craft; nowadays, the apathy of these daughters towards it is said to be threatening it with extinction. There are, however, male witches as well, and no witch may practise until he or she has been initiated by one of the other sex; initiation involves coition and is witnessed by the group. There is no further indication of coven or Sabbat, and apparently no popular belief concerning them. Witches, typically, perform their rituals naked; it must be noted, however, that nakedness plays a remarkably large part in Ozark folklore generally, and in the local forms of eccentric Revivalist Christianity.

There are points of similarity between this and Mr. Gardner's sect, and points of significant though slight difference. In the Ozarks, the parent of equal sex *instructs*, and someone of the opposite sex *inducts*, which involves intercourse in the presence of a (naked) coven. According to Mr. Gardner, the *instructor* should be a person of the other sex, though the parent of equal sex is a permitted exception; initiation is a formal ceremony, also performed naked but not involving

[11]This process is the explanation of the term "Scotch-Irish"; before the mass migration of Irish, Irish settlers tended to attach themselves to existing communities of Scots, and vice versa; so that in the New World there came to be a synthetic Scotch-Irish stock, intermarried and assimilated in speech and culture. This of course complicates the problem of tracking down any particular detail of this culture to its Old-World origin.

[12]Randolph, *Ozark Superstitions*, especially cap. 12. Cf. the same author's article, "Nakedness in Ozark Folk Beliefs," in *Journal of American Folklore*, 1953.

intercourse.[18] Either of these practices might be derived from each other, or both from a common original; the English version may differ from the American as an attempt to return to an original dimly remembered, and the American from that original as a reversion to still more primitive conditions, or a development by mere forgetfulness. In fact, I think we can see in this Ozark testimony the traces of the cult stripped to what its unlearned members considered its essentials, after persecution and enlightened scepticism between them had deprived it of both learned leadership and true continuity of tradition. We should learn little more, I fancy, if Mr. Randolph were to persuade one of his witch neighbours to tell him all; she would know only what her own ancestors had neither forgotten nor misunderstood. To her, almost certainly, the essential point would not be the religious ceremonies, if any, but the wart-cures and love-potions; but as she is accustomed to gain her ends by rituals that she cannot understand (because, in fact, they are irrational), naturally she may keep up a remembered fragment of Dianic worship, for she does not need to believe or disbelieve a word of it.

I imagine English witchcraft, if it survives in a form less artificial than we have been speaking of, survives generally at this level of intelligence, and that normally there is nothing self-consciously pagan about it nor any general feeling that an organization and a god are necessary. But probably there are groups known to each other, and faint oral traditions of coven and Sabbat in the past. The educated shaman's strength is that he has the knowledge to restore something convincingly like the substance of these dim memories; he can recreate a past and then speak with its authority. Who else has the authority to deny him?

I know of no indications, however faint, of the recent history of witchcraft in the rest of the area over which persecution raged. I should judge that any modern witch-master in France or Germany would almost inevitably be a Satanist and a celebrant of Black Masses, because the weight of literary tradition would leave him hardly any option. But there is at least one interesting clue from Italy, which seems to point to a distinct national tradition parallel to the one we have been considering. The evidence is contained in *Aradia, or the Gospel of the Witches*, published in 1899 by an American, Charles G. Leland. It is important to notice that this work was available in England at that date, and therefore could have been known to English

13Gardner, *Witchcraft Today*, p. 75.

revivers of the Dianic cult; for witchcraft was a cult of Diana to Mr. Leland thus early. He was a folklore student whose two main interests were sorcery and surviving pagan mythology, so he must have been happy to combine them. In the main, I gather, he relied upon Michelet; but he was fortunate enough to gain the confidence of a practising sorceress, and from her received the manuscript that forms the substance of *Aradia*. (I should note that it was in her writing, and may perhaps be allowed to bear out, thus far, the authenticity of the last text I referred to out of Gardner.)

Leland had, he says, heard of the text's existence in 1886; and most of the contents were already known to him, from evidence of the same informant which happened to chime in with the views of the egregious Michelet. The style appears to have been a problem to him, both in this manuscript and in others of his collection. I should say rather the mixture of styles, for at least three can be distinguished. One is exactly that of nursery rhyme, in short lines haphazardly rhyming, and indeed actual nursery rhyme is quoted. The main body of the "Gospel" was apparently written in prose in the original, but transposed by Leland into blank hendecasyllabics, again rather haphazardly. He seems to have felt metre more appropriate; and while I do not wholly agree with him (it makes the Italian read like a translation of the English translation), it is true that it is incredibly wordy and bombastic—though if anything surprisingly *lacking* in metre and rhyme—for a gem from the treasury of Folk tradition. What I mean is, it is not memorable. For the third style we rely on Mr. Leland, since he does not give the Italian; he says, "The language . . . as regards needless padding, indicates a capacity on the part of the narrator to write an average modern fashionable novel, even a second-rate French one, which is saying a great deal."[14] If one thinks of, say, Catulle Mendès or Gyp, the last comparison is hardly fair (though perhaps he reckoned them first-rate), but the interest of the criticism remains. He seems to have cut down the passage concerned to a quarter of its length; that is something like padding, and utterly uncharacteristic of the genuine traditional article. In fact, it seems as certain as in the case of Mr. Gardner's quotations that these texts are "art products," not "folk products," even if they are bad art.

The *vecchia religione*, as represented in its "Gospel," has much in it to interest us. The "Gospel" itself is calculated to settle the claims of witchcraft to be in fact the "old religion," and of Diana to be its presiding deity. Actually, the *Vangelo* says as much for, though less

[14]Leland, *Aradia*, p. 70.

about, Aradia, whom Mr. Leland, reasonably, identifies as Herodias; she is made out to be Diana's daughter and the special protectress of the *strege*, though of course subject to Diana's ultimate suzerainty. The father was Lucifer. The theogony, and commission given by Diana to Herodias to trouble the Christians, occupy the first chapter (I presume the division is Leland's). There follows what he calls the Sabbat or "Treguenda" (*sic*, for "Tregenda"); that is, a description of the witches' feasts, with forms of consecration for corn and salt, and invocations to Diana and *Cain*. This portion concludes thus (the Italian is not given): "And thus shall it be done: all shall sit down to the supper all naked, men and women, and, the feast over, they shall dance, sing, make music, and then love in the darkness, with all the lights extinguished; for it is the spirit of Diana who extinguishes them, and so they will dance and make music in her praise."[15]

The chapter is brought to an end, rather inconsequentially, with an invocation to Aradia.

The following chapter is perhaps the most interesting in the book, if only for its opening words: "Diana was the first created before all creation; in her were all things; out of herself, the first darkness, she divided herself; into darkness and light she was divided. Lucifer, her brother and son, herself and her other half, was the light."[16]

Diana desires the light for its beauty, and pursues Lucifer; she is likened, here and throughout the passage, to a cat. She seeks advice from "the fathers of the Beginning," who apparently were older than herself despite what has just been said, and they "told her that to rise she must fall; to become the chief of goddesses she must become a mortal." There is little of interest in the details of her incarnation (in which Lucifer accompanied her), except in the theogamy between them; Diana took the form of her brother's pet cat to gain entry to his bed. Afterwards she charmed away his anger by her arts, and the two of them spun a wheel, that seems to be Fate. Lastly, Diana revealed her identity to the (already existing) witches and fairies and so forth, and was accepted by them as their queen after demonstrating her power by turning the stars into mice.

The rest of the manuscript is taken up with spells. I will only single out one point, the emphasis on the herb vervain; because Mr. Gardner, speaking of ointments, seems to give vervain an importance not ascribed to it in any earlier guess at the ingredients.[17] Vervain is common in Italy, rare in England, almost unknown in Scotland. There

[15]*Ibid.*, p. 14.   [16]*Ibid.*, p. 18.
[17]Gardner, *Witchcraft Today*, p. 53.

are other minor correspondences between Leland's and Gardner's accounts, which lead me to the view that whoever was responsible for the English system may well have been using Leland; but they are nowhere close enough to amount to certainty.

Mr. Leland includes some other material, largely alternative legends of Diana; and Herodias, taking the collection as a whole, is hardly a prominent enough figure to justify the title. Indeed, she remains as shadowy as she always was, as she is in Burchard or Gratian; and in the "Gospel," as in the canonists, one is left with the strong impression that she exists to explain a discrepancy.

There are several incidental points of interest about the *Aradia* text, which we could only pursue at the cost of a digression. The salient point is clear; it is setting out to show witchcraft as a pagan survival, *la vecchia religione*, and revealing throughout a set of ideas borrowed at second hand from the Albigensians; it is, very largely, the Inquisitors' picture of the "Waldensianism" they had conflated in their minds out of two heresies with a little "Canon *Episcopi*" mixed in, the same that they called "Luciferian" in Germany and in north Italy would probably call "Patarene." Nothing is said about Diana in the *Vangelo* (though there is a version of the Endymion legend among the addenda) that implies more knowledge of her ancient character than that she was goddess of the moon. Imagine a writer who can make his Diana pursue his "Lucifer," and thinks of a cat! Why not a dog? I suggest, because he knew nothing of the old Artemis but wanted to bring cats in; because of the stories that the "Cathari" worshipped a cat. The passage relating to the division *of the goddess herself* into Light and Darkness is plain popular Manichaeism; the description of the *agape* of bread and salt, where Cain was invoked, and where indiscriminate fun and games went on indoors with the lights out is very unlike the northern Sabbat but exactly the kind of thing that was alleged against the "Waldensians" and "Luciferians." The place given to Lucifer in the *Vangelo* of course points the same way; I need hardly repeat that the heresy actually involved is Albigensianism as filtered through a propagandist's mind, not Waldensianism as the Poor Men of Lyons practised it or as it is practised today.

Either the Italian witches in the thirteenth or fourteenth century took up with heresy and imitated the practices ascribed to heretics, or this suspicion fastened upon them until they justified it because their recruits shared it, or some who undertook to supply them with a set of scriptures, in modern times, acted on the assumption that the suspicion was or had once been true. Probably all these took place to

some extent. The process must actually have robbed Italian witchcraft of any real pagan tradition it still preserved. Of course, the
Italian common people have long memories for old gods, and nobody
would be surprised to find pagan survivals there; but the Church's
saints and festivals have so exactly replaced the pagans that no mere
magician would be likely to trouble about the difference. Catholicism,
in Italy, has quite as good a claim to represent the old paganism as a
cult that talks about Diana but regards her as a kind of Aeon of a
very vulgarized gnosticism.

Of course, there is the phrase, *la vecchia religione*, which implies
a theory that witchcraft is both very old and a religion, but need not
imply that it was the general religion of Italy before Christianity
(though I admit it is probably meant to), and which only bears witness
to an opinion, not to a fact. The phrase is not actually a usual one for
witchcraft; and if it was its currency might be explained not by a
general assumption of its accuracy but by its neatness as a pun.
Vecchia, which as an adjective means simply "old," means "crone" or
"hag" when used by itself as a noun, and on that ground can be
applied to a witch as readily as the more technical *strega*. Of course
the phrase does imply a belief in the paganism of witchcraft; and in so
far as there have always been witches, the belief must be true, since
there were witches in pagan times. Perhaps Italians who use that
phrase believe that witches preserve pagan doctrines; and perhaps
they are mistaken. (According to Leland, the expression is the witches'
own; and of course those he had made contact with believed in its
truth, rightly or wrongly.)

I would have liked to speculate more at large on the provenance
of this Italian material; but it is not more than marginally relevant to
my purpose to do so, and so far as it concerns us its significance is
fairly plain. Mr. Leland's collection appears to have been the work
of several literate but not learned persons, its main specimen being
probably worked over more than once. The addenda show more
knowledge of paganism but do not profess as much knowledge of
witchcraft as the *Vangelo*. The aim of the latter, in its final form,
seems to be to bring out and emphasize the debased Cathar aspect
of Italian witchcraft, and no serious attempt has been made, in this
section, at convincing proof of paganism. Its source was probably anti-
Cathar and anti-sorcery propaganda, in which the two were already
confused together. Probably one could find cheap pamphlets of pious
authorship from which the necessary hints were taken. I am not,
however, excluding the possibility that the *strege* actually took up

with what they conceived to be Catharism in the Middle Ages, accepting the assurance of the Church that sorcerers and heretics were both worshippers of Lucifer (and Diana and Herodias). In that case the text would be drawn from genuine, though not prehistoric, witch traditions, and merely written up in modern times. The description of the *agape*, however, is in that case surely quite gratuitous, and the language, in places, surprisingly gnostic. The whole work reads much more as if one of its authors was consciously seeking to establish that the witch-cult was a cult of this particular nature, and grafted material calculated to prove it on to an existing straightforward book of incantations.

The English material supplied by Mr. Gardner smells too strongly of the lamp for us to exclude, in its case, the possibility of any influence available in the early years of this century, while what is traditional in it probably goes back to the same tradition as the Ozark sect. Italy and the Ozarks, however, can hardly have influenced each other; so it is worth enquiring what elements are common to both. In both, the witch, though typically a woman, belongs to a society also containing men. The purpose of the society is primarily ritual magic; certain rituals require nudity and intercourse between the members of different sexes. This is all; though it must be allowed the Ozark evidence is slight and very incomplete. (It may be added that the Ozark evidence should not be considered in isolation from the folklore of the region as a whole; in my view, from which the reader may well differ, it becomes less remarkable in its context than when taken separately, and less indicative of pagan survival.) As we knew before we started[18] that nudity and sexual intercourse, or abstention from it, can have magical significance; and as in the nature of the case sorcerers are likely to form secret societies when their activities are socially frowned on, or when their powers in their own eyes become so great as to be dangerous, this correspondence amounts to almost nothing, or at least to no indication of paganism beyond what is implicit in belief in magic.

It cannot be too often asserted that reliance on magic is incompatible with reliance upon a transcendent god, and that the magician, as such, can have no exclusive devotion to any one religion. He is bound to consider the gods as circumscribed within the scheme of the universe, whose laws he is ambitious to know, and knowledge of whose laws gives command over gods and men. Therefore, all worship

[18]From Frazer. The subject may be profitably pursued through the index to the *Golden Bough*.

when performed by a consistent sorcerer is something quite other from what we understand as "religion," whether or no we allow it to bear the name. It is pretty well inevitable that a magician will view with the strictest impartiality any profound change in the sphere of religion, because he will regard it as a private quarrel between gods, beneath the notice of his philosophy; if the outcome is important to him personally, that is merely because his power is not yet so great that he can afford to ignore the reigning deity. A simple-minded magician may indeed take sides, and probably most witches always did; but, even so, they were favouring one of the supernatural parties to a dispute, not claiming that his adversary did not exist, nor imagining that it would not be possible to come to a working agreement with that adversary, if he should prove the stronger. A convinced witch would not mean quite what we mean by the word "god."

Well, in that case obviously all witches are pagans to this extent, that they have nothing against using such pagan ceremonies as they happen to think useful. The history of the craft in its relations with the Church is probably at bottom a matter of rigid and insoluble cross-purposes, the witches simply not making distinctions fundamental to Christianity, the Christians not realizing that anyone could fail to make them. This does not exonerate witchcraft. In all probability its lack of moral content made it the refuge of the reprobate, and persecution that made it a crime made it a friend of criminals. Persecution, whatever its motive and however admirable the original principles of the victim may be, is seldom good for the character, and most of the world's depressed minorities have a right to our compassion but lack charm. The witch, as such, had no admirable principles, but was distinguished from her neighbours by her claims to secret sources of power, which if good were none the better for being a monopoly and if evil were nothing to be proud of. Her persecutors had an honest conviction of moral duty, but I am prepared to allow that persecuting is no better for human nature than being persecuted, and the zeal of many led them into very questionable courses; notably they tampered with the evidence, and became blind to the value of other virtues besides righteous zeal and judicial methods that did not automatically result in conviction. The spectacle is none the less melancholy for not being in the least unfamiliar.

We can hardly accept any account we have of the witches' activities, from whatever source it may come, entirely at its face value. Much that was later discovered to be false was accepted as evidence in the courts, not to speak of what obviously was false but was not discovered

to be so. And anything revealed by a professed witch must be received
with caution, because if it was not extorted by torture still it is bound
to be contaminated by her delusion. Witches, if sincere, are not wiser
than other men but more gullible; if not sincere, then they will find
their own fellows in the craft their easiest dupes. It is easier to
persuade a spiritualist than a non-spiritualist that you are a medium.

A witch is not a profound metaphysician. Her craft rests on basic
assumptions that cannot ultimately be justified by reason and do not
proceed from any authentic revelation. What she believes she believes
because she believes because she believes, and to her Right and
Wrong and first principles are alike irrelevant; at least to her witchcraft, if not to herself. So it is reasonable to suppose that most sorcerers in Christian times have retained more primitive religious
attitudes, seeing that belief in witchcraft is itself a more primitive
religious attitude. This might or might not mean that she would
retain specific pagan beliefs; it would mean that she would accept
Christianity, if at all, in what one might call a pagan sense. It is easiest
to suppose that to her, as to her neighbours, pagan memories would
grow dim as the generations went by; but that some trace of those
memories would remain, along with ideas from all sources, Christian
and heretical Christian included, to clutter her disorderly mind. Those
practices of magic that would look most heathen to the priest need
not have seemed so to her. Christianity has no room for magic, but it
is not altogether easy to appreciate the fact. The true magician is of
no particular religion; if he is ambitious to claim for his sect the
prestige of a religion, he will be the world's wildest syncretist, because
he has in these matters no standards of selection; there is no reason
for him to exclude anything.

Nobody, I suppose, would doubt the lavishly syncretic character
of the cult described by Mr. Gardner, or would claim that the goddess
with so many Greek names, but no Celtic ones, has undergone no
editing since the Before Time; and "what that Before Time was, I
think scarcely Sphynx can tell." And no informed person can doubt
that the whole content of Mr. Leland's *Vangelo* is post-Christian,
down to the use of Diana's name in conjunction with that of Herodias.
One might distinguish in both cases a possible pre-Christian residuum,
but it would be very slight and not very pagan; not very religious at
all. Indeed, this probably would be true to the original character of
magic; for the more firmly a magician believes in magic, the less awe
he can have of the gods, including the Devil in that category.

But magic could not continue to be practised in a society that feared the gods without becoming infected by that society's attitudes. Little as the witches may have meant by the word "god," they had to have one when everybody else did. Leaving the former paganism aside (and that was also a religion), Christianity has had a clear run of fifteen centuries more or less in Western Europe and had everywhere been established about a thousand years before the witch persecutions began. The persecutions are an ugly episode and produced much twisted thinking and many miscarriages of justice; and that experience also must have affected, one way or another, the witchcraft that survived. Let the reader make his own guesses; but before I close, it may be convenient if I set out mine.

First I must hazard those definitions I earlier tried to avoid. By "magic" I understand the science, pure or applied, of the occult; where the occult is taken to mean (for it could have other meanings) that sphere of knowledge, falling within the frame of the universe and bound by rules, that is of its nature knowable to man, but is of its nature not knowable by the ordinary techniques of co-ordinated sensory observation (the inductive method). The occult therefore ought not to include, but might accidentally be held to, whatever science might discover, but had not yet discovered; and in fact such knowledge might be come by, indirectly, through magic just as it might be conferred by revelation. It also does not include the sphere of whatever in the universe is not bound by rule, that is of pure chance, if any, and of free will, if any, whether of man or of a transcendent God; though it might be a fact of occult knowledge that no such free will existed. The universe is governed by occult laws, subject to magical control, in so far as it is not governed only by laws knowable to science (presumed inferior to magic) or by Divine Omnipotence (presumed superior). Actually, if there is Divine Omnipotence at all, and if it is the free will of a reasonable God (not Himself subject to rule except the law of His own nature), then there is no such intermediate sphere, for everything below Omnipotence must be knowable by reason or revelation or not knowable. All creatures are subject to the reasonable laws of the Creator, and only He can set them aside. There is the Course of Nature, there is Man's skill as Artifex as a special case within it, and there is Miracle, which only God can perform (for He alone works the effect, whether or no He does it through the agency of another). Magic, therefore, is a delusion, although magicians may sometimes have happened on scientific facts ahead of the scientists. In his specific activity the wizard cannot succeed, and therefore the reality of the powers claimed is no test whether he is genuine. The true magician or witch is that person who honestly, not being deranged, believes himself to be so.

The witch is a magician, whatever else he or she may be incidentally. He differs from other magicians in that his knowledge of the occult is transmitted by an oral, not a learned tradition. Typically, though not necessarily, the witch is female (and old and ugly); and in common parlance at least she is typically malign. It matters nothing to her character as witch that she should belong to a particular fellowship of witches or worship a particular god, except in so far as, in some countries at some times, fellowship with other witches and participation in the same rituals would affect the *bona fides* of her belief that she was a witch, as that society commonly understood the term.

Our own society in former ages came to accept both Christianity (and therefore belief in the Divine Omnipotence) and the reality of the witches' powers; rationalizing the combination by holding that these powers were not enjoyed by witches by virtue of occult knowledge but by the aid of the Devil; that is to say, the chief of the devils. By devils we understand fallen angels, that is, revolted ministers of God of an original nature higher than our own, and still enjoying (by God's permission) powers, not miraculous, but greatly beyond those possessed by Man. As, however, we are not compelled either by reason or by revelation (properly interpreted by reason) to believe that such creatures exist, and as, if they exist, their powers, though possibly greater than our own, must still be subject to scientific laws, we may assume that, whether witches relied on their own powers or those of the Devil, they were still deluded. Of the Devil I would further say that he can have no right to exclusive authority over the devils or over Hell, nor is there any reason to suppose that he enjoys it; the devils, having once revolted against Omnipotence, cannot be prevented from revolting against a lesser power. The Devil, however, was for much of the history of Western Christendom imagined as the arch-enemy of God (though ultimately powerless against Him), and as possessing powers, from the human point of view, almost as extensive. This view, however, though it is as old as the known history of witchcraft (for what that amounts to), is probably much younger, both altogether and in Western Europe, than witchcraft itself. I will now proceed to guess at the antiquity and development of this last.

In the very primitive beginnings of our culture, it is to be presumed that magic and religion were indistinguishable, and that everyone practised both for some time after a distinction was perceptible. I do not mean that necessarily they were jumbled together in a formless whole, for the thinking of primitive man is often more complex than our own on such subjects; but that a supernature that may have had an elaborate structure was not divided into just these two categories.

As soon, however, as any ritual system for influencing Nature was developed, there was probably from the first a division of ritual functions within society, some for men and others for women, and some for each trade that the first division of labour brought into existence. In course of time there developed, by stages we cannot usefully guess at, classes of rituals (probably more than one) that were the special property of groups of people whose trade, for one cause or another, brought them closer in contact with the *feared* Unseen than other people, and who were therefore themselves feared. These included a class of ritual experts, who derived their authority from their having originally specialized in very important or very difficult rituals and who became soothsayers of oracular status; they danced, on special occasions, in a costume originally designed for purposes of "sympathetic" magical control of deer (on which, in that stage of its evolution, the tribe had depended). There was also a class of wise-women distinguished by their knowledge of herbs, who practised what there was of medicine but who were able to apply the same knowledge to less admirable uses. The distinguishing features of their rituals were that they were mainly concerned with causing or averting harm to individuals; they were designed to clinch the effect of the remedy or poison, with which together they constituted the "spell," or else to protect the witch herself from the harmful effects of the powers she employed. The religion of this age was "animistic," that is, it ascribed a soul to every natural object and worshipped some of the more important of these animate objects (as well, perhaps, as other gods). Of all such things to which a kind of consciousness was ascribed, the most numinous, the nearest to real gods, were trees; the influence of the tribe's habitat in northern Europe, the strength and age which trees attain, and the comparative lack of economic exploitability in the greatest of them, most of all the well-known psychic "horror" they seem sometimes to exude (the original Panic), all this made the first "Celtiberians" tree-worshippers. That is to say, their attitude towards the spirits of trees was nearer the specific religious than the specific magical. In the highest development of the later Celtic culture in Britain and Gaul they produced, in Druidism, the cult of oak and mistletoe, an impressive and reasonably sophisticated religion to whose priests the Romans readily though ignorantly ascribed almost boundless learning. Long before that could have come about, before they consciously worshipped gods at all, the "Celtiberians" had divided the year by the coming and going of the leaves. The witches owed their position in this society largely to the close relation in which they stood to the most poisonous herbs that grew.

This relationship was specially manifest in their ability to take certain herbal venoms without ill effects and even with pleasure; the explanation being that they took externally a preparation whose two main toxic ingredients were antagonistic. These were belladonna and aconite, and their action in combination when rubbed into the skin was probably a numbing of sensory perception that conferred an illusion of freedom from gravity, confusion of distance, and so forth; also an excitation of the heart which might act as an aphrodisiac stimulus. The ultimate deleterious effect of this drug was too long delayed to be recognized. The experience thus undergone by the witches they construed as an induced spiritual ecstasy and came to value for its own sake, regarding themselves in consequence as spiritually privileged persons. This did not increase their popularity with their neighbours.

The craft, in most places, was confined to women and normally handed down from mother to daughter; but the more active members and the most eager and dependable recruits were the older and more ill-favoured, both because the work was light but needed great knowledge and because, being feared, it offered a substitute importance to the woman who was not loved or desired. The special risk its rituals involved or implied brought the craft into specially close relations with the oracular shaman, so that a kind of male leadership was externally imposed; while among the women the more active older members and those who actually possessed the arch-secret of the ointments tended to set up an internal rank system. Among the ritual dances of the group those performed naked under the influence of the drug, which probably were led by the masked shaman, came to be regarded as the most solemn and were performed by all the initiates, active or not, on the great occasions of the seasonal calendar.

I pass over a lengthy stage in the development of this culture, in which migration brought contact with other cultures and other worship already established over a large area of the Mediterranean and Atlantic seaboards; the witches with each culture-contact and each development in the sphere of religion had the opportunity to add to their repertoire of spells, but this is not a subject I am now concerned to unravel. (It is also possible, but I should judge unlikely, that contacts with the Levant may have involved contact between our witches and comparable classes elsewhere, for example, the sorceresses of Thessaly, who were famous in classical times.)

With the advance northward into territory that had become Celtic of anthropomorphic ideas conveyed largely from Greece by Roman agency, the spirit wherewith the witches in their ecstasy were inspired was reinterpreted as a god of more or less human attributes, and it came to be assumed that the shaman in dancing disguise represented him. They thus acquired a horned god of characteristics similar to those of the classical Pan or satyr and the Christians' devil, and probably derived from the same, or a parallel, ultimate source. This development was clinched by the advent of Christianity, which completed, north of the Alps, the process of Hellenistic anthropomorphosis. The conversion, however, also involved the legal suppression of specifically pagan practices, and as such, rightly or wrongly, the witches' dances were regarded by the Church. Actually, the witches continued to practise in secret what they themselves hardly regarded as conflicting with their religious obligations; for, with the typical impartiality of the sorcerer, and in common with the rest of the population, they accepted the religious dictates of their rulers and in time forgot all but the most external features of the former paganism—a paganism itself a novelty compared to witchcraft.

Witchcraft went underground, and where it survived survived in isolation. Its development in consequence varied considerably from place to place; in some districts it may have died out completely or been merged in one corpus of rural superstition, ceasing to be the mark of a distinct group. Elsewhere it preserved more of its old form, and in some places was still for a time under the control of male witchdoctors, though in time the line of these probably everywhere died out and its loss was mourned by the witches themselves until they forgot about it. Everywhere there would be an element of syncretism, but everywhere it would pursue a somewhat different course. The horned god, however, survived when most paganism had withered away because syncretism itself encouraged his survival, equating him with the Church's powerful Satan. The use of the ointment also was persevered in, because the ecstasy that could be worked up with its aid was still the witch's supreme emotional compensation and assurance of esoteric power. It often happened, however, that the true secret was lost by the death of one who had jealously guarded it, and so several variant formulae arrived at by guesswork came into use. Roughly the same set of dances were also generally retained, because they were the easiest part of witchcraft to learn and remember; there was nothing specially secret about them, and several dances that were not in origin peculiar to the cult were preserved by it when the moral opposition of the Church forbade them public performance. The craft at this stage, however, was in essentials merely engaged in the trade of customary empirical spell-peddling. As such it was more or less criminal, because it might deal in poisons, aphrodisiacs, and abortifacients, and because (to those who believed in it) it might curse as well as bless. It was therefore generally illegal, but the Church did not take it very seriously and most secular codes of law treat it as beneath their notice.[19]

The Church's law, however, did come to include a canon that seemed to speak of witchcraft, though its original intention was doubtful, its tenor rationalistic, and its authority probably spurious. This was the Canon *Episcopi*, adopted, with emendations, by Gratian out of Regino of Prüm and ascribed to the Council of Ancyra (which secured its general acceptance). The canon was really concerned to condemn as a delusion a legend current over much of northern Europe of a nocturnal cavalcade of the dead; in this cavalcade some living women (who may well have been witches) claimed to have taken part, a claim that was condemned as tending to paganism. The leader of the cavalcade was probably known in different places by names that alliterated with "Herzog" or a cognate formation, but elsewhere had been confounded with a German goddess whose name became "Habonde" in French, and was translated loosely by Regino as "Diana"; his commentator Burchard, having come into contact with another version of the legend, supplied "vel Herodiade" and Gratian accepted both. Thus the Church acquired a wholly mistaken belief in depraved female worshippers of Diana and Herodias, naturally equated with witches. Garblings of the canon by priests unfamiliar with its text who tried to obey its instructions had the effect of spreading this belief through Latin Christendom, and adding thereto the impression that these witches were capable of supernatural flight (which the canon mentioned ambiguously and implicitly denied).

[19]Church codes normally treated magic as wicked (because pagan) but a delusion. See McNeill and Gamer, *Mediaeval Handbooks of Penance, passim.*

The attitude of the Church towards sorcery and paganism was profoundly changed by the alarming success of the Cathar movement in the twelfth century. This was a dualist heresy broadly of the gnostic type, originating in Asia Minor, that penetrated the West from the Balkans at this time and was gaining ground in the South of France, in a region where the Church was in serious need of reform, because of the appeal it made to the more rigorist and old-fashioned believers who were out of sympathy with the then trend of religious thought. The same region also saw the rise at this time of another heresy, the Waldensian, a straightforward Back-to-the-Bible movement. These two were apt to be confused together in the minds of churchmen; and after the Cathars had been subdued by armed force (from 1208), and the Waldensians went into hiding in northern Italy and the Alps, a number of accusations both true and false originally attaching to each were applied indiscriminately to all covert religious groups. By a process of mental association accusations levelled at Jews, Cathars, and Waldensians in succession were applied to the supposed followers of Diana and Herodias, and the belief associated with these applied to surviving groups of the former. Thus, there was built up in the minds of churchmen, and specially of the Dominican Order whose main purpose was to root out heresy, a composite picture of the followers of Satan, which included both heretics and sorcerers. The salient features of this picture were that the sectarians parodied the rites of the Church, held nocturnal ceremonies marked by a mock-Mass and by sexual licence, worshipped the Devil, and paid him obscene homage in the form of a goat (or of a cat; an accusation of a type generally associated with the Jews, transferred to the Albigensians apparently as a result of popular etymology getting to work on "Cathar" and "Bougre").

The success of heretics was ascribed to sorcery; the success of sorcery was ascribed to the Devil; the Cathars as dualists were assumed to be devil-worshippers, and so were the pagans, since the Devil was the only possible reality behind their idols. All non-Christians, including Moslems, were assumed to be idolaters, following Biblical precedent (and adopting suspicions current among the Romans to assimilate the Jews to the same class). There is no real beginning or end to this farrago of cross-associations; but there is a circumference, and into its convenient compass all Christian dissidents and all sorcerers were bundled willy-nilly.

Academic speculation in this same period (the middle thirteenth century) had its attention directed towards Satan by the threat of dualism, and came to recognize the possibility of his possessing certain powers beyond those in the reach of man, and ascribed to him a desire to use these powers to gain acceptance by the morally depraved as a god. To the less analytical this was confirmation of the view that he was, in fact, a quasi-gnostic archon of the material world or a power operating independently of the Church's God. Among those who came specially under Dominican influence tending this way were the multitudes of poor clerks attending the University of Paris, of whom many were disappointed of academic or ecclesiastical success and swelled the numbers of the spoilt clerks who had taken to a vagabond life, and, under the names of *Goliardi, Eberhardini,* or *Vagi scholares,* were formed into a society or mock religious order for mutual aid and protection. This order is known to have existed by the beginning of the century; I presume that the organization as it developed was based (partly by parody) on the most obvious models, namely the rules of the mendicant friars.

Members of this order, in their wanderings about France and Germany, sometimes practised the trade of a charlatan or conjuror and sometimes attempted to exploit for gain their clerical status. Some came into contact with surviving groups of witches, and were able to impose upon them as representatives of a higher and more learned tradition of the art. Within the frame of the beggars' society they formed a secret group of witch-masters, and reorganized witchcraft as an offshoot of the "order," hence as a society framed ultimately on the Franciscan model; the local unit in both cases being the "conventus," ideally of thirteen members. They probably also imposed upon the cult, so far as they were able, the characteristics that their education encouraged them to suppose it must once have had, or ought to have in theory. Possibly some of them introduced the "Black Mass." This was a product of superstitious fear of the real Mass. Up to that date, it probably did not exist, but the enormous thaumaturgic potency imputed to the Mass, coupled with interpretations of the Cathar *agape* as the devilish parody of it, created a belief in the sorcerer's or Satanist's perversion of the Christian sacrament, which in its turn produced attempts to put the vague supposition into concrete form. Thus, the goliard witch-masters, who construed the cult as Satanic and who possessed the technical knowledge, though not usually the ordination, to celebrate a valid Mass, may sometimes have invented suitably diabolical perversions of it; but this does not seem to have been the general practice at this date, and where the Black Mass, in any form, is a feature of a coven's ceremonies, it is probably a later accretion from a time when the legend had had two or three more centuries to grow.

The concerted leadership then set up did not last; the sect immediately attracted vigorous persecution while the strength and intelligence of the goliards' order declined for unrelated causes. The numerous outbreaks of popular heretical fanaticism in the fourteenth century (which may perhaps be related to the emotional disturbance of the Bubonic Plague) may sometimes have taken their colour from local witch-societies and sometimes coloured them; but no new feature was thus added to the cult as a whole, since it had lost its effective unity. It did, however, become specially entrenched in an area—the northern Alps—noted for religious eccentricity then and later. The panic that was to develop in the sixteenth century spread from this area as a storm-centre and followed, roughly, the lines of demarcation of the Protestant and Catholic camps.

Organized and Satanic witchcraft only entered Britain in this period, largely under the influence of Puritan propagandists trained on the continent who presumed its existence and were concerned to put it down, and who therefore could not avoid publicizing its practices. The few indications of it in earlier trials are wholly to be written off as fabrications of political and personal spite designed to appeal to the ecclesiastical courts. In Scotland, political adventurers and learned kabbalists were able to make contact with a large number of local witch-groups who remained in the primitive condition in which the goliards had found their continental equivalents; and a fairly elaborate witch-society was set up, though it had only a short life since the central governing conspiracy (of the Earl of Bothwell's supporters) was almost immediately detected. Though covens continued to meet far into the seventeenth century, they were merely the *disjecta membra* of the organization where they were not spontaneous responses of traditional witches to the new popular education in witch methods disseminated by the clergy themselves. In this and all ages of persecution the actual incidence of the cult was greatly multiplied in popular imagination and probably the majority of victims were substantially if not wholly innocent.

In England, where evidence of the cult's existence is both very late and very local, it was probably the creation of isolated reforming magi adapting a local group to the suggestions of propaganda.

In many places, isolated groups survived the persecution period, but in an unrecognizable form, since the persecution had disposed of most of those who possessed any extensive knowledge either of the traditional secrets of the craft or of the concocted literate corpus of doctrine and ritual that had generally been grafted on to it at one stage or another, and perhaps more than once. The former, when it was lost, was lost irreparably; but the latter could be replaced by a new example of the same process. A new literate quack who gained the confidence of a coven could foist a new fabricated mystery upon it; and we know of at least one case where this has occurred.

The reorganization I suppose to have taken place in the thirteenth century was only the outstanding example of a recurrent process whereby a witch-group, lacking a leader, accepts at his own valuation a would-be wizard with his own theory of what the sect ought to be. At each reorganization something genuinely traditional has been lost, and something book-learned added. "Waldensian" analogy threw open ordinary membership to men; Franciscan parody suggested the rigid coven; calumnies on heretics and Templars made witches kiss the buttocks of a horned animal; the magus of the moral chapbooks supplied the compact, and mere verbal confusion suggested the Black Mass. Later ages have supplied the trappings of the literary paganism and the pantomime properties of Mysticism for the Million.

Perhaps there is some truth after all in the belief that witches can change their shapes. Witchcraft, as I believe, has changed its shape till it has no true shape left. Pursuing a phantom hope, how should it not follow wherever that hope might seem to stray? How could its footing be other than marshy, or its vision clear of vapours, when a jack-o'-lantern was its guiding light? It was once rational to fear witchcraft; though those who rested in a securer hope and a coherent faith did not fear it without folly or repress it without sin. It has never been rational to admire it; its ends are not admirable and its means are foolish. Those who seek here for a mystical profundity hidden from common men will seek in vain, and wander in the same fog hand-in-hand with the eager latter-day necromancer on their left and on their right the Comparative Religionist spying out the elder gods. If they should pick up ten moonstruck companions, let them form their own coven to prove their own points; it will be as traditional, as well-instructed, and as authentic as any there has been these thousand years.

APPENDIXES

The Blokula Scare

THE PANIC THAT added the word "Blokula-Häx" to the Swedish language deserves particular attention; and though it is admirably dealt with in Sir Walter Scott's *Letters on Demonology and Witchcraft* (Letter VII *ad fin.*) it may be convenient to say something more about it. The panic, which broke out in 1669 in the village of Mohra, is remarkable as having produced the most elaborate and detailed evidence of the practices of Satanism ever supplied by external witnesses, almost independent of confessions; and as being one of the clearest instances on record of pure malicious fabrication. As in the famous Salem case a few years later, the accusations were laid, and the most detailed accounts volunteered by young children who claimed to have been bewitched. Not content with accusing a very large number of persons of having put the Evil Eye on them, like children in so many other places in that age, these little monsters claimed to have been repeatedly spirited from their beds to attend the actual Sabbat, of which they gave circumstantial but very confused accounts. About three hundred children were involved, and about a hundred alleged witches, many of them near in age to the children themselves (including the children of the adult witches, who were uniformly accused with their parents and ultimately punished, by whipping if not by the stake). It would seem that children outnumbered adults at these Sabbats by about four to one, yet the witnesses made it abundantly clear that the occasion to which they were thus surprisingly summoned was a sexual orgy. In some cases the parents were prepared to swear that the witnesses had been asleep in their beds at the time they were supposed to be gallivanting through the night sky, but this circumstance was not allowed to interfere with the Course of Justice. The means of transport varied enormously; some travelled to the place of assembly by natural means, others rode on the backs of bewitched human beings (who waited in a trance at the hitching-post till their mistresses were ready to return), some flew on aerial goats, some on broomsticks, some on both; the elder witch would ride the goat, while her family were precariously balanced on a spit protruding from the beast's anus (a detail Scott could not bring himself to repeat). The place of assembly was the "Blokula," described as an unusually large and well-appointed house, standing by itself in an enclosed field, with a central room for feasting and numerous luxurious bedrooms surrounding it. The children gave most of their attention to the part of the rites that took place in these latter.

These are the peculiarities of the case. Nowhere else do we hear of such a variety of magical manifestations at the Sabbat; nowhere else do we hear of Sabbats night after night, nor of a special temple or palace set aside for the purpose. Of course, if this building had existed, it must have been possible to find it, in so thinly settled a country, and the magistrates who eagerly swallowed what these young neurotics told them ought to have looked. But perhaps they had sense enough to realize that it would not look like a building on the outside; "Blokula" is "Blue Hill." A blue hill is a faraway hill; and a faraway hill that turns out to be a kind of mansion is clearly the palace of the trold-king.

The rest of the evidence is presumably extemporized by rather inexpert liars with a very confused picture of witchcraft drawn from a wide variety of old wives' tales and horror pamphlets—the panicky lying of children frightened of being caught out in a previous lie, feeding their invention with the tales of terror with which children have always delighted to torment themselves. I doubt if malice was the original motive; more probably what began as a game ended by frightening some children into fits and set off a wave of infectious hysteria that spread through all the village, partly by way of emulous self-importance and dramatization. The emphasis on sexual depravity in the evidence thus concocted is not very surprising in view of the sleeping habits of the country and time; a neurotic horror of sex coupled with an unhealthy interest would be more natural than not among these children. It was, of course, the elders who were really to blame, both in feeding their children with tales of imagined terror and in believing the tales when they were fed back. But this also was only to be expected; parents generally have both too much imagination and too little where their children are concerned, and a fear of the imagination coupled with an imaginative world that is almost wholly fearful is characteristic of the northern peasant generally, nor by any means confined to him.[1]

(The source drawn on for this case by all English commentators including Scott—and myself, if it comes to that—seems to be the same, viz. Horneck, A., "An Account of What Happened in the Kingdom of Sweden in the Years 1669 and 1670," Appendix to Glanvil, Sadducismus Triumphatus, London, 1681. The reader should be warned that this is a translation of a lost German pamphlet.)

For those with Swedish at command, there exists a work by Emanuel Linderholm, De Storn Häxprocesserna i Sverige, which however I have as yet been unable to obtain.

---

[1]Although the Blokula scare is in several respects unique, it is instructive to compare it with the slightly earlier case (1620) of Anne de Chantraine, described in an appendix to the article "The Sixteenth Century and Satanism" by Emile Brouette, in Satan.

The Waldensians and Albigensians

CONTEMPORARIES, and many since their time, have managed to get themselves hopelessly entangled about the Albigensians and Waldensians. Let
me assert here for the sake of clarity that the two sects originated in the
same general area at about the same time, but have almost nothing else in
common. The Waldensians are easier to dispose of; they were, and are
today, straightforward nonconformists, Protestants before their time. There
is absolutely no mystery about them. Like many another Puritan sect, this
began as a movement to win the laity to a holier life, and only parted
company with the Church as a protest against the latter's lukewarmness
in supporting it. It was inspired by the Gospels in translation. Its founder
was a small burgher of Lyon, Peter Waldo, who having secured a copy of
the Scriptures encouraged study of them among his neighbours. The group
thus formed became convinced that the Church was neglecting its duty of
preaching and teaching and avoiding its responsibility for promoting a
moral life. They rated morality and preaching above the sacraments, and
challenged the authority of the Church as not grounded in Scripture. Their
opinions were, of course, condemned by the ecclesiastical authorities, and
as they refused to give them up they were forcibly repressed. They fled to
remote refuges in the foothills of the Alps, and there preserved their
existence down to modern times, never more than suffered to live by the
civil power and from time to time actively persecuted, but saved from
obliteration by the inaccessibility of their retreats. At the time of the
Reformation they came in contact with the Protestants of Geneva and,
reluctantly, accepted Calvinism. In the following century a recrudescence
of persecution inspired Milton's sonnet, "Avenge, O Lord, thy slaughtered
saints. . . ." A handful survived, in very primitive conditions of life, into the
nineteenth century; the liberalizing Piedmont of Cavour left them alone,
anti-clerical United Italy extended toleration, and the present Republic
recognizes them as a church. Latterly they have spread in handfuls over
north Italy, living the sober middle-class lives of their like in other countries, and building churches that are exactly like any other dissenters'
meeting-houses. They can be seen, they have written books, there is no
secret about them nor any need of confusion. Nor is there any reason to
doubt that they always were what they are now, Bible puritans. The
Inquisition was fully aware of this. But naturally when they were forced
to be secretive it was easy to spread dark rumours about their goings-on,

and these may have been partly true. All sorts of things may have been done under cover of Waldensianism; and it is possible this sect, like many others, proliferated in eccentric splinter groups. But the Waldensians as a body, as an organization, offer us neither mystery nor extravagance to seize hold on. They were humble people, and only accidentally heretics; and until their name came to be fathered on other sects to save the champions of the Faith the trouble of thought, they did not give rise to any fairy stories.

The Albigensians seem always to have inspired more horror, and rightly, for they were much more radically opposed to the Catholic faith, and they were greater and more dangerous people. As a result, and also because they do not survive, we are dependent on more prejudiced testimony, and their exact origins and beliefs are by no means clear. Broadly, we know that they had many points in common with the Bogomils and Paulicians, and probably derived their ideas from that source. Unfortunately, a good deal of obscurity hangs over these also.

In general terms, however, Paulicianism may be described as a spontaneous and independent re-creation of gnosticism. Its founder Paulicius (which was perhaps not his name, but that need not detain us) was a native of Asia Minor who came somehow into contact with the doctrines of the Persian heretic Manes, a dualist, and reinterpreted Christianity in this light. Thus, like the gnostics, he gave a Christian gloss to what was essentially Zoroastrianism at second hand. In the prevailing view, parallels to gnosticism proper or to the views of such analogous non-Christian sects as the Mandaeans, should not in this case be taken as pointing to a direct debt; and further parallels that might (with some distortion) be drawn between these and (for example) the Christian Scientists may be allowed to reinforce this opinion. This is only worth mentioning to show that the Bogomils had, in all probability, no long history behind them when they are first heard of, and were never in contact with any occult tradition of Babylon, Egypt or wherever.

According to Paulicius's followers (we cannot say how much he was personally responsible for) the Universe was divided between the Good and Evil principle, though it is unlikely that they thought of these as a perfectly symmetrical pair. The Evil principle was the Demiurge, the creator of the physical universe and its lord until the time of Christ. (It is convenient to borrow the gnostic expression "demiurge," though I imagine this sect did not employ it.) Matter was thus wholly depraved, and the object of the Christian revelation (distorted, of course, by the Church) was to free the Soul from its bonds. For this reason, Christ did not actually take human flesh; He either was a mere appearance of a man, or consented to inhabit the body of a quite distinct being, the miraculously sin-free man, Jesus; these two opinions are both common in gnosticism, and both emphasize that Christ Himself did not suffer on the Cross. As there was no Incarnation, the Atonement wrought no redemption of the physical world, but brought to man the means to free himself from its trammels. The Paulicians therefore rejected the sacraments of the Church; the more extreme condemned marriage and sexual intercourse absolutely, as well as most physical indulgences, and denied the authority of the state. Absolute abstention from the contaminations of the flesh was not, however, demanded of all. The sect recognized an outer class of mere believers and a class of full initiates, the Perfecti or Cathars (the "Pure"), who having received the rite called (in the West) "consolamentum," a kind of ordination, were considered incapable of sin but were obliged to observe a rigidly ascetic way of life.[1]

The belief in irrevocable salvation of the elect while still on earth is not unlike Calvinist orthodoxy, and is shared in essentials by many puritan and revivalist bodies. It certainly need not be construed as licence to offend against the moral law in the assurance of impunity after death; though naturally it could be so construed by hostile propaganda, and it is always possible that fanatics will try to put such a belief into practice or libertines use it as an excuse.[2]

The Paulicians fell early under the ban of the Eastern Empire because of their attitude to the State; they took refuge in Bulgaria for a brief space and there acquired the name of "Bogomil" ("Beloved of God"), as well as the name of "Bulgar" by which they were generally known in the West. Their sojourn in Bulgaria was brief, and Bosnia became their permanent home until, under the Turks, they accepted Islam. But already by the middle twelfth century[3] missionaries had penetrated to Languedoc; Albi became a Paulician centre, and the sect gained so many adherents among the lesser nobility of the County of Toulouse as to become almost the official religion of that region. It had its own hierarchy, and Cathar synods were on occasion attended by both French and Bosnian bishops. (The original Paulicians seem to have survived for some time in Armenia, out of contact with these offshoots, and their doctrines may have developed separately.)[4]

[1]Obolenski, The Bogomils; Runciman, The Mediaeval Manichee.

[2]Cf. the alarming experiments of some American revivalists in the nineteenth century, as described by Hepworth Dixon, Spiritual Wives, and Strachey (ed.), Religious Fanaticism.

[3]Probably not earlier. Certainly there are references to "Cathar" heretics in the West in the eleventh century, and the heresy already existed in the Balkans; but the name alone cannot be taken as conclusive. The Albigenses themselves were very seldom called "Cathars" by outsiders; and the word already existed, for a sect long extinct but recorded in the popular encyclopaedia of Isidore of Seville. Occasional use of the word by a chronicler before the age of controversy, applied vaguely to a religious dissident, may stem from this; and any other hypothesis will force upon us serious problems of chronology.

[4]The question of the relations of French and Balkan Catharism is a highly confused one, but the filiation of West to East seems sufficiently clear from inherent probability and from the word "Bougre," Bulgar, applied to the Albigensians. (This was the first sense in which the word was used as an insult.)

The Cathari were thus in effective control of a valuable enclave in the heart of Latin Christendom, and were disseminating opinions subversive of all states and of the whole essence of Catholicism. They had little in common with their neighbours the Waldenses; but there was probably a certain connection between the two movements, in that both weakened the Church in roughly the same catchment area of converts; the existence of each was of advantage to the other. The recovery of the Languedoc and Savoy for Catholicism became the most serious problem facing the Roman church in this age.

It may seem a little hard to understand how the aristocracy of what was, at this time, a relatively sophisticated corner of Europe could be attracted to a cult so inhumanly austere. But that is hardly how it would have struck a contemporary. Here we must go back to two points I glanced at earlier: the "feudalizing" of Christianity, and the rise of the cult of the Virgin. Both these have been discussed by Mr. R. W. Southern[5] in a manner I cannot hope to rival; but perhaps it may be convenient if I summarize, at the risk of over-simplifying, what might be called the state of fashion in the piety of the age.

In the centuries previous to this, which saw the rise of feudalism, thinking on a variety of subjects was, not unnaturally, permeated by feudal ideas; and in many ways this movement affected the Church itself and the attitude of laymen towards it. The concept of homage seems to have made possible the organization of the Cluniac order, the first of all religious orders to unite under one authority several scattered convents. This supplied the model on which the more federal systems of the Cistercians and Carthusians and the unified armies of friars could improve, and is thus, quite accidentally, in the ancestry of the coven, which however is original to the friars. More significantly, the relation of lord and vassal was taken as a type of the relation of God and Man, and this in at least two ways. It justified what seems to us the very arbitrary process of conversion by whole kingdoms at a time. If a man's lord took Christ as his own liege, renouncing Woden or Mahomet, it was the vassal's natural duty to follow suit; and it was a perfectly reasonable condition to impose on a defeated enemy that he should do fealty to the god of the victor. This social attitude already existed in the Dark Ages, though then it had not fused with other elements to make the Feudal System, and the behaviour of a Charlemagne or an Alfred towards their subjects and their pagan neighbours on the religious issue must be construed in the light of it. The same state of mind is evident in the general attitude towards the Crusades in Palestine and Spain; though, significantly, this will hold good only for the early stages of the movement.[6]

But for our purpose the most important instance is to be found in the prevailing view of theologians on the Atonement. At the beginning of the

[5]Southern, *Making of the Middle Ages*, cap. 5, especially p. 234ff.
[6]I am indebted to this point to Dr. H. D. Sacker of University College, London.

twelfth century one can say, broadly, that the Fall of Man and his subsequent redemption were both interpreted in feudal language. Adam had "defied" God in the technical sense and become Satan's man; all his progeny were, so to speak, "nativi" (villeins) of Satan, which is one possible significance of birth-sin. Satan himself was of course a rebel vassal of God's; but the ordinary morality of the time insisted that it was the man's obligation still to serve the lord who had his homage, whatever the rights and wrongs of that lord's quarrels, and it further insisted that war and rebellion were games to be played according to the rules; Satan still had his rights, including his right to his own people's service, whatever his relations with his suzerain.

God, therefore, when He took it in hand to free Man from the bonds of Sin, could not simply override Satan. He must put Satan in the wrong, and cause him to forfeit his fee and with it Man's service. To this end Christ was born, that Satan not recognizing His Godhead should exercise over Him a power not justified by any contract; whereafter he could be convicted of usurpation and disseized of his lordship over the World and the Flesh.

It will be seen that this view, which I have put very crudely, has points of resemblance with Albigensianism. It allows the Principle of Evil a certain independence, certain entrenched rights against the Good. It allows him a legally sanctioned dominion over the World. It suggests an element of trickery in the Incarnation, and casts doubt on the full humanity of Christ. Further, the "feudal" view of conversion does tend to make the soul's salvation the result of a single irrevocable act, done on earth, which however irrevocable may carry with it a host of special rules and obligations like the oath of a knight or a monk.

There would, therefore, be a good deal in Catharism that a member of the knightly classes in the twelfth century would find familiar. At a time when the Church was going through one of its periodic crises of decay and regeneration, an active heresy whose heretical nature was hardly obvious to the non-specialist and whose concepts were particularly close to those of the nobility could reasonably be expected to gain adherents in that class in a province of Christendom where the Church was internally weak. This is a point worth establishing, because of a widespread disposition to ascribe to the Albigensians both morals and opinions more sophisticated than they can have dreamed of; and this could be, indeed has been, a powerful red herring.

The Albigensians were not specially sophisticated; if anything, they were rather old-fashioned. Christianity as a whole in the Western Church of their day was leaving behind the crudities they would have shared with it in the previous century. It is one of the great advantages of the doctrine of the Trinity that it allows the idea of God to grow in "immanence" and "transcendence" at the same time; and this process was now taking place. Religion was becoming more *three-dimensional*, taking on a new depth of subjectivity, and if you like of sentimentalism. A new emphasis on personal experience was beginning to make the legalistic view of conversion and Christian duty impossible (which is perhaps reflected in the Waldensian movement). As against God the supreme liege-lord the idea of God the Creator was gaining ground. God was thus seen as absolutely other than, and sovereign over, His creation, in all its categories from archangel to woodlouse taking in devils and men. Moreover, the creation as His work and His dominion in which Satan had no rights, over which he could have no power but by God's permission, was seen to be good in its essence; the material universe was God's handiwork and could find therein its sufficient justification. This was the age of Bernard Sylvestris and the "humanism" of the school of Chartres; it was also, I believe, the age that saw the first emergence in literature, and in the writings of the most austere monastics at that, of a sense of the beauties of landscape.[7]

Perhaps no side to this tendency had a more profound effect than its emphasis on the full humanity of Christ. What this meant in terms of the doctrine of the Atonement does not, I think, now concern us; the humanizing effect on the Church's attitude to the world in general is important, but was not immediately apparent. It was, however, closely bound up with the cult of the Virgin, which from this time on became a more prominent part of popular Catholicism than devotion to the Trinity itself. The Virgin was far more obviously unlike the Cathars' God than Christ Himself; and she was its most serious rival, from the first and in the very stronghold of Catharism, as an inspiration for the world of secular chivalry. But on every side, and in ways too numerous to mention here, the friendly yet infinitely august Church Triumphant of Catholicism at its best was arising to drive out the narrow flesh-loathing and, so to speak, militant quietism of an older generation of monastic saints. This was, I suppose, the most important thing that happened in the twelfth century. It did not, of course, happen all at once, nor was it the invention of a few great men, though one can mention names that certainly played a large part in it: Anselm and Ailred of Rievaulx and Bernard of Clairvaux and Bernard Sylvestris and Abelard should not be passed over in silence, and it is worth running through such names if only as a reminder that most of them were professed religious—monks—who in questions of the Christian life were not less but more austere than the preceding, the "Cluniac" generation. The Church was not making any kind of compromise with the World, the Flesh, and the Devil in its new sympathy with the world of Nature.

At the same time, of course, the new movements did not overthrow the old ideas; they were not, they never have been, completely successful. They bore fruit in the most unlikely places; and they bore the most unlikely fruit. St. Francis, perhaps the extreme representative of the religious ten-

[7]Notably St. Bruno; see Southern, *Making of the Middle Ages*, pp. 167–8, and cf. the monk Walter Daniel, quoted by Sir F. M. Powicke, "Ailred of Rievaulx" (in *Ways of Mediaeval Life and Thought*).

dencies of this age, was to inspire both heretics and ferocious heresy-hunters. The cult of the Virgin, in every succeeding age, was to kindle the one spark of human feeling in the austerest of men; it was to inspire many of the most moving and many of the most atrocious products of religious art; and it gave rise, from the first, to the most a-moral of miracle stories. Religion was becoming anthropomorphic as never before, and transcendental as never before in Europe; Christianity, as an ultimate consequence, was to be represented as easier than falling off a log and too difficult to be achieved at all. In my own opinion both these views are correct; but putting them into practice has its dangers.

I need not probably go into details concerning the origin of the Order of Friars Preachers, except to say that its form was determined by the coincidence in date of St. Dominic's life with that of St. Francis and with a period when the heresies of the Languedoc were the chief internal danger of the Western Church. In a general history of that church it would also be necessary to trace how the Catholic offensive against the Albigensians marks a stage in the degeneration of the Crusade from a spontaneous wave of enthusiasm and self-dedication in the cause of the Holy Sepulchre to a device of Papal politics. Suffice it to say that the area of Albigensian predominance was subdued by force of arms, in the early thirteenth century, by crusaders who had the double incentive of absolution and real estate, and was submitted thereafter to a Catholic terror of which the Dominicans were (latterly) the principal agents. In the middle of this process, in 1215, the Fourth Lateran Council produced its official answer to Catharism and for the first time laid down Catholic doctrine relating to the whole question of evil, and in particular to the Devil. The fact that these definitions were made as a consequence of the Cathar threat is, of course, not without significance for our purpose.

A Short Glossary of Words
Sometimes Treated as Technical Terms
of Sorcery

Adept　　　　A full initiate; treated as a technical term only in very modern and fabricated systems of *magia*, such as the post-Renaissance Rosicrucians, who recognize several degrees of initiation on the Masonic model.

Alchemy　　　of course actually has nothing to do with sorcery at all. It was once perfectly serious science, though derived from Hellenistic philosophical speculation about the nature of the universe rather than from observation. However, its main objects—to transmute base metals into gold and to discover the secret of human immortality—were akin to those pursued by the learned magi, and continued unsuccess drove many alchemists into superstitious practices; let alone that they relied on astrology, which they and many sensible men in their times regarded as science. A confusion between alchemy and magic is therefore not unreasonable, and doubtless the more "philosophical" magicians were alchemists also.

Arcana　　　Secrets, and could be a variant of "occult" (except to booksellers, who use it to mean pornography). A technical term only in divination by the Tarot q.v.

Beltane　　　and *Samhain* were solar festivals of ancient Ireland; they have no known connection with witchcraft, except in the minds of those Britons—beginning, I think, with John Buchan—who assume that the witch-cult was of British, and therefore Celtic, origin; which is most improbable.

Blokula　　　Legendary meeting-place of witches in Sweden; sometimes confused on this account with the Brocken. (See above, appendix A.)

Brocken　　　Legendary meeting-place of witches in Germany (e.g. in Goethe's *Faust*). A mountain in the Hartz, to which superstitions attach on account of the strange optical phenomena observed in its mists.

Coven	from *conventus*, a cell of the witch-cult ideally of thirteen members; possibly confined to Scotland.
Dianus	Cognate form of "Janus" and masculine of "Diana"; from a root very common in the names of gods, quite possibly means simply "god" and became attached to the two-headed god of Beginnings and Endings only by accident. The god of a dying-king cult according to Frazer; never applied to the witch-god before Margaret Murray.
Esbat	Word collected by De Lancre from the evidence of Basque witches and taken by him to mean an occasion of less ceremony than a Sabbat q.v. Quite possibly it is the word "Sabbat" misunderstood, though it plainly might be a back-formation from it. Not recorded as used by witches anywhere else. Adopted by Miss Murray in a sense private to her theory, and by myself to mean a regular meeting of a witch-group at intervals more frequent and occasions less ritually important than such major festivals as Hallowe'en.
Familiar	In popular belief over much of Western Europe (not only Britain as is sometimes stated), an attendant devil appointed by Satan to serve a witch, usually taking the form of some small animal. Tradition on this point is exceptionally confused.
Goetia	and *magia* are used by some to mean "black" and "white" magic respectively. The original contrast seems to have been between "native" and "exotic" magic, *goes* (Greek) being roughly our "witch" while a *magus* was a Persian priest, popularly supposed to be a magician. The nearest modern equivalent (in Western eyes, not in fact) would be a Tibetan Lama or someone of that kind; but it seems most convenient to employ these terms to express the dichotomy between the humble, unlearned wise-woman tradition on the one hand and the complex of literate superstitions, the Faustian Occult, on the other. This use is justified by the fact that Zoroaster, the first real magus, is often linked with Hermes Trismegistus as the legendary founder of this "learned" tradition.
Grimoire	Name applied in the last few centuries to supposed magical manuscripts in the "learned" tradition.
Hallow	Shibboleth whereby one may recognize those who derive some part of their ideas from the nineteenth-century mystagogue Arthur Waite, who used the word to mean "a sacred object, esp. a relic; an article having a ritual

purpose." Many people who ought to know better now use the word in this sense; if they must use ME fossil words, the one they want is "Halidom." "Hallow," if it still existed, would mean "saint."

Imp   Son or daughter; nowadays, "of the Devil" always understood. Hence, no connection with such creatures as fairies, pixies, and so forth; not a folklore figure at all (nor a technical term; but I mention it because I have used it).

Incubus   Not, as Barrat supposed, the name of a devil; but any devil who takes male flesh for the purpose of sexual intercourse with a human female. The corresponding term *succubus*, for a devil who takes the female role, is better known in this connection because the corresponding belief is more prominent in legend. *Incubus* and *succubus* are only ordinarily used of fiends specially summoned from the Pit to gratify a mortal's lust, and on the whole the more lustful mortals are men. The word could be stretched to cover the case of the devil at the Sabbat, but would not naturally apply to it.

Kabbala   "cabbalistic" etc. Originally, the mystic tradition in Judaeism, and the texts in which it is contained. Some of the language of alchemy may be borrowed from it, but its association with magic is due to the usual misapprehensions about the nature of the Jewish religion.

Ligature   Induced partial impotence, especially impotence of a man towards his own wife. It was a question much discussed by the theologians whether this was possible, and if so whether it constituted a ground for nullifying the marriage. Its connection with witchcraft is less clear than it might seem, though H. C. Lea certainly regarded it as crucial. The thing, of course, occurs; in the Middle Ages it was taken to be the effect of sorcery, but not necessarily of the devil (till all sorcery was so defined), nor the work of witches rather than other practitioners of magic. The witch might employ it to avoid her husband's embraces when bound for the Sabbat, but this was not the case with which the theologians were concerned or the question of nullification would not have arisen.

Magia   See *Goetia*.

Necromancy Literally, raising the dead for purposes of divination, but also used generally for Black Magic.

Osculum Infame The kiss upon the hindquarters of the Devil in the form of a beast, supposed to be demanded of the Satanist on

initiation and to be a principal feature of the ritual of
the Sabbat.

Pentacle   A five-pointed star, drawn in five lines enclosing a penta-
gon. Widely celebrated as a mystic figure, belonging
principally to the *magia* tradition. Drawn, with propitia-
tory rituals, on the floor, its inner and outer angles mark
out the two concentric circles of protection within which
the magus may feel secure when raising the Devil.
Modern witches, according to Gardner, use it to mark
out the ring for their dances; but this is an untraditional
detail.

Sabbat   Presumably from "Sabbath," which is how the word was
usually written until recently. A major festival of
witches; generally used for all their gatherings, but used
by me in contradistinction to *Esbat*, q.v., to mean an
assembly held on a date, such as Walpurgisnacht, that
was itself of ritual significance and not arbitrarily chosen.

Sabazia   Festival of Sabazius, the Thracian god of profligacy;
suggested by Michelet as the origin of "Sabbat." The
suggestion deserves no more credence than any other of
the same author on this subject, on which he relied
entirely on his imagination.

Sorcery   In origin, divination by drawing lots, *sortilegium*; but so
generally used for all magic whatsoever that it would be
pedantic so to confine it. As, however, this origin is still
obvious in the French language, which has no other
word for witchcraft than *sortilège*, it may well have
influenced the thinking of French writers on the subject.

Succubus   See *Incubus*.

Tarot   (origin of word obscure) A pack of cards developed c.
fifteenth century for the special purpose of divination.
Now associated with gypsies, but they are not likely to
be the inventors. It is divided into two Arcana, a Greater
and a Lesser, of which the former is simply a primitive
playing deck while the latter consists of 21 additional
Court cards. The symbolism of these has never been
satisfactorily explained, and probably is not systematic,
but appears to derive in part from Alchemy. The Tarot
thus represents a point of contact between *magia* at its
most philosophical and *goetia* at its most fraudulent,
bypassing witchcraft as I understand it.

Tregenda   (Italian) A large number (lit. 300), used especially of
swarms of devils and lost souls on such occasions as
Hallowe'en, and sometimes transferred to the occasion
itself; hence can be used for "Sabbat."

Volta	Peasant dance of the Alpine region, original of the waltz; formerly associated with witches, and held immoral on three grounds: (*a*) the close embrace of the couples; (*b*) their free and unco-ordinated movements; (*c*) the fact that it was danced widdershins, an "unlucky" direction that witches are supposed usually to follow in their rituals. All these, of course, are features of modern ballroom dancing, but were unknown in polite society till the late eighteenth century.
Walpurgis	(German) and *Walpurgisnacht*. The eve of St. Walburga's Day (May Day).
Widdershins	"Against the sun," anti-clockwise. Therefore left-handed motion; the superstition against it may derive from the unluckiness of the left hand quite as well as from respect for the Sun.
Witch	Origin of the word unknown, but most unlikely to be from the root of "wise." Probably cognate with German *Hexe*, and both these, like *Stryx*, probably in origin onomatopoeia for "screech-owl"; the witch, we may suppose, having a similar characteristic cry. A closer connection than this between witches and owls would be intriguing to establish but there is little basis for it; the mental association would be rather with the male magus (by way of Pallas Athene, goddess of wisdom).
Wizard	on the other hand, does mean "a wise man," and can apply to the magus; it is not the masculine equivalent of "witch," though doubtless it could properly apply to a male witch also.

Bibliography

IN VIEW OF the variations of meaning of words such as "witchcraft," no bibliography of this subject can be more than a selection. The following list includes works actually used, including references to side-issues raised incidentally in the text or notes, and some works included mainly as examples of the classes to which they belong. I indicate those among the latter which I consider to be worthless.

Among basic standard works I ought to mention:
DUCANGE. *Glossarium mediae et infimae Latinitatis.*
MANSI. *Sacrorum Conciliorum Amplissima Collectio* (1759–   ).
The Cambridge Mediaeval History (now rather out of date and undergoing revision).
The Oxford History of England (ed. G. N. Clark), 1936–1961.
Dictionnaire de Théologie Catholique.

And among collections:
MIGNE. *Patrologiae Cursus Completus,* Series Latina, Paris, 1844 (MPL), especially volumes:
    LXXXII, Isidore of Seville, *Etymologia;*
    CXXXII, Regino of Prüm, *De Disciplina Ecclesiastica Libri Duo;*
    CLXXXVII, Gratian, *Concordantia* &c.;
    CCX, Alanus ab Insulis, *Opera.*
The Rolls Series and printed Calendars of the public records, published by the Record Commissioners for the British government.

AHMED, ROLLO. *Black Art,* London, John Long, 1936 (introduction by Dennis Wheatley). Specimen of credulity by a modern would-be magus: Yoga, Atlantis, Knights Templar, and the whole bag of tricks.
ALAIN DE LILLE or ALANUS AB INSULIS (MPL ccx). *Contra Haereticos Libri Quattuor,* Bk. 1 (attacking Albigenses).
AMANN, E. "Luciferiens," in *Dictionnaire de Théologie Catholique.*
ANON. *Sir Gawain and the Green Knight.* See especially the edition by J. R. R. Tolkien and E. V. Gordon, Oxford U.P., 1925 and 1952.
BAECHTOLD-STÄUBLI, HANNS. *Handwörterbuch des Deutschen Aberglaubens,* Berlin and Leipzig, 1927–42 (10 vols.).
BAMBERGER, BERNARD J. *Fallen Angels,* Philadelphia, 1952.

BARRET, FRANCIS. *The Magus* or Celestial Intelligencer, &c., London, 1801.

BAVOUX, F. *La Sorcellerie en Franche-Comté*, Monaco, 1954.

—— *Hantises et Diableries dans la terre abbatiale de Luxeuil d'un procès de l'inquisition (1529) à l'épidémie demoniaque de 1628-30*, Monaco, 1956.

BONIFACE VIII (Pope). *Registres*, ed. G. Digard for the French Schools at Rome and Athens, Paris, 1904.

BUDGE, SIR ERNEST A. W. *Babylonian Life and History*, London, 1925.

BURCHARD OF WORMS (MPL cxl). Penitential of.

BURCHARDT, JACOB. *The Age of Constantine the Great*, Basel, 1852; trans. Moses Hadas, New York, 1956 ("Religion in Roman Gaul"; cf. Duval, below).

BURR, G. L. *Narratives of Witchcraft Cases*, New York, 1914.

—— (ed.). *The Witch-Persecutions*, vol. 3, no. 4, of the Translations and Reprints series, Philadelphia, U. of Pennsylvania, 1897.

BUTLER, E. M. *The Myth of the Magus*, Cambridge U.P., 1948.

—— *Ritual Magic*, Cambridge U.P., 1949.

CAMDEN SOCIETY PUBLICATIONS. *Proceedings against Dame Alice Kyteler*, 1840. (Mainly the narrative of Robert Leatherhead, Bishop of Ossory.)

CAMPANELLA, T. *De sensu rerum et magia* (ed. Adami), Frankfurt, 1620.

CAMPBELL, G. A. *The Knights Templars*, London, Duckworth, 1937.

CHADWICK, N. K. (ed.) and others. *Studies in Early British History*, Cambridge U.P., 1954.

CLARK, SIR G. N. (ed.) and others. *The Campden Wonder*, London and New York, Oxford U.P., 1959.

COLLINGWOOD, R. G. and MYERS, J. N. L. *Roman Britain & the English Settlements* (vol. 1 of the Oxford History of England), Oxford U.P., 1936.

CONSTANT, ALPHONSE LOUIS. See LEVI, ELIPHAS.

COULTON, G. G. *Five Centuries of Religion*, Cambridge U.P., 1923-50 (4 vols.).

DAVIES, R. TREVOR. *Four Centuries of Witch Beliefs*, London, Methuen, 1947.

DELCAMBRE, ETIENNE. *Le Concept de la Sorcellerie dans la Duché de Lorraine au xvie et au xviie siècles*, Nancy, 1948.

DELRIO, M. *Disquisitionum magicarum libri sex*, Mainz, 1612. (An Anti-Sadducee classic.)

DENOMY, ALEXANDER J. *The Heresy of Courtly Love*, New York, D. X. McMullen, 1947. (Neo-Thomist moral theology.)

DIXON, W. HEPWORTH, *Spiritual Wives*, London, 1868.

DUVAL, P.-M. *Les Dieux de la Gaule*, Paris, Presses Universitaires de France, 1957.

EWEN, C. L'ESTRANGE. *Witch Hunting and Witch Trials*, London, Kegan Paul, 1929.

—— *Witchcraft and Demonianism*, London, Heath Cranton, 1933. (The most intensive modern studies on English and Scots trial records.)

FLORES HISTORIARUM (Chronicle, Roger of Wendover), London, Rolls Series, 1886–9.

FRÄNGER, W. *The Millennium of Hieronymous Bosch* (trans. Eithne Wilkins and Ernst Kaiser), London, Faber, 1952 (see p. 176, note 22).

FRAZER, SIR J. G. *The Golden Bough*, London, Macmillan. The first version is that of 1890; that most often referred to in bibliographies, that of 1922, but this is sometimes now replaced by the abridgement of 1954.

GARDNER, GERALD B. *Witchcraft Today*, London, Rider, 1954 (introduction by Margaret Murray).

GIRALDUS CAMBRENSIS or GERALD DE BARRY. *Itinerary through Wales* (Latin) in *Opera*, Rolls Series, vol. 6, London, 1868; trans. W. L. Williams, London, Dent (Everyman's), 1930.

GIVRY, GRILLOT DE. *Witchcraft, Magic and Alchemy* (trans. J. C. Locke), London, Harrap, 1931. (A profusely illustrated compendium, totally uncritical.)

GRUNZWEIG, A. "Les Incidences Internationales des Mutations Monetaires de Philippe le Bel," in *Le Moyen Age* (Brussels), 1953, vol. 59 (see cap. 6, n. 19).

Handwörterbuch des Deutschen Aberglaubens. See BAECHTOLD-STÄUBLI.

HANSEN, JOSEPH. *Zauberwahn, Inquisition und Hexenprozess im Mittelalter und die Entstehung der grossen Hexenverfolgung*, Munich and Leipzig, 1900.

—— *Quellen und Untersuchungen zur geschichte des Hexenwahns und der Hexenverfolgung im Mittelalter*, Bonn, 1901.

HERSKOVITS, M. J. *Acculturation: The Study of Culture-Contact*, New York, Augustin, 1938. (A very general survey of anthropological work done in this field.)

HÖFLER, O. *Germanisches Sakralköningtum*, vol. 1: *Der Runenstein von Rök und die Germanische Individual-Weihe*, Tubingen, 1952. (Additional material on the Cavalcade of the Dead.)

HOLE, CHRISTINA. *Witchcraft in England*, London, 1945. (Rather in the Murrayite vein.)

—— *A Mirror of Witchcraft*, London, Chatto & Windus, 1957. (Sensible. Consists mainly of selections from original sources.)

HOOKE, S. H. (ed.) *Myth, Ritual and Kingship in the Ancinet Near East*, Oxford U.P., 1958. (Sums up the present state of the question on post-Frazerian views of sacred kingship and on "patterns of culture" generally.)

HORST, G. K. *Zauberbibliotek*, Mainz, 1821–6 (6 vols.).

HUBERT, H. and MAUSS, E. "Esquisse d'une Théorie Générale de la Magie," in *L'Année sociologique*, 1902–3.

HUGHES, PENNETHORNE. *Witchcraft*, London, Longmans Green, 1952. (Dissident Murrayite; well informed but highly eccentric. Good bibliography.)

HUXLEY, ALDOUS. *The Devils of Loudun*, London, Chatto & Windus, 1952 (see p. 34, note 8).

—— *The Doors of Perception*, London, Chatto & Windus, 1954.

JAMES VI and I (King). *Daemonologie*, Edinburgh, 1597; reprinted, London, John Lane, 1924.

JUNG, C. G. *Psychology and Alchemy*, Zurich, 1944; trans. R. F. C. Hull, vol. 12 of Collected Works in Bollingen Series, New York, 1953.

KITTREDGE, GEORGE LYMAN. *Witchcraft in Old and New England*, Cambridge, Mass., Harvard U.P., 1929.

KLEIN, HERBERT. *Die älteren Hexenprozesse im Lande Salzburg*, Salzburg, 1957.

KNOX, REV. R. A. *Enthusiasm*, Oxford U.P., 1950. (Caps. 5 and 6, on mediaeval heresies.)

KRAMER, or INSTITORIS, JACOB. See SUMMERS, MONTAGU.

Lanercost, Chronicle of, ed. J. Stephenson for the Bannatyne Club, Edinburgh, 1839.

LEA, H. C. *History of the Inquisition in the Middle Ages*, New York, Macmillan, 1888.

—— *Materials toward a History of Witchcraft*, Philadelphia, U. of Pennsylvania Press, 1939. (Posthumously published, unfinished, and very awkward to use but unsurpassed as a collection of sources.)

LELAND, CHARLES G. *Aradia, or the Gospel of the Witches*, London, David Nutt, 1899.

LEVI, ELIPHAS. *Transcendental Magic* (trans. A. E. Waite), London, Rider, n.d.

—— *History of Magic* (trans. A. E. Waite), London, Rider, 1913. (One of the most influential of modern synthetic magi. Source mainly the Kabbala.)

LEWIS, C. S. *The Allegory of Love*, London, Oxford U.P., 1936.

—— *Miracles: A Preliminary Study*, London, Bles, 1947.

LIZERAND, G. (ed.). *Le Dossier de l'affaire des Templiers*, Paris, Champion, 1923. (Replaces Michelet.)

LOVETT, E. *Magic in Modern London*, London, 1925. (Journalism.)

McNEILL, J. T. and GAMER, H. M. (eds.). *Mediaeval Handbooks of Penance*, vol. 29 in the Records of Civilization series, New York, Columbia U.P., 1938.

MAITLAND, F. W. *Roman Canon Law in the Church of England*, London, Methuen, 1898. Cap. 6, "The Deacon and the Jewess."

MALINOWSKI, BRONISLAW. *Magic, Science and Religion*, New York, Free Press, 1948.

MAURY, A. *La Magie et l'astrologie dans l'antiquité et au moyen âge*, Paris, 1877.

MAUSS, E. See HUBERT, H.

MICHELET, JULES. *La Sorcière* (ed. L. Refort), Paris, Didier, 1952; trans. A. R. Allinson, *The Sorceress*, London, 1905; American title, *Satanism and Witchcraft*.

—— (ed.). *Procès des Templiers*, Paris, 1841–51 (2 vols.).

MURRAY, MARGARET A. *The Witch-Cult in Western Europe*, Oxford U.P., 1921.
—— *The God of the Witches*, London, Faber, 1934.
—— *The Divine King in England*, London, Faber, 1954.
—— "Witchcraft" in *Encyclopaedia Britannica*.
—— Note in *Folklore*, Dec. 1952.
NEUMANN, ERICH. *The Great Mother: An Analysis of the Archetype* (trans. R. Mannheim), New York, 1955.
NOTESTEIN, W. *History of Witchcraft in England*, Washington, American Historical Association, 1911.
OBOLENSKI, PRINCE DMITRI. *The Bogomils*, Cambridge U.P., 1948.
PAPINI, G. *Il Diavolo: appunti per una futura diabologia*, Florence, Vallecchi, 1954. (Neo-Gnostic.)
PERERIUS, B. *De magia, de observatione somnis et de divinatione astrologica libri tres*, Cologne, 1598.
PERNOUD, REGINE. *La Vie et mort de Jeanne d'Arc*, Paris, Hachette, 1953; trans. J. M. Cohen, *The Retrial of Joan of Arc*, London, Methuen, 1955.
PEUCKERT, W-E. *Geheim Kulte*, Heidelberg, 1951.
PIERRE DE VAUX DE CERNAY or PETRUS SARNENSIS. *Historia Albigensis* (ed. Guebin and Lyon), Paris, Société de l'Histoire de France, 1926.
POOLE, A. LANE. *From Domesday Book to Magna Carta* (vol. 3 of *Oxford History of England*), Oxford U.P., 1951.
POWICKE, F. M. *Ways of Mediaeval Life and Thought*, London, Odhams, 1949.
RANDOLPH, VANCE. *Ozark Superstitions*, New York, Columbia U.P., 1947.
—— "Nakedness in Ozark Folk Belief," *Journal of American Folklore*, 1953.
REGINO, ABB. PRÜM. See MIGNE.
RHODES, H. T. F. *The Satanic Mass*, London, Rider, 1954.
RIEZLER, SIGMUND. *Geschichte der Hexenprozesse in Bayern*, Stuttgart, 1896.
ROUGEMONT, DENIS DE. *La Part du Diable*, New York, 1942; (trans.) *Talk of the Devil*, London, Eyre & Spottiswoode, 1945.
RUNCIMAN, STEVEN. *The Mediaeval Manichee*, Cambridge U.P., 1947.
—— *History of the Crusades*, Cambridge U.P., 1951–4 (3 vols.).
RYMER, T. *Foedera*.... (Edition of 1705 employed in referring to Miss Murray's references.)
SACKVILLE-WEST, VICTORIA. *Saint Joan of Arc*, London, Michael Joseph, 1948 (revised ed.).
Satan (collection, translated from *Etudes Carmelitaines: collection de psychologie religieuse*). London and New York, Sheed & Ward, 1951.
SCHRAMM, P. E. *History of the English Coronation* (trans. L. G. Wickham Legg), Oxford U.P., 1937.
SCHWOB, MARCEL. "Le Sabbat de Mofflaines," in *Le Roi au masque d'or* (vol. 3, *Œuvres*, Paris, 1927). (Fairly typical literary approach.)

SCOT, REGINALD. *Discoverie of Witchcraft*, London, 1584; ed. Summers, London, 1930. (Best known as a classic of scepticism and the immediate occasion for King James's *Daemonologie* which attacks it, but also contains a compendium of information on popular beliefs, not all of it critically treated.)

SCOTT, SIR WALTER. *Letters on Demonology and Witchcraft Addressed to J. G. Lockhart Esq.*, London, John Murray, 1830. (Really a series of articles in the *Family Library*, which Lockhart edited.)

SOUTHERN, R. W. *The Making of the Middle Ages*, London, Hutchinson, 1953.

SPEE, FRIEDRICH VON. *Cautio Criminalis*, Frankfurt, 1631–2; German trans., J. F. Ritter, Weimar, 1939.

SPRENGER, HEINRICH. See SUMMERS, MONTAGU.

STENTON, F. M. *Anglo-Saxon England* (vol. 2 of *Oxford History of England*), Oxford U.P., 1943.

STRACHEY, RAY CONN. *Religious Fanaticism*, London, Faber, 1928; essentially reissued as *Group Movements of the Past and Experiments in Guidance*, London, Faber, 1938. (Mainly an edition of the papers of Hannah Whitall Smith; but Miss Strachey's own contribution throws more light on "enthusiastic" sects.)

SUMMERS, REV. MONTAGU. *History of Witchcraft and Demonology*, London, Kegan Paul, 1926.

—— *Geography of Witchcraft*, London, Kegan Paul, 1927.

—— (ed.), SPRENGER, H. and KRAMER, J. (Institoris), *Malleus Maleficarum*, London, Pushkin Press, 1928.

—— (ed.), GUAZZO, *Compendium Maleficarum*, London, John Rodker, 1929.

—— *Popular History of Witchcraft*, London, Kegan Paul, 1937.

THORNDIKE, LYNN. *History of Magic and Experimental Science*, New York, Macmillan and Columbia U.P., 1923–58 (8 vols.). (Exclusively concerned with the learned, not the popular, tradition.)

TIEDEMANN, D. *Disputatio de quaestione quae fuerit artium magicarum origo*, Marburg, 1787.

TRACHTENBERG, J. *Jewish Magic and Superstition*, New York, Berhman, 1939.

—— *The Devil and the Jews*, New Haven, Yale U.P., 1943.

WADDELL, HELEN. *The Wandering Scholars*, London, Constable, 1927.

—— *Mediaeval Latin Lyrics*, London, Constable, 1929.

WAITE, A. E. See LEVI, ELIPHAS.

WILLIAMS, CHARLES. *Witchcraft*, London, Faber, 1941.
　　Cf. his novels, especially:

—— *War in Heaven*, London, Faber, 1930.

—— *All Hallows' Eve*, London, Faber, 1944.

WILLIAMSON, HUGH ROSS. The Arrow and the Sword, London, Faber, 1947. (Ingenious but unconvincing theories about the Knights Templar.)

Index